FROM PARIS COMMUNE TO PERESTROIKA
State, Classes and Revolution

FROM PARIS COMMUNE TO PERESTROIKA

State, Classes and Revolution

H. SRIKANTH

With a Foreword by
Prof. MANORANJAN MOHANTY

GIAN PUBLISHING HOUSE
New Delhi-110002

GIAN PUBLISHING HOUSE
4-C Ansari Road
New Delhi 110002

ISBN 81-212-0326-0

PRINTED IN INDIA

Published by Mrs. Gayatri Garg for Gian Publishing House, New Delhi-110002.
Laser typeset by : Ocean Laser Prints, Delhi-110051
Printed at Goyal Offset Printers, Delhi.

Dedicated to

Com.KRISHNA CHAKRABORTY

Who taught me the fundamentals of

MARXISM-LENINISM

and

SHIBDAS GHOSH'S

Thoughts

Foreword

Marxist theory faces enormous challenges today. The changes in Eastern Europe, the repression in China's Tiananmen Square and the unfolding restructuring of the Soviet Union have raised questions about the prevailing notions in those societies and in some other quarters about the state, the communist party and the mode of socialist construction. The debates on all these issues have become intense day by day. While many communists have taken an about turn in Eastern Europe and adopted liberal democratic philosophy, some Marxists have held on to their earlier formulations steadfastly. Many others are reformulating their understanding of Marxist ideas trying to reconcile the original premises with the developing human condition. This book in many ways belongs to the last category though in some respects it may appear to take the second line. Either way it is a serious theoretical exercise that must be commended.

Among the questions raised in the recent debates the central one concerns the problem of bureaucratic authoritarianism in socialist systems. The leaders of communist parties understood "dictatorship of the proletariat" as a self-defence mechanism against the enemy classes that justified not only denial of freedom of expression and association to all others but suppression of all opponents. On the other hand, this concept entailed in the Marx-Lenin framework, a series of measures to transform the society in the image of the proletariat, i.e. spread the values of equality, freedom solidarity, rationality and creativity. For this purpose the communist party was to mediate between the workers and the rest of the society, by persuasion and exemplary performance, by proving through competition with other groups that it had a more substantial perspective on freedom and democracy than the bourgeoisie. The state as the political organisation of society with workers and their allies exercising power was to promote this process of democratisation. The coercive organisation in the state apparatus should be reduced gradually as the state became more and more democratic. Thus through democratic and participatory planning under the state auspices conditions for freedom for the working people should have expanded.

On the other hand, the leaders of the socialist regimes after assuming power went about using the state machine to achieve the same goals as the capitalists set for their societies after the industrial revolution. Releasing of the productive forces from the shackles of exploitative capitalist system was the call of Marx. But he said this as a measure to curb alienation of labour and indeed of human beings and to enlarge the realm of freedom. The capitalists aimed at increasing production and create a climate of expanding consumer needs that continuously generates further demands. It did not matter if this process produced new structures of domination in society, disrupted natural environment and attacked cultural sensibilities. The socialist leaders thought that they had to *first of all* achieve the levels of production and technology prevailing in the Western capitalist societies and *then* think about another goals. These other goals were never attempted seriously. On the one hand, the common people of Eastern Europe began to demand the same amenities of life as in the West since they had no commitment to alternative socialist values of freedom. On the other hand, the centralisation and bureaucratisation of the polity under the party leadership created more and more alienation in society. Finally, the revolt against the authoritarian regimes came.

The social basis of state power is no doubt characterised mainly by the class or classes who dominate the mode of production, but it is intermingled with many other structures of social domination like caste, ethnicity, race, gender and religion. That communists would automatically overcome their ethnic and caste identities and socialist policies would necessarily guarantee the fulfilment of ethnic and other aspirations have been challenged in course of practice. Each of these categories has to be taken as an autonomous factor and tackled through special policies both in course of revolutionary movement from day one and through state policies. At the same time those who exclusively stress either of these categories cannot integrate their struggles with the overall democratic and socialist transformation. Here class analysis is helpful in linking up various structures of a domination. Thus Marxist theory of the state has to dialectically relate various forms of structural domination with class contradictions.

The capitalist industrial revolution was a liberative movement in the first phase of its progress. Thereafter it generated more and more exploitative relations. Throughout this century struggle against that process is continuing in various ways all over the world. In the process the capitalist systems have also evolved to absorb various challenges. The socialist movement was an alternative to capitalist mode of life and society. By adopting policies within the same paradigm the communist leaders took the wrong direction. The third world leaders too have the same temptation. But everywhere the people's movements are challenging that paradigm of the capitalist industrial revolution which continued to spread alienation. At this time a reaffirmation of Marxist theory in this scholarly work is a welcome contribution to the debate.

Manoranjan Mohanty

Dept. of Pol. Science
University of Delhi
Delhi.

Preface

From the *Communist Manifesto* of 1848, Marx and Engels travelled a long way to perfect their own understanding of the state in general and the capitalist state in particular. Whereas their keen observation of class struggles in France and Germany gave them a clear idea of the autonomous role that the capitalist state can play in the civil society, their study of political economy helped them in comprehending the dialectical relationship that the state as an element of superstructure has with its economic base. Efforts made by Marx and Engels to examine the impact of overseas expansion of capitalism enriched their understanding of different noncapitalist social formations in the world. However, a real turning point in Marxist analysis of state took place during the days of Paris Commune of 1871, when the French workers and other labouring masses could take over and retained political power for more than seventy days. That new experience reaffirmed Marx and Engels' faith in the possibilities of socialist transformation through the dictatorship of the proletariat. Since then, Paris Commune continued to inspire international working class movement.

Though Marx and Engels did not live long enough to see any revolution taking place, the rich literature they left to posterity guided the proletarian revolutions in the 20th century. In the era of imperialism, Lenin enriched and perfected Marxist theory of state and correctly guided the Russian revolution which could establish the first socialist state in the world. By correctly handling the international contradictions his successor, J.V. Stalin could establish communist regimes in the Eastern Europe. Again, by applying Marxism to the concrete conditions in semi-feudal and semi-colonial China, Mao-tse-tung proved the possibilities of socialist transformation even in the underdeveloped countries of the world. All these developments, at one time, gave the impression that the world socialism was not a distant reality.

However, to the utter disappointment of the Marxists and their admirers, the post-war world witnessed new developments which the traditional Marxists never dreamt of. In the capitalist world the bourgeoisie could devise new methods of control which could effectively neutralise the potentialities of the revolutionary forces. The renewed resilience in the post-war capitalist world gave birth to a number of bourgeois and petty-bourgeois theories which began to question the very relevance of Marxism in the advanced capitalist societies. Within the developing world, excepting a few countries like Cuba and Vietnam all others preferred to remain non-socialist. In one sense, the emergence of a non-aligned movement foiled Marxists' expectations of revolutionary transformations in the colonies and semi-colonies. Marxists who had to accept that the prospects of revolutions in the advanced capitalist countries and the Third World societies were not so bright, were also forced to swallow the fact that all was not well with the socialist world. Conflicts within the socialist camp and controversy over the correct path of socialist development created a lot of confusions in the minds of the admirers of socalism. It is so disgusting to note that every time a new development takes place in the socialist countries, the Marxists find themselves on the horn of a dialemma as to whether they should disown it as revisionism or accept it as creative application of Marxism.

Thus the Marxism of the late 20th century finds itself cornered from within and from without. In such critical conditions how did the contemporary Marxist theoreticians respond to the challenges? How far they succeeded in giving a satisfactory Marxist analysis of the post-war developments ? Do they have any solutions to overcome the present crises or confusions? Can the Marxists who dream of world socialism ever succeed in achieving their goal? These are some of the questions which agitate all the scholars interested in socialist studies. Keeping these questions in mind this book made a modest attempt to critically evaluate some of the recent Marxist interpretations of the post-war developments in capitalist, socialist and the Third World countries. While pointing out the logical consistencies in their theories and praxis, the book attempted to give a systematic Marxist interpretation of the state, classes and prospects of revolution in different social formations.

The first chapter points out certain critical questions that the Marxists are expected to answer. It summarises the view-points of the critics who argued that Marxism has lost its relevance in the advanced capitalist countries. The chapter also refers to the inadequacies and confusions underlying Marxist interpretations of the changing Third World scenario. Finally questions that the recent trends in socialist countries pose to the Marxists are also highlighted.

After pointing out the apparent contradictions in the classical Marxist interpretation of the relationship that the state has vis-a-vis the classes and the economic base, the second chapter introduces the Anglo-American empiricists who tried to defend Marxism from the onslaughts of bourgeois theories. While evaluating the relevance of Ralph Miliband's analysis of the capitalist state, the chapter attempts to answer : (1) Why state in capitalist society be called capitalist state? (2) How the capitalists and the state elite are linked to each other? and (3) How much autonomy the state enjoys vis-a-vis the ruling classes?

The next chapter aims to understand the structural Marxist interpretation of the capitalist state. In course of evaluating the contributions of structural marxists like Althusser and Poulantzas, the chapter throws light on certain aspects relating to the Marxist understanding (1) the autonomy of political; (2) the constitution of classes and class struggles in the capitalist state and (3) the autonomous role of the state in liberal and fascist countries.

In the fourth chapter an attempt is made to comprehend the economic role of the state in capitalist societies. In course of evaluating the view-points of the German Derivativists and other marxist political economists, the chapter highlights (1) the necessity of state intervention in economy; (2) anatomy of welfare state; (3) the process of capitalist reproduction and (4) the impact of commodity fetishism on the appearance of the state in capitalist societies.

The fifth chapter makes efforts to comprehend the relationship between the nature of the ruling classes and the process of economic development in the Third World. In the light of conflicting interpretations of Chinese communists, Russian Marxists and Dependency theorists, this chapter discusses (1) the nature of state and classes in the Third World, (2) their relationship with imperialism and (3) the prospects of Third World development in the context of changes in the world order.

The Sixth chapter critically evaluates the economic and political reforms initiated in the USSR in the name of 'Perestroika'. Keeping in view the official interpretations of the reforms carried out in China and Russia, efforts are made to throw light on (1) the relevance of the dictatorship of the proletariat and party control, (2) the role of classes in socialism and (3) cultural revolution and economic development in the socialist setups.

In the final chapter an attempt is made to understand the prospects of world revolution. While comprehending the nature of contradictions inherent in each system, we tried to assess the obstacles underlying socialist path of development. After making an objective analysis of the present stage of development in the advanced capitalist countries, socialist societies and the developing nations, efforts have been made to discover the options opened for the Marxists to overcome the obstacles and realise their dream of establishing a classless and stateless communist society.

Having briefed the contents of the book, it now becomes my responsibility to state a few limitations of the work. The main purpose of the book is to study the nature of state, classes and prospects of reveolution in the post-war world. The book discusses and critically evaluates some of the contemporary Marxist theories of the state only to get clear insights into the dynamics of state in each social formation. Hence, contributions of certain Marxist theoreticians could not be given a place in the book in spite of their substantial contributions to the theory of Marxism.

It should be admitted that as regards the Third World, we could only give general guidelines necessary to comprehend the nature of state, classes and economy in the developing countries. But the comprehensive study of any particular Third World state was attempted to substantiate our view-point. Paradoxically, while the necessity is to analyse the recent trends in different socialist countries, the book only highlighted the political and economic reforms initiated in the USSR in the name of Perestroika. Though we could arrive at certain general conclusions on the questions of socialist path of development, dictatorship of the proletariat and the dominance of party and bureaucracy in socialist set-ups, there is the necessity of studying the developments in China and East Europe separately. Despite all these limitations, we hope, the book will be found very useful for the scholars interested in comprehending the relevance of Marxist theory of state, clasess and revolution in the post-war world.

H. Srikanth

Acknowledgements

Writing the book, *From Paris Commune to Perestroika* is indeed a pleasant experience in my academic career. I never expected that I would be approached to take up the responsibility of writing on such theoretical issues of contemporary relevance. Considering my own abilities the topic that I had to deal was not an easy task. Hence at this moment, I do not have any hesitation to say that I could not have completed the work without the help of my teachers, friends and well-wishers.

On this occasion, it gives me immense pleasure to express my gratitude to my teacher and mentor, Prof. Sisir Bhattacharya for his valuable guidance and invaluable suggestions. Since almost all chapters of the book are written under his direct guidance, it would not be an exaggeration to say that in one sense, he is the co-author of the book.

I am extremely grateful to my teacher Prof. R.V.R. Chandrashekhar Rao, the present Vice-Chancellor of the Andhra Pradesh Open University for his warm affection and sincere encouragement. I also owe a lot to Prof. G. Haragopal. Infact I had to take great care in this book to reflect on many provcative remarks he used to make on different issues related to recent developments in socialist societies and the Third World Countries.

I should also thank my friend — M. Thimma Reddy, L. S. Reddy, Anniah, P. Sudhakar, Saikumar and many others who helped me in so many ways in the completion of this work.

Further, I should admit that my methodological approach and my understanding of state, classes and revolutions are much influenced by the thoughts of Com. Shibdas Ghosh. I am indebted to the leaders of Socialist Unity Centre of India (S.U.C.I.) who enriched my understanding of Marxism, Leninism by clarifying a number of theoretical questions that I encountered in my research.

In addition to these people who are directly associated in writing this book, there are many other persons who encouraged me by creating an atmosphere of understanding and hope. In this regard, I am forced to remember a short interlude I had with the American Marxist writer, Prof. Bertell Ollman. His honest appreciation of my understanding of Marxism and his critical evaluation of my research work helped me in acquiring necessary confidence in my abilities to think and write.

Another key person who has been a source of inspiration to me is Prof. Manoranjan Mohanty. To see that I make a place for myself in the academic world, he took pains to introduce me to many leading intellectuals and academicians in India. My sincere thanks are due to him for writing the Foreword to my book.

I will be doing a great injustice to myself if I forget my parents who suffered silently and sacrificed everything they have, only to see that I would become what I really wanted to become.

Finally, I express my sincere thanks to M/s Gian Publishing House for publishing my work in such a short span of time.

Contents

Chapter I

KEY QUESTIONS ON STATE, CLASSES AND REVOLUTION

Lenin, to whom goes the credit of giving practical shape to the ideas propounded by Marx and Engels, in one of his lectures at the Sverdlov University observed : "the question of the state is a most complex and difficult one, perhaps one that more than any other has been confused by bourgeois scholars, writers and philosophers".[1] The statement does not seem to be exaggerated when one looks at so many parallel theories of state and society that appeared and continued to appear in the name of liberal interpretation. The classical Marxists claimed that they were the first to expose the myth of 'state' by establishing its true relationship with economy and the classes which the economic base gives birth to. Comprehension of the dialectical interactions between state and civil society and state and economy are projected as essential keys to unlock the mystery of human society divided into classes. They argued that because of their correct understanding of the state, classes and economy they could shape the future of the world through revolutionary praxis. Such claims appeared to have relevance in the first half of 20th century when the communism won substantial victories against the bourgeois world. Rapid progress that a backward country like Russia achieved in a short span of time and the communist revolutions that broke out in many other parts of the world strengthened the impression that communism, Marxism has universal validity.

However, such a belief could not hold ground for long. After the death of Stalin, the so-called 'orthodox' Marxist-thories of state and society came under sharp criticism. It was argued that in the changed social, political and economic conditions of the post-war world where alignments of class forces inside the nations and of nations within the international framework seem to have gone against the predictions of classical thinkers, Marxist theory of state has lost its validity as well as utility in the modern era. In addition to usual bourgeois or petty bourgeois critics, the theory and practice of marxists of all nations created many doubts about the contemporary Marxism. Since all new interpretations appeared in the wake of changed national and international conditions, no serious scholar interested in Marxism can ignore the imperative need of taking note of all those developments which are usually cited to show that the Marxist approach is no more useful in explaining the dynamics of the modern world. Hence before reacting to those critics, a brief study fo the challenges that they posed is essential.

Marxism and the Advanced Capitalist Societies

Keeping in view the necessity of understanding the critics' viewpoint, one may first look at the way the critics attacked the basic tenets of Marxist theory of the state in advanced capitalist societies. Many critics argue that Marx in his time could not foresee many changes that took place after his death. Marx lived in the era of competitive capitalism ridden with crises in producation and market. It is said that he was very much moved by the degrading conditions of workers, their problems of poverty, unemployment, alienation, exploitation and oppression resulting from the anarchy of capitalist system of society during the first stage of its development. He could only see, so it is alleged, the competitive era leading to the era of monopoly, but failed to foresee beyond that. In political field, the Chartist movement in England, 1848 revolutions in Europe and Paris Commune of 1871 created in him the impression that the state continues to be an instrument in the formation of class, and class contradictions are inevitable in capitalist society and that they necessarily lead to the victory of the proletariat in all the advanced capitalist countries. But the historical events that followed belied the basic predictions of Marx. The countries which turned socialist so far are those which were then semi-feudal and semi-capitalist states (e.g. Russia) or semi-feudal and semi-colonial states (e.g. China, Vietnam, Cuba *etc*). Even hundred years after the death of Marx one is not sure whether atleast in the near future there would be intensification of class struggle which would lead to proletariat's capture of state power in all the so-called advanced capitalist societies. "Western industrial societies have remained unchanged since Marx, because they have not experienced revolutions".[2] These failures of Marx's premises, it is argued, stemmed from the limitations of his own period which made him unable to foresee the future development of capitalist society.

In course of development of capitalist form of economy, the period of free competition gradually paved way for the concentration of capital in a few hands and thereby giving birth to the monopolies. These monopolies with all the resources and information at their disposal about the market conditions, and environment and positions ownership of raw materials *etc.* could overcome to a great extent the problems of overproduction and other crises related to them. At about the same time, the state which once acted as a direct instrument of the capitalist society suppressing workers agitations, changed its character. The state which kept itself, in the main, away from the economic sphere during the era of free competition began slowly but positively interfering in the economy to protect the national interest. The state enacted factory acts decreasing the working hours and increasing the pay, which went in favour of the working class. From the second quarter of the twentieth century the tendency of the state to take over and nationalise important basic industries hitherto held by a few individuals increased. Further, to quote Sydney Webb. "Every one of these functions, with those of the army, navy, police and courts of justice were at times left to private enterprise and was a source of legitimate individual investment of capital. Step by step the community has absorbed them wholly or partially and the area of private exploitation has been lessened".[3] The liberty of the private property owner to oppress the propertyless began to be circumscribed, obstructed and even forbidden.

The great depression of 1929 necessiated overall planning for the entire nation. Then many Marxists underestimated the ability of the bourgeois state to adjust itself in response to the demands of the time and considered that capitalist crises would continue to be a regular phenomena. They considered that there existed only two alternatives—Fascism or Socialism. But this conception proved to be worng when the state itself started replacing the private monopolies to undertake the responsibility for effective planning to overcome the economic problem affecting the nation. In course of time having understood the necessity of state planning even the traditional economists stopped talking about the *laissez-faire* economy. Here worth mentioning is the contribution of Keynes. As one commentator says, "to those equally repelled by politics of Stalin and Hitler—Keynesian middle way came almost as a deliverance; promising full employment and J.S. Mill too"[4] Keynes attributed the capitalist crises to oversaving by rentiers and financial institutions. To restore profitability and full employment without sacrificing political and economic freedom, he proposed certain fiscal and monetary measures which involve filling up of the gap between investment and consumption through governmental intervention in the form of social policy.

Keynes believed that these public affairs should and could be managed by an elite of clever and disinterested above class, public servants or technocrats.[5] Introduction and implementation of Keynesian economics imparted stability to the capitalist system. The unplanned capitalist sectors producing for unknown markets, that creating at times the problems of depression, industrial crash, unemployment, immiserisation *etc*. gradually sought to be overcome by planned economy.

Social policy implemented by the bourgeois welfare states provides material benefits to a large section of the poor people. A considerable percentage of the state budget is allotted to the welfare activities.

Lindblum democratic and communist regimes do not differ greatly in percentage of gross national product, allotted to social welfare measures.[6] Contrary to Marx's expectations, development of capitalism did not lead to immiserisation of the masses.[7] Rather as Bernstein viewed, the working conditions and material benefits enjoyed by the workers increased their economic status and well being.[8]

The status of the working class improved in political field also as for example by the formation of trade unions. The states legalised trade unions and within the bounds of law granted them the right to go on strike to realise their legitimate rights and demands. Labour courts have been established to settle the disputes between the workers and capitalist or say between the labourers and the owners concerned. Workers' right to participate in the decision making process is also conceded in many of the public as well as private sectors. Geiger who describes the change as "institutionalization of class conflict" says "the tension between capital and labour as a class struggle is recognized as a principle of the structure of the labour market and has become a legal institution of society... the methods, weapons and techniques of the class struggle are recognised- and also thereby brought under control. The struggle evolves according to certain rules of the game. Thereby the struggle has lost its worst sting, it is converted into a legitimate tension between power factors which balance each other"[9] More than all these, introduction of universal adult franchise, much to the dislike of the dominant classes was a great political achievement of the working class. Now the working class is allowed to have its own parties. These parties can contest in the elections and can capture governmetal power. Even communists of to-day are allowed to form ministries. Sincerely, one can observe significant changes in the method of recruitment to the civil services. The criterion for recruitment to any state service has nothing to do with one's class or birth. Persons who have the requisite talent and ability can compete and get into any post in any field. In some countries the states made necessary provisions for reservation in education and employment for socially and economically backward sections with intention to uplift them into the national mainstream. All these developments indeed democratized the state and its government.

It is argued that this process of democratisation, is not limited to social and political spheres alone. Even the economy has undergone remarkable changes, gradually giving up its old robber-baron face. The present day economic system in advanced countries especially in the U.S.A is radically different from the one that was experienced by Marx in his days. Though private property as such is not dissolved, the real significance of private ownership of production has been disappearing. Unlike the classical epoch where entrepreneur is both the manager and the owner, the modern epoch is characterised by the separation of ownership and control. Most of the big firms, which have come to stay in these countries consist of some thousands of shareholders. Moreover the scientific and technological advances of the present day industrial societies make the problems of the modern industries very complicated. As such no capitalist, can run the firms efficiently without the active support from the scientists, technocrats operating executives, production managers, plant superintendents and other administrators. Though the formal ownership is still in the hands of the capitalists, all modern firms in reality are run and controlled by these professional managers. James

Burnham called this new phenomenon as 'managerial revolution' asserts : "Ownership means control; if there is no control there is no onwership.... If ownership and control in reality are separated, then ownership has changed hands to the 'control' and the separated ownership is a meaningless function."[10] As such the managers become prime movers of the industrial society. Managers have their origins in different classes—they may not be the product of bourgeois class. But having become the managers they enjoy more autonomy in running the firms than the real owners of the concerned firms. Due to technical complexity of mangement process the managers receive high pay and social status. Their outlook, is expected to be different from that of the owners. They would be more humane and would show more interest in efficient administration of the firm rather than exploitation of the workers. These groups of managers have emerged as a new homogeneous class in the society. In place of the owners of capital, this new class is now assuming the status of the dominant class so much so that it makes Burnham say that in society towards which we tend today, "the managers will in fact, have achieved the dominace, will be the ruling class."[11]

Another recent development in capitalism is impersonalisation and democratisation of capital. Modern giant firms consist of a large number of shareholders. These shareholders in turn select the board of directors. These shareholders or directors may come and go but the institution continues without identifying itself with any individuals in particular. Similarly it is argued that in most of the big firms even the workers will be given shares so that they too can enjoy a share in the profits of the firm, along with the capitalist shareholders. As such capitalism of the capitalists is now tending to become people's capitalism.[12]

Here one may also mention a new stratum called by Leaderer and Marchask as "the new middle class" that emerged within the industry of modern societies. With the growing intervention of the state in the economy the power and authority of the bureaucrats to administer the affairs of the industry has increased in very large measure. It is held that these bureaucrats or white collar employees constituting of this 'new middle class' generally come from the petty bourgeois or from the working class families. In course of their work, they develop special identity and entertain particular interests of their own. This emerging bureaucratic capitalism is not an exclusive reserve of the rich people any longer. Though many Marxists did not consider bureaucrats as an inevitable class or special class in the capitalist societies, Milovan Djilas' analysis of the growth of political bureaucracy in the socialist setups,[13] gave an opportunity even for the non marxists to justify their claim that bureaucrate are becoming a powerful class in all advanced industrial societies.

In course of time, along with other changes, even the psychological makeup of the workers transformed Marx's expectation of 'class in itself' becoming 'class for itself'—a homogeneous class conscious working class was never accomplished. Calling Marx as "a genuine child of his century" Dahrendorf says that the "working class of today, far from being a homogeneous group of equally unskilled and impoverished people, is in fact a stratum differentiated by numerous subtle and not-so-subtle distinctions".[14] Further he quotes Andre Philip who says—"Everywhere, the working class differentiates itself more and more, on the one hand into occupational groups, on the other into three large categories with different, if not contradictory interests—the skilled craftsmen, the unskilled labourers, and the semi-skilled specialist workers".[15] Just as the different factions of the capitalist class vie with one another these different groups of the same working class are now involved in bitter competition to secure as much as possible within the existing system. It is said that both the classes, capitalists and workers have now learnt to co-exist in the interest of the nation as a whole. As a result, the class antagonisms are petering out and the need for violent revolution is becoming unnecessary. What is found is the workers themsleves are becoming bourgeois in their habits, and culture. Opportunism, economism, social Darwinism and national chauvinism have come to replace the united, uncompromising, revolutionary international spirit among the workers.[16] It is apparent that the workers in these countries by and large align themselves with the bourgeois or social democratic parties. Here the communist parties exist merely for name sake. These trends in working class make Emmanuel Aghiri conclude that a *de facto* united front of the workers and the capitalists of the well-to-do countries—with the workers here taking vanguard positions—directed against the poor nations co-exist with effective and sometimes violent trade union struggles over the sharing of the loot.[17] Trends like these in the working class movement make one doubt about the possibility of the victory of the communists in these advanced capitalist societies though the possibilities are no more. In the present changed conditions, "the pleasing simplicity of Marx's view of society has become a nonsensical construction even to the labourers sometimes. If ever there have been two large homogeneous, polarized and identically situated social classes, these have certainly ceased to exist today, so that an unmodified Marxian theory is bound to fail in explaining the structure and conflicts of advanced industrial societies".[18]

Corresponding to these social, political and economic developments, there emerged a number of theories and ideologies interpreting the modern developed capitalist countries and making forescasts for their future shape.

Pluralism[19] the predominant ideology in the U.S. and the U.K. considers that advanced capitalist countries are pluralistic, in the sense that they consist of a number of competing groups each with some influence in its own sphere, none without any power, competing with one another to promote their own interests. In such societies there exists no ruling class and that the state which responds to the pressure exerted by different groups and classes is not a state of any particular group or class as such.

Neo-corporatist theories [20] which are now replacing the pluralist theories hold the view that the state has become very dominant in the modern societies and that its intervention and mediation are accepted by all the classes. As such both the capitalists and the working class are absorbed in the corporatist structures. Middleman makes the point very clear when he says that corporatism is "a system of interest in which the constituent units are organized into a limited number of singular, compulsory, non competitive, hierarchically ordered and functionally differentiated categories, recognized or licenced (if not created) by the state and granted a deliberate representational monopoly within their respective categories in exchange of observing certain control on their selection of leaders and articulation of demands and supports".[21]

The more popular theory and still very influential is the theory of welfare state. According to welfare state theorists the modern state is not merely a police state. It is a state that looks after the welfare of all sections of the people. It aims at satisfying all basic socio-economic needs of all classes of people from the 'cradle to grave' and from ' womb to tomb'. Now the state provides citizens such diverisfied services as midwifery, nursery, education, boarding, vaccination, medicines, public amusements and entertainments. The state also make the provisions for minimum pay, unemployment relief, bonus, pension, housing allowance and many other subsidies for the poor desiring labouring masses. It takes welfare measures for primary producers, workers, general consumers and other backward sections of the society. Unlike police state of the era of free competition, the modern welfare state actively intervenes in economy, and regulate it in the interests of the nation. While undertaking the social policy, it also works to extend social and political democracy. Such a state realises, says Myrdal in *Beyond Welfare State*, "a type of society which would have satisfied even that angry philosopher Karl Marx, who gave such an uncompromising expression of old liberal version".

Along with these theories, there continues revisionist tradition starting from Bernstein and also social democratic thinking from the period of Lassale to the Fabians and the from them to the philosophy of the Labour Party, which believes in evolutionary, piecemeal, step by step approach to socialism—the goal which can be achieved by the working class, that too by using the existing capitalist state as a means to achieve the desired end. To this, one can add Khruschevite's revisionist theory of 'national democratic revolution' as a way to socialism, which they think, can be realised by an alliance of the workers and progressive national bourgeoisie in a peaceful parliamentary way.

Marxism and Contemporary Socialist Practice

Confusions regarding the Marxist conception of state are not created merely by the bourgeoisie and petty bourgeois theoreticians. Theory and practice of present leadership in the socialist states are also responsible for creating confusions among the admirers of Marxism. Absence of an all acceptable authorities like Lenin, division of international communist movement into different blocks and various experiments that each socialist country—tried sum total of all these events raised many questions regarding the true character of state and civil society in the socialist setups. In fact recent developments in communist giants like China and the USSR force one to question whether those countries which proclaim themselves as socialists adhere to the basic tenets of marxism. Here it may be mentioned that the Chinese Communist Party (CPC) in the year following the Marx's death centenary claimed that some aspects of Marxism became obsolete in solving the problems of modern socialist societies. About a decade after the so-called "modernisation" and "de-Maoisation" programmes, the new leadership faces the wrath of lakhs of Chinese students who squatted in the historic Tiananmen square demanding extension of democracy. It is reported that considerable number of citizens including the workers and a few army men supported the students movement without even having fair understanding of their goals. As the malady would have it, the students appealed for intervention of Soviet authorities—hitherto branded by the Chinese leadership as revisionists and social imperialists—in getting 'glasnot' introducted in Socialist China. There was erosion of prestige and credibility of the Party and its present leadership. Unable to convince the students, the state had to use coercion against its own people in the name of suppressing the counter revolution. Whereas the entire bourgeois world condemned it as a 'brutal coercion', the communists and their sympathisers outright failed to come to a consensus on this issue. Though there are people who justify the official stand of the CPC, many considered it as something opposed to the socialist practice. Apart from the question as to whether the students movement can be branded as 'counter revolutionary' or not, what happened in China recently evokes serious questions regarding the proletarian state, party and civil society in the socialist setups.

Perhaps the problems become more complicated when one had to digest the experiments taking place in the U.S.S.R. in the name of 'socialism'. Now, the winds of 'perestroika' and 'glasnost' flowing in full swing in the Soviet Union succeeded in creating a world-wide debate on the future of socialism in the world. Criticism of Russian socialist system by the Western intellectuals is not a new phenomenon. But now one can see, perhaps for the first time, the General Secretary of the CPSU, Mikhail Gorbachev himself speaking about economic stagnation, cultural degradation and bureaucratic oppression in the socialist Russia. Holding all his predecessors—exept Lenin—responsible for such state of affairs, Gorbachev, the New Messiah, calls for 'perestroika' and 'glasnost' as if what was constructed so far was not socalism and what existed so long was not socialist democracy. Though he promises to bring 'Lenin' back to the Soviet Union, many of his ideas appear to have no base in the classical Marxist literature. For example, as against the Leninist conception of party as the vanguard of the proletariat and the state as an instrument of the dominant classes, Gorbachev supports Khruschev's interpretation of state as 'the state of all' and communist party as 'the party of all people'. In fact many of his ideas on contemporary international politics reminds one of the convergence theorists who express belief in the fusion of capitalist and socialist systems. Unlike Lenin, he makes all wars an anathema and prescribes 'peace' as precondition for settlement of all international problems. Not "antagonistic contradictions" but "peaceful competition" is his motto. In place of the Marxist dream of "the world communist movement" he argues for interdependent world system. To quote him, "the prevailing dialectics of present day development consists in combination of competition and confrontation between the two systems and in a growing tendency towards interdependence of the countries of the world community. This is precisely, the way, through which the struggle of opposites, through arduous effort, groping in the dark to some extent, as it were, that the controversial but interdependent and in many ways the integral world is taking shape".[22] From perestroika Gorbachev expects "freedom to reign supreme in the coming century everywhere in the world. We want people of every country to enjoy prosperity, welfare and happiness. The road to this lies through proceeding to a nuclear free, non-violent world".[23] Whereas the entire bourgeois world started hailing the humanist content of Gorbachev's theory and practice, the world communists find it very difficult to endorse Gorbachevism as the Leninism of the era of developed socialism.

With such developments occurring in China and the USSR, economic failures engendered serious crises in political hegemony of the socialist regimes of the East Europe. These East European countries which have experimented with the process of liberalisation long before China and Russia had thought of them, are now facing all the problems which are common to capitalist societies. When their neighbours are finding it difficult to solve the multitude of the internal problems, the Euro-Communists of the Western Europe, as usual, remain "international" and "national" in deeds. They reject Leninist conception of the party and the dictatorship of the proletariat and dream of an appropriate moment where they can pass over to socialism with democracy, a multiparty system, parliaments and representative institutions independent trade unions and freedom for opposition.

Marxism and the Third World

In more than any other field, inadequacies of Marxist analyses are clearly visible in comprehension of the nature and dynamics of the developing societies. Marx, Engels and Lenin wrote extensively on the impact of imperialism on the colonies and semi-colonies. All of them believed that the contradictions that imperialist penetration create within the colonies and semi-colonies will ultimately help the world socialist movement. Hence during their time, they encouraged national liberation struggles. However none of these giants were alive to see the process of decolonisation which ultimately gave birth to the Third World. Even for Stalin, it was too short a time to predict the role of newly independent nations. he thought that in spite of formal political independence, countries like India are bound to act as puppets of the former imperialists. For many years, the same idea held sway in China. Belief in the primacy of contradiction between imperialism and national liberation struggles drove Mao Tse-tung to become a champion of anti-imperialist struggles in the post-war world. Chinese theoreticians of the sixties believed that the economic and political conditions in all the developing societies were akin to the one that existed in China before revolution.[24] The position however changed after the 10th Congress of the CPC when China recognised the political independence of many developing countries. During the seventies, the Chinese coined the Three Worlds Theory where they reposed high faith in the revolutionary potentialities of the Third World.[25] But all these changes in their interpretations are not accompanied by production of factual data. In this respect, the intellectuals of U.S.S.R. are better positioned, in the sense that they undertook vigorous empirical research to understand the complexities of political and economic conditions in the underdevloped countries. However, like Khruschev,[26] they predict peaceful transition of these countries to socialism through people's or national democratic revolutions. Apart from Chinese and Soviet Marxists, there emerged the 'Dependency School' whose intellectuals[27] concentrated mainly on the relationship between the metropolis and the satellites. They being mostly economists, much attention was not given to the questions relating to the nature and dynamics of states in the Third World.

Though all these streams claim to follow the Marxist methodology their theories, in the main run parallel to one another. None of them acquired the dominant position to be able to disprove other competing versions. The social formations in the developing societies appear to be so complex that any generalisation of the nature of the state, dynamics of the classes and development of economy appears to be unwarranted. Under such circumstances the question as to how one should proceed to gain a correct understanding of the state in the Third World should be a concern of all those who are interested in developing Marxist framework for the developing world.

In Search of Marxist-Leninist Framework

In view of the multitude of questions that critics as well as the followers of Marxism raised on various aspects relating to the dynamics of the state in different social formations, a world-wide debate on the vital questions concerning Marxist theory of state becomes indispensable. Different trends in theory and practice that we could record so far gives us an impression that Marxism is a rigid theoretical framework which failed to cope with different changes witnessed in the post-war world. If Marxism is a dogma — as its critics would argue—it has to lose its validity like any other ideologies and philosophies. Now, if there are still people who consider Marxism as a scientific theory of state by answering all questions that the critics as well as the followers have raised all these years. To be able to meet the challenges that confront them, the contemporary Marxists should be in a position to update and enrich the treasure house of Marxism. In view of the absence of a ready-made Marxist theory of the post-war state, it is necessary to have a dialectical interaction among different Marxist theoreticians. It is sad to note that in the recent years, the so-called communist parties in India, for the sake of petty organisational interests, gave up the tasks of making independent theoretical enquiries into vital issues involved in the world communist movement. However, in the West many Marxist intellectuals and politicians came forward to defend marxism from all kinds of onslaughts. It is true that their reaction to the critics is not always based on scientific understanding. The debate at times gives birth to conflicting opinions, vulgar misinterpretations and unwanted confusions. Yet the importance of the debate should not be undermined. Knowledge cannot develop in isolation. It is out of dialectical interaction among different ideas and ideas with the material world that real knowledge about anything may be sought.

Keeping all these points in mind, an attempt is made in this book to introduce the contributions of contemporary Marxist intellectuals who have made sincere attempts to understand the dynamics of state in different social formations. With intention to give a comprehensive out look on the questions concerning the state, ruling class and economic development in different social formations, the book would critically evaluate the contributions of contemporary Marxist theoreticians like Ralph Miliband, Nicos Poulantzas, German Derivativists, Dependency theorists, the Russian Marxists and above all their new spokesman i.e., Gorbachev. While reviewing different interpretations their methodological fallacies and conceptual inadequacies are pointed out and possible alternatives explored. Such exercise is ultimately aimed at acquiring a correct understanding of state's relationship with economy and classes in this ever changing national and international conditions. While trying to examine the multidimensional role that the state plays, efforts are made to examine whether the state acts as an instrument of the dominant classes or acquiring an element of autonomy vis-a-vis the classes and the economic base. Questions relating to the form and content of the state and institutions and functions of the state organs are taken up in discussing various categories of state. The contradictory influences that economic development exerts on the dynamics of state and classes and the way they respond to the economic pressures are briefly analysed. All these tasks are undertaken by approaching, wherever felt essential, the classical Marxist literature on state, classes and economy.

Notes and References

1. Lenin, V.I., *Selected Works Vol III,* Progress Publishers, Moscow, 1977, p. 200.
2. Dahrendorf Ralf, *Class and Class Conflict in Industrial Society,* London, Routledge and Kegan Paul, 1976, p. 131.
3. Webb, Sydney, *Fabian Essays,* Boston, The Ball Publishing House, 1909, pp 42–43.
4. Hirsh Fred, *Social Limitations to Growth,* London, Routledge and Kegan Paul, 1977, p. 126.
5. Skidelsky, Robert in Crouch Colin, *State and Economy in Contemporary Capitalism,* London, Croomhelm, 1979, p. 65.
6. Lindblum,. C.E. *Policies and Markets,* New York, Basic Books, 1977, p. 124.
7. It should be mentioned that Marx spoke of relative immiserisation, not of absolute misery.
8. Gieger Theodor, quoted in Dahrendorf, *op.cit.,* p. 65.
9. Gay, Peter, *The Dilemma of Democratic Socialism ?* New York, Collier Books 1962, pp. 127-128.
10. Burnham, James, *The Managerial Revolution,* New York, 1941, p. 92.
11. *Ibid.*, p. 72.
12. Galbraith, J.K, *New Industrial Society,* Harmondsworth, Penguin Books, 1969, also Stratchey J., *Contemporary Capitalism*, New York, 1956.
13. Djilas, Milovan, *New Class: An analysis of the Communist System*, New York, Thames and Hudson, 1957, p. 38.
14. Dahrendorf, *op.cit.*, p. 48.
15. Philip Andre, *La Democratic Industrialle*, Paris, 1955, p.2.
16. Cf. Bhattacharya Sisir, *Social Darwinism in India's Welfare State*, Hyderabad, 1984, Chapter I.

17. Arghiri, Emmanuel, *Unequal Exchange*, Monthly Review Press 1972, pp. 182-183. Also refer, Bhattacharya Sisir, *op.cit.* pp. 10-12.
18. Dahrendorf, *op.cit.*, p.57.
19. Refer Richardson J.J.& Jordan U J, *Governing Under Pressure,* Martin Robertson, Oxford, 1979; Dahl R.A. *Who Governs,* New Heaven, Yale University Press, 1961 and also Latham E., *Group Basis of Politics*, Cornwell University Press, 1952.
20. Refer Middlemas, K. *Politics in Industrial Society*, Andre Deusch, London, 1979, Schmitter, P. "Still the Century of Corporatism?" *Review of Politics,* 36, 1974, Panitch, L, *"Recent Theorisation of Corporatism"*, *British Journal of Sociology*, 31 (2), 1980.
21. Middlemas, K., *op.cit.*, pp. 93-94.
22. Gorbachev, *Political Report of the CPSU (CC) to 27th Party Congress*, Novosty Agency, Moscow, 1986, p. 26.
23. Gorbachev, *Perestroika*, Collins, London. 1987, p.254
24. See News from Hsinhua News Agency, August 3, 1967, reproduced in Banarjee. Sumantha, *India's Simmering Revolution : The Naxalite Uprising*, Select Service Syndicate, New Delhi. 1984.
25. Editorial, *Peking Review*, No. 45, Nov. 4, 1977, Reproduced in Chen, *China and the Three Worlds*, Macmillan, Michigan, 1979, pp. 100-121
26. Khruschev, N.S., 'Report to the 20th Congress of the CPSU', February 1956; also his 'For New Victories of the World Communist Movement', *World Marxist Review*, No. 1, 1961, p.22
27. See Dos Santos, Theotonio, 'The Structure of Dependence', *American Economic Review*, 60, No. 2, May 1970, pp.231-236; Baran, Pual, *Political Economy of Growth*, New York, Monthly Review, Inc., 1957; Cordoso, F.H.& Faletto, E, *Dependency and Development in Latin America*, University of California Press, London, 1979; Frank, A.G., 'Dependency of Underdevelopment' in Rhodes, Roger, I. *Imperialism and Underdevelopment: A Reader*, MRP, 1970; and also his, *Lumpen Bourgeoisie and Lumpen Development*, MRP, New York, 1972.

Chapter II

STATE IN THE CAPITALIST SOCIETIES
Instrument or Independent?

In the first chapter, the arguments of different schools that have indeed become real challenges to the ideological validity of Marxism are discussed. It is unfortunate that though some of the works of Marx and Engels refer to politics and 'state', they do not give well formulated theory of the capitalist state, particularly of late capitalism, as they give of the capitalist economy. Lenin basing himself on Marx and Engels wrote *The State and Revolution* to expose the revisionist interpretations and to re-establish the need to destroy the exploitative class state. But the present work discusses very little about the specific character of the capitalist state. However, Lenin's some other works viz. *Imperialism the Highest Stage of Capitalism, Dictatorship of the Proletariat* and *Renegade Kautsky* and the pamphlets *On State, A Caricature of Marxism* and *Imperialist Economics* help one to understand the nature and dynamics of capitalist state in the era of imperialism. There was a long slumber after Lenin—the only exception being Gramsci's contribution—in the development of Marxist theory of state in capitalist societies. It is unfortunate that Stalin who made substantial theoretical contributions to certain fields, did not pay much attention to enrich Marxist theory of the capitalist state in the light of changed economic and political conditions of his days. After him, almost upto the seventies, the trend of looking at state as a mere tool in the hands of the ruling classes, a machine that can be manipulated by them at their will, prevailed the Marxist theory as the classical Marxist view of the state.

Although one may argue that in reality no great Marxist thinker starting from Marx to Mao, viewed state so mechanically, every student of Marxism comes across numerous expressions in the classical Marxist literature which gives an impression that the state is a simple tool in the hands of dominant classes. For example, as the famous statement in Manifesto of the Communist Party reads: "Each step in the development of the bourgeoisie was accompanied by a corresponding political advance of that class...the bourgeoisie has at last, since the establishment of modern industry and of the world market, conquered itself, in the modern representative state, exclusive political sway. The executive of the modern state is but a committee for managing the common affairs of the whole bourgeoisie".[1] In *The German Ideology* Marx and Engels assert that the state "is nothing more than the form of organisation which the bourgeoisie necessarily adopt both for internal and external purposes, for the mutual benefit and guarantee of their property and interests".[2] Engels in *The Origin of the Family, Private Property and the State* says "The state of antiquity was above all the state of the slave owners for the purpose of holding down slaves, as the feudal state was the organ of the nobility for holding down the peasant serfs and bondsmen and the modern representative state is an instrument of exploitation of wage labour by capital".[3] In his letter to Cuno, Engels writes, "State power is nothing more than the organisation which the ruling classes—land onwers and capitalists have provided for themselves in order to protect their social privileges."[4] One can find similar expression in Lenin's writings. To quote him from *The State and Revolution* : "According to Marx, the State is an organ of class rule, an organ for the suppression of one class by another, it is the creation of order, which legalises and perpetuates their oppression by moderating the conflict between the classes."[5] Elsewhere he says, "As long as there is private property, even if it is a democratic republic state is nothing but a machine used by capitalists to suppress the workers".[6] Such like expression, if read without taking into consideration the contexts in which these were made, would give an impression supporting the instrumentalist view of the state.

Whereas the above quotations seem to say that the state is a puppet of the ruling class, not enjoying any kind of independence, one may get puzzled to see the same thinkers talking elsewhere about the independence of the state. The ability of the state to dictate terms to the members of th ruling class was analysed by them. It is also found that they were aware of the situation in which the state had to give concessions to the working class as against the interests of the members of the dominant class. Marx in *The Eighteenth Brumaire of Louis Bonaparte* considered that the state which was once instrument of bourgeoisie later became independent of all classes. To quote him "Under the absolute monarchy, during the first Revolution, under Napoleon, bureaucracy was only the means of preparing the class rule of the bourgeoisie. Under restoration, under Louis Philippe, under the parliamentary republic, it was the instrument of the ruling classes, however it strove for the power of its own. Only under the second Bonaparte does the state seem to have made itself completely independent. As against civil society, the state machine has consolidated its position so thoroughly....".[7] Further "France therefore seems to have escaped the despotism of a class only to fall back beneath the despotism of an individual, and what is more, beneath the authority of an individual without authority. The struggle seems to be settled in such a way that all classes equally impotent and equally mute fall on their knees before the rifle butt".[8] But when does such a situation arise ? Engels answers: "By way of exceptions however periods occur in which the warring classes balance each other so nearly that the state power as ostensible mediator, acquires for the moment, a certain degree of independence of both. Such was the absolute monarchy of 17th and 18th centuries, which held the balance between the nobility and the class of burghers. Such was the Bonapartism of the first and still more of the second French Empire, which played off the proletariat against the bourgeoisie and the bourgeoisie against the proletariat. The latest performance of this kind, in which the ruler and the ruled appear equally ridiculous is the German empire of Bismarck nation : here capitalists and the workers are balanced against each other and equally cheated for the benefit of the impoverished Prussian cabbage junkers".[9] But Marx maintains that the phenomenon of Bonapartism is common in all countries where the bourgeoisie has lost its power of ruling and the proletariat has not yet achieved the power.[10] All these reveal that the relative autonomy is not peculiar to exceptional situations. To quote him again from *Critique of the Gotha Programme*, "It is by no means the aim of the workers to set the state free.... Taken in its grammatical sense, a free state is one where the state is free in relation to its citizens, hence a state with a despotic government... today too, the forms of state are more or less free to the extent that they restrict the freedom of the state."[11] What do these statements actually mean?

One may get confused reading two diametrically opposite views expressed by the same thinkers. Their answers seem to pose more questions than what they answer. What is correct : Is the state simply a tool of the ruling class ? Can it be independent of all classes? Is such 'independence' or 'freedom' of the state a general phenomennon or the product of few exceptional conditions, the disappearance of which again makes the state an instrument of the ruling class ? Can any reconciliation between these two extreme assertions be achieved? These important issues were not seriously examined by the Marxist thinkers of the earlier generations. But the debate that was initiated in the West during the late sixties and early seventies of this century sought to fill the gaps in earlier interpretations of Marxism. Initially major attempts to present the instrumentalist view of the capitalist state and to reestablish the validity of class theory of state even in the present era of modified capitalism were made by Ralph Miliband. His first Book on this subject, *The State in Capitalist Society*, published in 1969 attracted many Marxist thinkers. it regenerated interest in the hitherto neglected area of study. He was then supported and followed by many commentators in Britain and the U.S.A. But in course of time his views and approach came to be criticised by many Marxian thinkers and many more new interpretations have come to surpass Miliband's contributions. An analytical and critical evaluation of his works and approach may be a starting point for scholars interested in understanding the nature and the dynamics of the modern capitalist state.

Miliband's approach to the study of the Capitalist State

Many scholars [12] called the approach of Miliband as 'Instrumentalist' as if he considered the state as a simple tool that can be manipulated by the ruling class. In reality, Miliband did not see things so mechanically and he also accepted autonomous role of the capitalist state even in his first book *The State in Capitalist Society* and more so in his *The Capitalist State in Britain*. In view of the complexities involved in his intereprtation, before one attmepts to understand his methodological approach.

Miliband in his first book, *The State in Capitalist Society* undertakes an empirical study of six advanced capitalist countries and based on the facts gathered he refutes and exposes bourgeois criticism and the hollowness of their theories of state and politics. The method he adopts to assert the validity of the marxist view of the state precisely consists of the following steps :

1. To establish the existence of the ruling classes and then understand their interests and power.

2. To understand the nature and dynamics of state and government and then

3. To study the concrete mechanism that got established between the state elite and the members of the ruling class, thus making the state a class state, not the state of all people.

Marx in his *Critique of the Gotha Programme* observes 'the present day state changes with a country's frontier. It is different in Prusso-German empire from what it is in the U.S. The present day state is therefore a fiction .....Nevertheless, the different states of different civilised countries, in spite of their motley diversity of form, have this in common, that they are based on modern bourgeois society, only one more or less capitalistically developed. They have therefore also certain essential characteristics in common. In this sense it is possible to speak of the present day state, in contrast with the future in which the present roof will have died off".[13] Miliband seems to follow this sequence in his approach. Though he starts with an observation that each of the advanced capitalist countries has its peculiar features, he asserts that despite that diversity there exists certain similarities among the advanced capitalist countries. All these societies have technologically advanced economic base with industrial production taking superior position when compared to agriculture. Here the main part of the economic activity is performed on the basis of private ownership, and control of means of production. They also have public sector owning a wide range of industries and services, and this sector acts as the largest customer of private sector. In all these societies, the state increasingly intervenes in economy by means of regulation, control, coordination and planning. Such increasing intervention of the state, in spite of its assurance given to the small capitalists, accelerates the domination of economy by the giant trusts[14]. It is precisely based on these similarities that Miliband considers it possible to study the nature of the state, dynamics of the classes and their relation to the state elite.

Existence of the Classes :

Miliband then proceeds to show us that in all such industrialised capitalist countries there exist groups of people occupying different positions constituting themselves as different classes. The important of all classes include the working class, the capitalist class and the petty bourgeoisie. He proposes certain variables necessary for the objective determination of different classes.

Miliband argues that a crucial notion for the determination of working class according to Marx is that of productive work. The productive worker is one who produces surplus value. To quote Miliband, "As far as classical Marxism is concerned, the working class is basically constituted by industrial wage earners, factory workers, the modern proletariat".[15] However, Miliband extends this definition to include even mental labourer who gets exploited by those who employ him. But in this category he avoids including managerial staff, white collar workers, executive personnel of higher ranks. Here introducting the criterion of subordination, Miliband gives his own definition of the working class. As he says, "The working class is therefore that part of the collective labour which produces surplus value, from a position of subordination, at the lower ends of the income scale and also at the lower ends of what might be called the "scale of regard."[16]

Similarly, Miliband admitting that he uses the words 'capitalist class' and 'bourgeoisie' inter-exchangeably, defines capitalist class as "the class which for Marx, was so designated by virtue of the fact that it owned and controlled the means of production and economic activity as general, the great manufacturing, financial and commercial interests of capitalist enterprises."[17]

In all western capitalist countries one can find a vast number of the workers and a small number of capitalists. Along with them, there exists the middle class which consists of professionals, small manufacturers, artisans, artists and small peasants.[18] Miliband, like Marx, argues that class consciousness is necessary for each class to become a class for itself. He believes that classes become class conscious in course of their struggle with other classes. Groups of people may exist as potential classes in spite of the absence of class consciousness among their individual members.

Supremacy of the Ruling Class

After stating that there are classes in the advanced western states Miliband undertakes the job of attacking the pluralists who consider that in these western societies both labour and capital are equally powerful and hence no one class can permanently influence the other or the state. To the pluralists, all western democratic countries are pluralist societies which do not have any ruling class. Miliband shows the hollowness of their arguments by proving empirically that a wide gulf exists between the capitalist and workers due to difference in their economic positions and this in turn leads to variations in the ability of the weaker classes to influence the state. Miliband shows that in all these countries the income and wealth of the capitalists continue to rise. In Britain 1 per cent of the population owned 42 per cent of personal wealth in 1960, 5 per cent owned 75 per cent and 10 per cent of population owned 83 per cent. In U.S.A. 2 per cent of American families in 1953 accrued 29 per cent and that 1 per cent of adults owned 76 per cent of corporate stock.[19] Its superior economic strength makes the capitalist class act as a powerful pressure group influencing the governmental policy at all levels. Commenting on the way that business can influence parliaments he says "business and other propertied interests have immeasurably greater resource than any other interest to shape the legislative mind and will and to influence the legislative process. The pressure may be direct and personal and it may take a multitude of forms or it may be exercised *via* public opinion by means of grass roots campaign".[20] Miliband also speaks of the capitalist's personal ties with the ministers, civil servants and other important members of the state elite. He stresses on the monetary contribution that capitalist makes to the conservative and even social democratic parties in order to influence their mode of operation in favour of private property. So powerful are the demands of capitalism that the capitalists interests are sold as national interests. Because of its superior position in economy capitalist class gets power to influence ideological institutions—churches, educational institutions, press, media, parties and sometimes even trade unions. By using them capitalist class spreads the ethos and values that confirm to the protection and promotion of the capitalist interests. Lack of knowledge and ability, on the part of the workers makes the competition imperfect and unequal.

In his first book *The State in Capitalist Society*, he calls the capitalist class as the ruling class. One can observe it when Miliband says, "In the Marxist scheme, the ruling class of capitalist society is that class which owns and controls the means of production and which is able by virtue of economic power thus conferred upon, to use the state as an instrument for the domination of society".[21]However, in his next book,

Marxism and Politics, he expands the definition of the ruling class and "includes many people who fulfil specific professional and other functions on behalf of these 'interests' and who are in various ways—by virtue of income, status, occupation, kinship *etc*. associated with them".[22]

In a society where the ruling class exists, the subordinate and intermediary classes in these regimes are forced to accept the existing social order and confine themselves within its limits. In view of this, all talks of democracy, pluralism, meritocracy in reality, becomes a hoax. To quote him, ". . . it has remained a basic fact of life in advanced capitalist countries that the vast majority of men and women in these countries have been governed, represented, administered, judged and commanded in by people drawn from other economically and socially superior and relatively distinct class".[23]

Against Managerialism

Miliband's definition of the ruling class naturally drives him to answer managerial theorists who believe in the predominant role of managerial class in the so-called post-capitalist societies. In reality the tendency to separate control from ownership was viewed by Marx long ago. In his *Capital Vol.III* he notes that the stock companies in general "have an increasing tendency to separate this work of capital... the mere manager who has no title whatsoever to capital whether through borrowing it or otherwise, perfroms all the real functions pertaining to the functioning of capitalist, only the functionary remains, and the capitalist disappears as superfluous from the production process".[24] Later, Lenin very clearly spoke about the emergence of financial oligarchy, that the powerful fraction of the capitalist class divorced from production processing on interest secured from the accumulated finance capital.[25] Thus the extreme tendency of separation of ownership from management was first explained by the Marxists; not by any managerialist.

Marx never considered that capitalist entrepreneur in any real sense controlled the economy as a whole, except in a secondary sense.[26] According to Marxism, it makes little difference whether ownership and control are united or separated. What are important in Marx's analyses of capitalism of attacking the managerialist view from that angle, Miliband undertakes to counter the argument with empirical data by showing that :

1) most of the managers are also big or small shareholders within the industry;

2) most of them come from elitist background with little scope for the members from the bottom to join this class;

3) just like the capitalist, the manager is motivated by the desire to secure highest possible profits and it is owing to the selfishness inherent in the capitalist mode of production itself; and

4) even if there exists difference between the managers and the capitalists, they are only tactical in nature and are generally overshadowed by a basic community of interests.

Miliband attempts to prove his assertions with empirical data. He points out that control and ownership of one hundred and fifty out of five hundred largest corporations in the U.S.A. are in the hands of individuals or the members of a single family and approximately seventy family named companies are still controlled by the founding families.[27] On the basis of other studies, he shows that managers are often shareholders in their enterprises and hence the so-called separation of manager from the means of production is not altogether valid.[28] Then he argues that the managers in their administration aim to gain the highest possible profits for their enterprises. These highly paid salaried sections educated at public schools are drawn in the main from the upper middle class and upper class families and have thus respective fathers in business concerns.[29] After submitting such necessary facts and figures, Miliband comes to the conclusion that there is no good reason to accept the validity of the thesis that the advanced capitalism produced a 'new class' which is radically distinct from the capitalist onwers.

Though the facts supplied by Miliband are correct it is doubtful if this is really the Marxist method of refuting the theory of 'managerialism' Miliband himself remarks that managing the industries for securing maximum profits is not a matter of selfishness in the soul of entrepreneur or manager or rather that selfishness inherent in the capitalist mode of production and policy decision that it dictates.[30] But he neglects to study the dynamics of the capitalist mode of production which necessitated separation of control from ownership. Do they make any significant differences or changes in the system if they are not motivated by profit considerations ? Moreover his stress on the relations between the capitalist-manager and the workers in the changed conditions. Here worth mentioning are the views of Harry Braverman. Braverman in his book *Labour and Monopoly Capital* shows that the so-called scientific management "is an attempt to apply the methods of science to the increasingly complex problem of the control of labour in rapidly growing capitalist enterprises".[31] Braverman holds that management leads to the organised study of work, division of work into its simplest elements and synthetic improvements of the workers performance of each of these elements. The principle of managers assuming the entire burden or gathering together of all traditional knowledge dissociates labour process from the skills of workers. Also, the centralisation of the mental work in the planning leads to dehumanisation of the labour process by reducing the workers to the level of mindless automations or animals. In such a system the workers not only lose control over instruments of production but also lose hold over their own labour in further promoting the interests of capital.

State Elites and Servants of Government

According to Miliband the state stands for a number of particular institutions which constitutes its reality. The institutions of the state system include government, bureaucracy, military, police, judiciary, sub-central government and parliamentary assemblies. The state power lies in these institutions and this power is exercised by the elites who occupy superior position in various branches of the state machinery.[32] This superior power controls even the ideological institutions. Having identified the state and then the state elite running the state machinery, Miliband considers that for the purpose of analysing the role of the state, it is necessary to understand the nature of the state elite that wields the state power as a distinct and separate entity.

To counter the bourgeois theory that the state is an independent and impartial authority and then to prove that the state and its institutions are only the allies of capital committed to maintain and defend the structure of power and privilege inherent in the system-Miliband again follows empiricist method. He examines power elites in different state organs and then comes to certain general conclusions. They include : (1) most of the officials in the army, bureaucracy and judiciary occupying important positions are drawn from business and other propertied professional classes and hence they are generally committed to bourgeoisie values and beliefs. They will be conservative in their outlook and behaviour. The state takes much precautions in recruiting to the sensitive posts only those elites who conform to the value bias of the existing system; (2) because of these aspects, the state elites cannot work as neutral parties especially when they are to deal with conflicting interests of the capital and labour. When such a situation arises they openly act on behalf of the interests of the propertied classes. Miliband quotes different sources supporting his claims that—"Officialdom, whether civil or military is hardly neutral", it speaks and inevitably it speaks as an advocate of private property. Also, "it is difficult for the judges to put an impartial position between different disputants, one, of your own class and one not of your class".[33] These statements are supported by Miliband with concrete facts. Due to the inferior position that the working class occupies in economy, social status, education and experience, it cannot effectively influence the state policy for promoting its own interests. (3) Similarly, the governments of these countries are mostly composed of men who entertain belief in the validity and virtues of the capitalist system. Even if they hail from the working class they consciously or unconsciously act in such a way that their role ultimately go in favour of the interests of capitalism. Generally, the majority in parliament is constituted by representatives who are conservatives. Nowadays the bourgeois parties developed as conscious vanguard of the class they represent. They serve more effectively the interests of the bourgeoisie than communist parties of many countries could do as vanguards of the working class.[34] When there is a crisis in the system, the social democratic parties do come to power with revolutionary slogans. But once they come to power and form the government they become moderates and begin to take up the activities which bring some kind of compromise between labour and capital. Their own dependence on capitalists forbids them from taking any revolutionary step which can go against the interests of all the private property owners. They take up only the activities acceptable to the capitalist class. Various activities that it undertakes in the name of national interest ultimately benefit the capitalists. Since their conception of national interest is inextricably lined with the fortunes of capitalist enterprise. Even if communist parties come to power at the centre or at local level in coalition with such social democratic parties, this arrangement yields no radical results except further legitimacy to the capitalist system.[35] (4) Miliband also speaks of the growing state intervention in the economy, which is giving an impression that the state can work in the interests of the workers, at times even against the wishes of the members of the capitalist class. Miliband attempting to expose the myth of interventionist state explains that the bureaucratic intervention is meant to alleviate the evils produced by unrestricted private economic power. Even the laws made for the protection of labour conditions, establishment of labour courts, *etc*., are the conditions necessary for the smooth working of the capitalists systems. Speaking of the governmental intervention in industrial conflicts Miliband writes, "They enter that conflict in the guise of a neutral independent party concerned to achieve not the outright defeat of one side or the other, but a reasonable settlement between them. But the state intervention in negotiation occurs in the shadow of its known and declared propensities to invoke its power of cocercion, against workers, if conciliation procedures fail".[36] Other than the necessity to check the workers, the capitalists depend on the state for subsidies markets and other bounties. To quote Miliband, "State intervention in economic life in fact largely means intervention for the purpose of helping capitalist enterprise.. In no field has the notion of welfare state had a precise and opposite meaning than here, there are no more persistent and successful applicants for public assistance than the proud giants of private enterprise system".[37]

Miliband further observes that with the ever increasing state intervention, bureaucrats and technocrats come closer to businessmen, financiers and industrialists. Wherever there exist private, public and mixed sectors side by side, exchange of managers from one sector to another becomes a common phenomenon. At times managers of private sectors are invited to head the public sectors. Like C. Wright Mills, Miliband considers that with the growing importance of the military and consequent militarisation of economy industrial-military-bureaucratic complexes appeared in all advanced capitalist countries bringing big business and top military officials together.[38] In such countries even nationalisation and welfare measures are undertaken only so long they do not pose any kind of threat to the dominant classes. Miliband clearly writes;"civil servants concerned with economic decision making intervention and regulation can ill afford to ignore the fact that attitudes and actions which are capable of being construed as 'anti business' are bound to antagonise powerful and influential people and are not likely to be particularly popular with political office holders".[39]

All these observations are the inferences from facts of life. Such inter-personal relations between the state officials and businessmen were exposed by the classical Marxists also. Engels in his mature work, *The Origins of the Family, Private Property and the State*, observes that in the democratic republics the wealth exercises its power indirectly but effectively. "On the one hand in the form of direct corruption of officials of which America provides the classical example, on the other hand in the form of an alliance between government and stock exchange".[40] Lenin in his *State and Revolution*, explaining the days of honeymoon of the Mensheviks with the bourgeoisie in the coalition government points out how Mr. Palchinsky acted as the representative of the bourgeoisie in the cabinet for a reward of 1,20,000 roubles per annum.[41]

But the matter may not be that simple. Lenin himself points out ideological outlook of the state elites and their personal relations with the businessman are not sufficient to call any state as the bourgeoisie state. Supposing the state apparatus and the governmental positions are filled by men drawn from working classes or the communist parties committed to the cause to working class, does the character of the capitalist state change simply by this feature? If the governmental officials refuse to be guided by the capitalists, does the state cease to be the state of the capitalists? Lenin answers "A democratic republic is the best possible political shell; it establishes its power so securely, so firmly that no exchange of persons, institutions and parties in bourgeois democratic republic can shake it".[42] Nicos Poulantzas says in a different language -—"The relation between the bourgeois class and the state is an objective relation... if the function of the state in a determinate social formation and the interests of the ruling class in their formation coincide, it is by reason of the system itself; the direct participation of the members of the ruling class in the state apparatus is not the effect... of this objective coincidence".[43]

Question of 'Relative Autonomy of the Capitalist State'

Though Miliband gives an account of Marx's view of independence of the Bonapartist state in his first book *The State in Capitalist Society* itself,[44] his method of treatment regarding the problems of the capitalist state, as explained above, gives an impression that personal connection between the state elite and the ruling classes make the state a puppet which cannot enjoy any kind of exceptional forms of state such as those of the Bonapartism and Fascism.[45] While answering to the criticism of Poulantzas, Miliband clarifies that he also subscribes to the idea of relative autonomy of the capitalist state and that according to him the fascist state was only the extreme case of relative autonomy of the state.[46] Though it appears that both of them subscribe to the idea of relative autonomy of the capitalist state, Miliband's subsequent contributions—*Poulantzas and the Capitalist State (1973), Marxism and Politics (1977),* and *Capitalist Democracy in Britain* (1982) show that he differs from Poulantzas in his treatment and analyses of Bonapartism and Fascism on the basis of which both of them studied the aspect of relative autonomy.

Miliband says that Marx and Engels gave considerable importance to the relative autonomy of the state in exceptional circumstances. This aspect was neglected by the Marxists who followed Marx. Referring to Marx's famous statement in the *Manifesto of the Communist Party*, that "the executive of the modern state is a committee for managing the common affairs of the bourgeoisie", Miliband cautions that it should not lead one to the conclusion that the state is a mere tool in the hands of the ruling class. The state is no doubt a class state but it does not always act at the behest of the class. In fact, in order to be a class state it should enjoy a degree of autonomy from the ruling classes.[47] Miliband in his book *The State in Capitalist Society* itself notes that the capitalist class is not a homogeneous class and that it includes within it different factions-monopolist, non-monopoly and small scale sectors—all involved in a bitter competition for supremacy. Yet he says—"Business, it could be said, is tactically divided but strategically cohesive, over most of the larger issues of economic policy and over other large national issues as well, it may be expected to present a reasonably united front".[48] But one can observe loss of faith in his book *Marxism and Politics*, wherein he finds the necessity of state to mediate and reconcile the factional interests. To quote him "in so far as that class is not monolithic and it never is, it cannot act as an agent, and it cannot simply use the state as its instrument. In this context there is no'it' capable of issuing coherent instructions".[49] Hence the relative autonomy of the capitalist state. According to Miliband relative autonomy refers to the degree of freedom which the state (there the state is seen merely as an executive power) has in determining how best to serve what those who hold power conceive to be national interest and, which in fact involves the service of the interests of the ruling class.[50] The degree of relative autonomy is in direct relation to the freedom which the executive power and the state in general enjoy vis-a-vis the civil society. The relative autonomy is more in societies where the executive power is less checked either by the elements within the state system or the forces of civil society for example, institutions and the pressure groups of both the dominant and subordinate classes.[51] Relative autonomy is a characteristic feature of all forms of capitalist societies, more so in dictatorial forms. Such relative autonomy is to be understood by differentiating class power and state power and then focussing on the forces and circumstances which make it to be more or less.[52]

Miliband's view of Bonapartism and Fascism

As against the view of Poulantzas who holds the Bonapartism is the religion of the bourgeoisie, Miliband considers it to be only an exceptional form of state. "Bonapartism", he says, "is not the religion of the bourgeoisie at all—it is its last resort in conditions of political instability so great as to present a threat to the maintenance of the domination which is the central part of the order".[53] According to Miliband, Bonapartist state is characterised by extreme inflation and concentration of executive power personified in one individual. The executive power is backed by immense bureaucratic and military organisation. The power and authority of the legislature are eroded. Such a state stiffles and suppresses the life of civil society and compels "all classes fall on their knees, equally mute and equally impotent, before the rifle butt".[54]

The state however, is not a supraclass state. As Marx states, "the state power does not hover in the mid air".[55] Miliband quotes from Marx to prove that the Bonapartist state enjoying a considerable degree of independence is only the state of the bourgeoisie. Indeed one can observe such an expression in Marx's *The Civil War in France*: "...... after their one heroic exploit of June, the bourgeois Republicans had to fall back to the near of the 'Party of order' —a combination formed by all rival fractions and factions of the appropriating class in their now openly declared antagonism to the producing classes. The proper form of their joint stock government was "the parliamentary republic, with Louis Bonaparte for its President".[56]

Again Miliband quotes Marx :

"The restraints by which their own divisions had under former regimes still checked the state power, were removed by their union, and in view of the threatening upheaval of the proletariat, they now used that state power mercilessly and ostentatiously as the national war engine of capital against labour".[57]

Based on these and other views expressed by Marx and Engels, Miliband concludes that the Bonapartist state in spite of its high degree of independence is only a class state.

To Miliband, Fascism and Nazism are only the extreme forms of Bonapartism. The fascist state like the Bonapartist state, Miliband asserts, is the state of bourgeoisie. Even in his first book, *The State in Capitalist Society*, Miliband analyses the philosophy and practice of the fascist state and shows how this exceptional phenomenon could help the bourgeoisie in spite of its rhetoric of total transformation of the society. Miliband shows from Mussolini's speech and Hitler's programme of 1933 that the fascist state respects private property and the state intervenes only to protect the weak, inefficient and unorganised sectors posing danger to the survival of the system.[58] The data produced by him show that between 1933 and 1936 in Germany the net profits of the capitalists rose by 433 per cent while the wages remained static and even fell slightly. The average income of the tax payers, managerial and entrepreneurial business rose by 46 per cent between 1934 and 1940. Fascist state nationalised labour and hired it out to capital at cheaper rates. During the war period, it could mobilise millions of slave labourers of occupied territories for promoting the German industries.[59]

In spite of all the benefits it could provide to strengthen the capitalist system, one should not conclude the fascist state is a simple tool used by the German bourgeoisie. The fascist state is a greater degree of independence from the bourgeois class, and the business under fascism had to submit to a far greater degree of state intervention than it liked. Officials in the fascist state were drawn from the middle classes and they could not be used by the class as it wished. Miliband syas, "the dictators while working to safeguard the capitalist order were extremely well placed to determine on their own, how they would do so and to take decisions of crucial national importance quite independently."[60] In such a system though "the capitalists were benefited, they had to pay a high political price for the immense advantages which were conferred upon them by the fascist regimes. For, while they retained many powerful positions and influence, they had to submit to a dictator over which they had no genuine control. Having helped the dictators to rob all other classes, they found their own drastically curtailed and in some crucial areas, notably foreign policy altogether nullified".[61]

Though Miliband's analysis of Bonarpatism seems to explain the phenomenon logically, much more clarity is necessary to tackle the inadequacies created by Marx and Engels' writings about the Bonapartist state. How can the supremacy of Bonaparte who "represents a class, and the most numerous class of French society at that, the small holding peasants[62]" over the "party of order" leads to the conclusion that the state became independent of classes? How do contradictions between the declining legislative power and the expanding executive authority within the state machine be justified to assert that the state is independent of civil society? How can this view of relative autonomy of the state be reconciled with the 'equilibrium of classes' or 'impotency of all classes to rule' which Marx and Engels speak of? Miliband's answers to these questions are inadequate. One finds in *The Eighteenth Brumaire of Louis Bonaparte* that Marx at times uses the state power and the executive power interexchangeably. As a matter of fact, the executive or government, whatever be its form is only a branch of the state apparatus. In the Bonapartist state the executive assumes a dominant role. The government which should run the day to day affairs of the state by handling various contradictions within the civil society and discharge its duties properly needs to be independent of various social forces. This independence of government or executive should not be identified with independence of the state as such.

Even after accepting that the relative autonomy is a characteristic feature of all forms of capitalist state, one may doubt the validity of identifying fascism with the Bonapartist state. Marxist understanding demands concrete analysis of the concrete conditions. Is there no difference in social, political and economic conditions between the Bonapartist state of the era of *laissez-faire* and the fascist state of the era of imperialism and proletarian revolutions? Can the problems of capital accumulation, the birth of state monopoly capitalism, the state's increasing role in ideological spheres, historical background of Italy and Germany, different class forces in their interactions and the peculiarities of fascist party and its ideology be ignored in the Marxist analysis of the fascist state ?

Conclusion

Miliband's style is simple, lucid and very impressive. He very effectively puts forward his own views and supplements his thesis with empirical data. By his empiricist method, he exposes the hollowness of the bourgeois theories of pluralism, managerialism and welfare state. He takes the criticism of bourgeois commentators seriously and makes sincere attempts to understand the nature and dynamics of the state in capitalist society.

The influence of his works has created much impact on most of the intellectuals in England and in the U.S.A. His method was used by many scholars to fight the bourgeois conceptions and to establish the reality of the class character of the state. For example, William Domhoff in his *State and Ruling Class in Corporate America*, very effectively throws light on the mechanisms by which corporate sectors influence the public view, political view and thereby policy making process itself. In India also the works of Sanjeeb Mukherji's *The Bourgeoisie and the State in India*, Debesh Roy Chowdhary's *The Role and Character of the Indian State* and Babulal Fadia's *The Pressure Groups in Indian Politics* seem to run on these lines.

A few more comments may be made. Though Miliband did not mention the name of Bukharin in his first book *The State in Capitalist Society*, the method and content of the book seems to be a sophisticated improvement of Bukharin's approach and views about the capitalist state as given in his book *ABC's of Communism*. Empirical investigation is not alien to Marxism and it is better for the materialist dialecticians not to look at things at high levels of abstractions. Marx, Engels and Lenin provided rich empirical proofs to support all their arguments. However, shortcoming in Miliband's *The State in Capitalist Society* is that he is silent at the level of theory and he uses empirical data without adopting Marxist problematic. One can indeed observe at empirical level the personal relations between the state elite and the ruling class members. But this proof is not enough to call any state a class state. What is important is to understand the internal necessity of the external dimensions within the system. Miliband does not investigate what is beneath the surface of the capitalist system. His identification of the Bonapartist state of the competitive era of imperialism and proletarian revolutions, for the reasons noted above appears unscientific. He ignores the impact of the capitalist mode of production and its problem of capitalist accumulation and markets on the nature, form and function of the capitalist state. Ironically in his "Introduction" to *Marxism and Politics* criticizing fragmented study as alien to Marxism he says—"The notion of economics as free from politics is an ideological abstraction and distortion".[63] It is indeed true. But what Miliband ignored was that similar expressions should have been made even to the notion of politics as free from economics.

In spite of these drawbacks, Miliband needs to be appreciated for initiating the debate which in course of time regenerated interest among many scholars giving birth to plenty of rich literature which attempted to uphold the relevance of Marxian philosophy which was then under a seize from all sides by the bourgeois conceptions and interpretations as described in the preceding chapter.

Notes and References

1. Marx ,Karl & Engels, Frederick, *Selected Works Vol.I*, Progress Publishers, Moscow, 1976, pp 110-11.
2. Marx, Karl and Engels, *Ibid.*, p.77.
3. Engels, Frederick, *The Origins of the Family, Private Property and the State*, Progress Publishers, Moscow, 1977, pp 168-69.
4. Marx and Engels, *Selected Works Vol.III,* Progress Publishers, 1977, p.425.
5. Lenin V, *Selected Works Vol.II*, Progress Publishers, Moscow, 1977, p.242.
6. Lenin, V. *The State- A Lecture at the Sverdlov University 1919*, Progress Publishers, Moscow, 1973, p.21.
7. Marx and Engels, *Selected Works Vol. III* Progress Publishers, Moscow, 1976, pp 477-78.
8. Marx and Engels, *Ibid.*, p. 476.
9. Engels, *The Origins of the Family, Private Property and the State,* Progress Publishers, Moscow, 1977, pp.168-69.
10. Marx, Karl, *The First International and After in Political Writings Vol.3* London, Pelican, 1974, p.208.
11. Marx, Karl, *Critique of the Gotha Programme*, Progress Publishers, Moscow, 1978, pp 25,35.
12. See Wright E.O. "Class Struggle and the Capitalist State" in Qinney Richard, *The Capitalist Society*, Illinois, The Dorsey Press, 1979, p.288, Also Ham Christopher and Hill Michael, *The Policy Process in the Modern Capitalist State*, Harvester Press, 1984, p.33.
13 Marx, Karl, *Critique of the Gotha Programme,* Progress Publishers, Moscow, 1978, pp.25-26.
14. Miliband,Ralph, *The State in Capitalist Society*, Weidenfeld and Nicholson, 1970, p.13.
15. Miliband, *Marxism and Politics*, Oxford University Press, 1978, p.25.
16. Miliband, *Ibid.*, p.24.
17. Miliband, *Ibid.*, p.26.
18. Miliband, *op.cit.*, p.17.
19. Miliband, *Ibid.*, pp.25-26.

20. Miliband, *Ibid.*, p.169.
21. Miliband, *Ibid.*, p, 23.
22. Miliband, *Marxism and Politics, op.cit.*, p.26.
23. Miliband, *The State in Capitalist Society, op.cit.*, p.62.
24. Marx, Karl, *Capital Vol. III*, Progress Publishers, Moscow, 1977, pp.387-88.
25. Lenin V, *Imperialism the Highest Stage of Capitalism*, Progress Publishers, Moscow, 1978, p.57.
26. Blackburn, Robin, *Ideology in Social Sciences*, Fontana. Collins, 1972, p. 168.
27. Miliband, *The State in Capitalist Society, op.cit.*, p.30.
28. *Ibid.*, p. 36.
29. *Ibid.*, p. 37.
30. *Ibid.*, p.34.
31. Braverman, Harry, *Labour and Monopoly Capital*, Monthly Review press, 1974, p.85.
32. Miliband, *The State in Capitalist Society, op.cit.*, p.54.
33. *Ibid.*, p.141.
34. *Ibid.*, p. 152.
35. *Ibid.*, p.97.
36. *Ibid.*, p.80.
37 *Ibid.*, p. 78
38. *Ibid.*, p.131; see also Mills C.W. *The Power Elite*, Oxford University Press, 1977, pp. 275-76.
39. Miliband, *Ibid.*, p. 128.
40. Engels, *The Origins of Family, Private Property and the State*, Progress Publishers, Moscow, 1977, p.169.
41. Lenin, *Selected Works Vol. II*, Progress Publishers, Moscow, 1977, p. 246.
42. Lenin, *Ibid.*, p. 247.
43 Poulntzas, Nicos, *The Problem of the Capitalist State* in Blackburn Robin *op.cit.*, p. 245.
44. See Miliband, *The Capitalist Society, op.cit.*, p. 93.
45. Poulantzas, *Problem of Capitalist State* in Blackburn Robin *op.cit.*, p.247.
46. Miliband, *Captalist State - A Reply to Nicos Poulantzas* in Blackburn. *op.cit.*, p. 260.
47. Miliband, *Marxism and Politics,* Oxford University Press, 1978, p.67.
48. Miliband, *The State in Capitalist Society, op.cit.*, p. 67-68.
49. Miliband, *Marxism and Politics, op.cit.*,
50. Miliband, *Ibid.*, p. 83.
51. Miliband, *Ibid.*, p.84.
52. Miliband, *Poulantzas and Capitalist State*, New Left Review, No, 182, 1973, p.2.
53. Miliband *Ibid.*, p.88.
54. Miliband, *Marxism and Politics*, *op.cit* p.77.
55. Marx and Engels, *Selected Works Vol.I* Progress Publishers, Moscow, 1976, p. 4478.
56 Marx and Engels, *Selected Works, Vol.II* Progress Publishers, Moscow, 1977, p.218.
57. *Ibid.*, p. 218-219.
58. Miliband, *The State in Capitalist Society, op.cit.*, pp.88-89.
59. *Ibid.* pp. 90-91.

60 *Ibid.*, p.94.
61. *Ibid.*, p.93.
62. Marx and Engels, *Selected Works Vol. I, op.cit*. p.478.
63. Miliband, *Marxism and Politics, op.cit.*, p.6.

Chapter III

CAPITALIST STATE, POLITICS AND CLASS STRUGGLES

Structures vs. Praxis

While analysing Miliband's contribution to the theory of state in the preceding chapter, we observed that the question of relative autonomy of the capitalist state should not be reduced to the interpersonal relationship between the state elite and the members of the capitalist class. Marx's materialist conception of history looks at the state as a superstructure formed on the given base. Hence understanding of the dialectical relationship between the base and superstructure is of utmost importance for all those who want to study the nature and dynamics of the capitalist state.

According to Marx and Engels what distinguishes men from animals is their capacity to produce their means of subsistence. Marx in his *Preface to a Contribution to the Critique of Political Economy* writes, "In the social production of their existence men inevitably enter into definite relations which are independent of their will, namely relations of production appropriate to a given stage of their material forces of production. The totality of these relations of production constitute the economic structure, the real foundation on which arise a legal and political structure and to which correspond definite forms of social consciousness".[1] But what and how the men produce are determined by the material conditions. "The way in which men produce their means of production depends primarily on the nature of the actual means of subsistence that find in existence and have to produce".[2] By these one can derive that the method of production refers to economic structure and it includes relations of production and productive forces with a motive force of production. The mode of production is something which exists, it is not merely a theoretical tool introduced by Marx and Engels to understand the social structure. Engels says in *Anti Duhring*, "there could be no question of building the laws of dialectics into nature, but of discovering them in it and evolving from it".[3] The same could be said of the mode of production.

The significance of the mode of production is described by Marx in *The German Ideology*: "this mode of production must not be considered simply as being the reproduction of the physical existence of the individuals. Rather it is a definite form of expressing their life, a definite mode of life on their part. As individuals express their life, so they are. What they are therefore coincides with what they produce and how they produce. The nature of individuals thus depends on the material conditions determining their production".[4] Further, the mode of production of material life conditions the general process of social, political and intellectual life. In fact, it is on this base, as its by-product arises the entire superstructure composing of legal, political, religious, artistic or philosophic institutions and their corresponding thinking. The social structure includes the base as well as the superstructure.

If one concludes that social structure refers to both the base and superstructure, then the question arises as to how they are related : Is the superstructure a mere reflection of the given base ? Or can it be independent of the economic base, so that the study of any component of the superstructure can be done without relating it to other components of the social structure ? Whereas the acceptance of the first one makes the study economically deterministic, the second one leads to superficial and compartmentalised study. Marx and Engels oppose both. They say, "neither legal relations, nor political forms could be comprehended whether by themselves or on the basis of a so-called general development of human mind, but on the contrary they originate in the material conditions of life, the totality of which embraces within the term, 'civil society'.[5] Engels wrote to J. Bloch "According to the materialist conception of history, the ultimate element in history is the production and reproduction of real life. More than this, neither Marx nor I have ever asserted. Hence if somebody twists this into saying that economic element is the only determining one, he transforms that proposition into a meaningless abstract, senseless phrase. The economic element is the basis, but various elements of the superstructure—political forms of class struggles, and its results to wit constitutions established by the victorious class after a successful battle etc. Judicial forms and even reflexes of all these struggles in the brains of the participants, political juristic, philosophical theories, religious views, and their further development into dogmas also in many cases preponderate in determining their form. There is an interaction of all these elements in which amid all the endless host of accidents, the economic movement finally asserts itself as necessary".[6] Though the base and superstructure become an inseparable whole in the social movement, Marx and Engels recognised that each element is relatively independent and that each one has its own identity. For example, Marx says in his *Preface to A Contribution to the Critique of Political Economy* : "The changes in the economic foundation lead sooner or later to the transformation of the whole immense superstructure. In studying such transformations, it is always necessary to distingusih between the metarial transformation of the economic foundations of production which can be determined with the precision of natural science, and the legal, political, religious, artistic or philosophic—in short, ideological forms in which men become conscious of this conflict and fight it out".[7] Stressing the active and positive role played by the state, a component of superstructure, Engels wrote to Schimdt in 1890, "Society gives rise to certain common functions which it cannot dispense with. The persons appointed for this purpose form a new branch of the division of labour within society. This gives them particular interests, distinct too from the interests of those who empowered them, they make themselves independent of the latter, and the state is in being. . . (this) new independent power, while having in the main to follow the movement of production, reacts in its turn, by virtue of its inherent relative independence—that is, the relative independence once transformed to it, and gradually further developed upon the conditions and course of production".[8]

From this discussion, one may come to the following conclusions about the dialectical relationship between base and the superstructure—(1) whereas the economic structure, meaning the mode of production is the base, the superstructure is composed of political, legal, ideological institutions and their corresponding thinking. (2) In course of historical development, different components of social structures interact with one another, thus making the base and superstructure an inseparable whole.

(3) Though each element of the superstructure is relatively independent of the base, and each one has necessary ability to consolidate or even change the base, its own nature and dynamics will be generally consistent with the economic movement. With this general understanding one may attempt to analyse the contribution of Poulantzas to the theory of capitalist state.

Nicos Poulantzas, who was already introduced as a critic of Miliband in the preceding chapter, developed a new theoretical approach to the study cf capitalist state. Poulantzas was the product of Structural Marxist school, popularised in France, by Louis Althusser. Poulantzas's debates with Miliband and publication of his own works in English (*Political Power and Social Classes, Fascism and Dictatorship, Classes in Contemporary Capitalism*) made him popular with most of the Marxian writers, especially in England and France.

Appreciation of Poulantzas's works is somewhat difficult, because it requires a good grounding in structuralism and structural Marxism. Hence before evaluating Poulantzas's theory of the capitalist state which he has developed in the structural Marxist tradition it is necessary to know basic contributions of structuralism.

Structuralism

French structuralism is an anthropological study made popular by Claude Levi Strauss.[9] It became highly influential among the anthropologists in contemporary western Europe. Structuralism being antipositivist, dialectical and a historical ignores causality, origins and historical processes. It is against all psychologism and sociological teleology.

Structuralism attempts to explain the collective conscience in terms of a pan human, neurologically based unconscious mental dialectic.[10] Following Durkheim, structuralists consider it possible to think of totality of thing with the help of 'molds' or structures present in human mind. These structures are not be confused with visible social relations. Structures constitute a level of reality not visible but present behind social relations, determining their appearance, dynamics and logic. Structural analysis precisely aims to discover these hidden structures.

Levi Strauss himself discovered 'the structure of generalised exchange' in his analysis of complex Australian Maori marital relations. His method involves finding in the collective mind of the pairs of 'binary opposition' which constitute the structures and 'mediators' or 'resolutions' produced as a result of the contradictions between these paired oppositions.

Structuralist analysis is opposed to empiricism, "Social structure has nothing to do with empirical reality, but with models built up after it."[11] The collective conscience is to be explained by grasping its meaning not by quantifying its relationship with other phenomena. Structure is a part of reality, but not of empirical reality. Structures according to the structuralists, are never directly visible and decipherable at the empirical level, but have to be "discovered by theoretical labour in the production of hypothesis and models".[12]

According to the structuralists, origin and evolution of a system can be analysed only after understanding the logic and mechanism of these structures. Though Levi Strauss himself admits the undoubted primacy of infrastructure, his critics point out that to him social phenomena "are nothing but objectivated systems of ideas" and that "mind has to be the ultimate explanation". Marvin Harris names such structuralism as "a synchronic form of Hegelian idealism, a stationary dialectic—a dialectic lacking in time and space".[13]

Structural Marxism

Despite the criticism against Levi Strauss on different grounds, his version of structuralism profoundly influenced a section of Marxist intellectuals in France. Though Levi Strauss was not a Marxist he had great respect for Marx. In fact he considered Marx, who first analysed the structures hidden behind capitalism as the founder of structuralism. Many intellectuals who were disgusted with historicist and existentialist approaches turned their attention towards Levi Strauss and his Marx, with a new outlook. The result was the emergence of a new school of thought called structural Marxism. A new research strategy adopted by it combines some aspects of structuralism with aspects of dialectical materialism.

Though some of the structural Marxists criticise Levi Strauss as essentially an idealist and as one who paid only lip service to the ultimate determination of superstructure by infrastructure, their points of concurrence with Levi Strauss in sharing aggressive antipositivism, blatant disregard for evolutionary movement and contempt for evolutionary methods brought them closer to Levi Strauss and his structuralism. In fact, structural Marxists found a significant degree of continuity between Marxism and structuralism. To them both Marx and Levi Strauss understood the difference between outward appearance and inner reality and then discovered the existence of hidden structures that obey internal dialectical laws of change. Both of them consider that all structures are determined ensembles of relations composed of specific elements, hence it is useless to insist on reducing one structure to another.

Structural Marxists, following Althusser consider that there is an epistemological break in Marx's thought and hence the Marxists should give greater importance to Marx's mature works than his earlier works, where Marx was still basing his social theory on the consciousness of individuals or on historical and evolutionary sequences. Only in later works causation is viewed quite differently. This makes the mature works distinct. "Causation or determination" in *Capital* he termed as "structural causality".[14]

Structural Marxists share the view that Marxism is not historicism and that Marx believed in the primacy of the study of structures over that of their genesis and evolution.[15] Basing on the architecture of *Capital* they argue that Marx instead of starting with the theory of capital, first sets up the definition of a group of categories necessary to study the system of commodity production. He defines and discusses categories such as value, exchange value, commodity, money, capital and labour. Preparation of this ground enables Marx to analyse the internal structure of the capitalist system and understand the mechanism of the production of surplus value through the capital-labour relations. Only then, he takes up the problem of primitive accumulation, where he discusses the emergence of free workers and capitalists—two important classes necessary for capitalist mode of production. This study of genesis of the structure is made possible only under the guidance of a pre-existing knowledge of that structure.[16]

Structural Marxists consider that Hegelian dialectics has nothing to do with Marxian dialectics. This idea of Althusser, as he developed in his article *Contradiction and Overdetermination* is worth understanding. Marx says : "With him (Hegel) the dialectic is standing on its head. It must be turned right side up again; if you would discover the rational kernel within the mystical shell".[17] According to Althusser when Marx says 'turning right side up again' he meant complete dissociation of his dialectics from Hegelian dialectics. Althusser points out the difference between Marx and Hegel. In Hegelian totality the mode of articulation of circular unity of equivalents is determined by self-development of the Idea. In his system, there exists only one contradiction *i.e.* the contradiction between the essence and phenomena of Idea and civil society. But this is not the case with Marx, Engels, Lenin, Stalin and Mao. Marxist totality is a complex unity of separate and specific levels which may be relatively autonomous of one another in a given historical social formation.[18] Based on the analysis of Russian revolution as given by Lenin and Stalin, Althusser argues and mere presence of workers and capitalists will not lead to revolution—only accumulation of contradictions at different levels within the whole structure and their fusion into 'ruptural unity' provoke a revolutionary situation. Further, quoting from Mao's work *On Contradiction*, Althusser argues that among the different contradictions, there exist primary and secondary contradictions and within each contradiction, there remains primary and secondary aspects of contradictions. In other words there is uneven development of contradiction and hence there exists a dominant contradiction essential to the unity of the complexity itself. Then Althusser introduces two concepts, 'displacement' and 'condensation'. The first one describes the exchange of roles between the contradictions and their aspects and the second one denotes the identity of opposites in a real unity. As such Marxist contradiction is not univocal. It "reflects itself complexly-structurally-unevenly determined". To this Althusser used the term 'over-determined'.[19]

Althusser is a bitter critic of economic determinism which reduces everything to the economic base. Structural Marxists argue that secondary contradictions are not the pure phenomena of the principal contradiction, that the principal is not the essence and the secondary so many of its phenomena. Each structural whole consists of so many structures which are irreducible to any one structure. Althusser argues that Marx distinguished between relations of production and forces of production, and never reduced one to another. This irreducibility should not be confined to economic structure since other social structures also have their own content and mode of functioning.[20] In all social formaition, secondary contradictions are necessary conditions for the existence of principal contradictions. Similarly superstructure is not the pure phenomena of the structure, but is a condition of structure's existence. Quoting Engels' letter to Bloch (1980), he says that in historical development of society, all levels of superstructure play an important role and that whereas the economy is only determinant in the last instance, dominant role may be taken by politics, religion, kinship or any other structure. Substitution of one phenomena for another ignoring the reality of social system amounts to 'vulgar materialism'. To put it in Althusser's words—"It is economism (mechanism) that sets up the hierarchy of instances once for all, assigns each its essence and role and defines universal meaning of their relations, it is economism that identifies roles and actors eternally; it is economism that identifies... in advance the determinant contradiction which for ever assimilates aspects such as forces of production, economy, practice to principal role and aspects such as relations of production, politics, ideology, theory to secondary role..."[21]

These ideas, are, in a sense, related to the structuralist concept of mode of production. Critics pointed out that structural Marxists like structuralists pay only lip service to the ultimate determination of superstructure by infrastructure. In fact few of them pack everything into infrastructure. To quote Godeliar, "a formerly superstructural element will become part of the relations of production".[22]

To this criticism structural Marxists reply that the capitalist mode of production (CMP) which Marx constructs is not cpaitalism which exists. It is a set of logically connected relations which explain the inner link between various surface phenomena. Engels's letter of Bloch (1890) is interpreted to mean that the mode of production is composed of different levels or instances, the economic, political, ideological and theoretical. As such by CMP, they mean "not what is generally considered as economic, but a specific combination of various structures and practices, which appear as so many instances or levels *i.e.* as so many regional structures of this mode".[23] In such a system different structures though not equally powerful, articulate and influence one another. Each articulated element in the complex whole has its own history, developmental trajectory and independent time scale. Hence the structural whole is viewed as the conjunctural fusion of several articulated elements with different natures.

Finally, in order to analyse Poulantzas's contribution, it is relevant to examine Althusser's and Balibar's idea of the capitalist mode of production. They think that Marx bases his study of capitalism on genealogy of different elements, (instead of focussing capitalism as gradual unfolding of one system to another through a series of contradictions). Marx's works provide three elements and two relations indispensable for all modes of production. The three elements include : (1) the worker or direct producer, (2) means of production and (3) the non-worker appropriating the surplus labour. The two relations derived from the combination of these elements include : (1) a relation of property referring to relations of production and (2) a relation of appropriation referring to relations of labour to means of production and productive forces.

What distinguishes capitalist mode of production from pre-capitalist mode is precisely the specific combination of these elements. In feudal mode of production, though the worker is not the owner, his labour and the instruments of production are unified and hence the surplus labour which can be distinguished in time and space can only be extracted by the intervention of non-economic pressure. But in the capitalist mode, the worker is divorced from both the actual ownership of property and also the instruments of production and hence here the surplus value is extracted by the ruling class without any direct need for regular political intervention.[24]

In the light of this analysis of the contributions made by different structural Marxists who preceded Poulantzas, one may take up and critically analyse Poulantzas's theory of capitalist state.

Politics as an autonomous field of Study

Following Althusser, Poulantzas asserts that in the CMP the political is relatively autonomous of the economic. But unlike Althusser, Poulantzas assigns both the determinant and dominant roles to the economic.[25] Again, though Poulantzas is opposed to Balibar's view of capitalist mode of production because of his concentration on what is generally called economic, Poulantzas uses Balibar's views for constructing a regional theory of politics.

Poulantzas sees a fundamental difference between precapitalist and capitalist modes of production. Whereas precapitalist modes of production are characterised by non-homology, in the C M P, one may "witness a combination of homology between the relations of property and of real appropriation; a homology which is set up by the separation of the direct producer from the means of production in the relation of real appropriation".[26] Further, in the precapitalist modes of production, surplus product is extracted by non-workers by other than economic pressure.[27] But surplus value in capitalism can be extracted by the capitalist in the economic process of production itself without any necessity of depending on political intervention.

Based on these peculiarities of capitalism, Poulantzas argues that since capitalism is characterised by instances, political and economic relatively autonomous of each other, regional theory of separate instances is possible. According to Poulantzas, Marx's *Capital* is his study of economic instance in the C M P. Just as Marx demonstrated the possibility of the study of economics separately, one may attempt to study politics and state as specific regions of study. Such study, Poulantzas argues, is both possible and desirable.

Poulantzas's view of Classes

Though Althusser speaks of political practice, in his works he did not give much importance to the role in classes and class struggles. But Poulantzas in his theory of capitalist state recognises their significance. However, he differs considerably from what is generally called classical Marxist view, Poulantzas is a bitter critic of economistic, historicist and functionalist interpretation of 'class and class struggles'. According to Poulantzas it is insufficient to determine classes by relating them to the economic level alone. The relations of production are not enough for constitution of classes. To quote Poulantzas, "a class can be considered as a distinct and autonomous class, as a social force inside a social formation, only when its connection with the relations of production, its economic existence, is reflected on the other levels by. . . pertinent effects".[28] As such a social class can be identified either at economic level or at the political or at the ideological level and can be located with regard to particular instance.

Interpreting Marx's terminology, Poulantzas argues that 'social formation' refers to 'structural level' and 'society' to 'the field of social relations'.[29] Structures and practices are two particular systems of ordered connections with structures of their own. Social classes always cover opposing class practices. They do not manifest within the structure. They are manifestations of the global effect of contradictions of different structures within the relations of production. Relations of production refers to structure, hence classes which include class practices should not be located within this structure.

Poulantzas identifies in Marx's tests two types of struggles-economic struggle and political struggle; and two types of interests-economic and political. Here also Poulantzas cautions not to identify economic, political and ideological struggles with economic political and ideolgoical structures.[30] Dominance of one structure, say political, in the era of state monopoly capitalism need not automatically lead to dominance of political practice. Poulantzas considers that economic struggles and political struggles are not one and the same. Poulantzas argues that though economic struggles of the working class create an impact on other levels, they are ineffectual in political sense.

One may have a look at Poulantzas's view of petty bourgeoisie. His general stand that not merely relations of production, but reflection of one's place in economy, in political and ideological level through pertinent effects takes Poulantzas to a new height in his interpretation of the petty-bourgeois class. Along with groups such as peasants and artisans, Poulantzas includes in the class of petty bourgeoisie all those non-productive salaried employees working in banks, insurance corporations, sales and advertising departments, on the pretext that they do not produce but only help in realisation of surplus value. Though all of them may not occupy same position in economy, they can be included under one class because all of them exert similar effects or force in political and ideological levels. This view of petty bourgeoisie become important in his analyses of fascism.[31]

Capitalist State : State apparatus and State power

Poulantzas defines capitalist state as a factor of unity in a capitalist formation, composed of specific and relatively autonomous levels.[32] His whole conception of the nature of capitalist state is based on this functionalist definition. According to classical Marxism, the state includes the repressive apparatus which includes military, police, judiciary, bureaucracy, legislature and government *etc.* Later Gramsci, who assigned the role of ideological hegemony to the state defined the state as political society plus civil society. Though Althusser opposes Gramsci on certain grounds he seems to have accepted this contribution of Gramsci. This becomes clear when we look at Althusser's definition of the state as repression plus ideology.[33]

Poulantzas criticises Althusser's definition on the ground that it limits the possiblity of understanding the role of modern state in all fields. Especially understading of Lenin's theory of state monopoly capitalism and revolution become impossible with such definition. However, Poulantzas also considers that ideological institutions can become a part of the state apparatus. He maintains that along with repressive character of the state, Marxist analysis should cover its political and ideological role also. As such Poulantzas' system of state is composed of several institutions of which certain have a principally repressive role and others principally ideological role. Poulantzas uses the terms 'State repressive apparatus' (singular) and state 'ideological apparatuses' (plural) to denote that the repressive apparatus has internal unity and cohesion, whereas ideological institutions enjoy relative autonomy. The state ideological apparatuses which includes churches, political parties, schools and even family to an extent become a part of the state system by assisting reproduction of society and thereby maintaining class domination.[34] Though Poulantzas recognises the increasing economic role of the modern state, he does not include economic institutions as part of the state system, on the ground that Marxism defines state as political organiser and that extraction of surplus value is not the basic function of the state.[35] Further, Poulantzas clearly states that the relations between repressive apparatus and state ideological apparatuses and also the relations among various branches in each of them will change from time to time depending on the objective necessities.

The complex structure of state allows the capitalist state to bring unity of the power bloc by accommodating various classes and class fractions within it. Generally, the hegemonic class or class fraction will have access to the nucleus of the state *i.e.* the repressive state apparatus. Other non-hegemonic classes and fractions of the power bloc are allowed to control other branches of the state system.

This view indirectly shapes Poulantzas's definition of power. Poulantzas defines power as the capacity of a class to realise its specific objective interests. Poulantzas considers that this power is, however, limited by the field of practices. It depends on the capacity of other classes to realise their interests. These class interests are to be located not in structures but in the field of practices. Based on such view of power, Poulantzas argues that the institutions of state do not have any power of their own. They are only the political power centres of the classes. Since power concentrated in an institution is a class power, the institutions must be considered according to thier impact in the field of class struggles. However, it should not lead to the conclusion that the state institutions are mere puppets of one or the other class of a capitalist society. To quote Poulantzas, "State power is not a machine or an instrument, a simple object coveted by various classes, nor is it divided into parts, which if not in the hands of someone, must automatically be in the hands of other; rather it is an ensemble of structures".[36] As such, state institutions enjoy relative autonomy, but this is not due to the fact that they have the power of their own. What make state institutions relatively autonomous of classes is their relation to the structures.

Relative Autonomy of the Capitalist State

Poulantzas's stand against instrumentalist theory of state leads him to examine the relative autonomy that the capitalist state enjoy vis-a-vis classes and class struggles. By relative autonomy, Poulantzas does not mean that the state becomes independent of all classes and hence it is possible for the state to act as a neutral authority. As he says, relative autonomy of the state "in the last analysis is only that autonomy necessary for the hegemonic organisation of the dominant classes; *i.e.* it is only that relative autonomy which is indispensable for the unambiguous power of these classes".[37]

How is relative autonomy of the state made possible? Firstly, by the separation of political from economic in the C M P. Secondly, by the specificity of the constitution of classes and class struggles in the C M P and social formation.[38]

Why does relative autonomy of the state become necessary ? It becomes necessary for the state to be able to act as a factor of unity in a capitalist formation composed of specific and relatively autonomous levels. This attribute assigns to the state the character of unity proper to the institutionalised power which by presenting a specific internal cohesion to the state institutions prevents the strained relations between classes and fractions of the power bloc from becoming self destructive.

The relative autonomy has nothing to do with equilibrium of classes of 'catastrophic equilibrium'. Poulantzas considers it to be a general feature of the state in the capitalist mode of production. Particular combination of classes only determine the extent of relative autonomy and it never precludes relative autonomy of the state as such at any time. This view of relative autonomy is based on Poulantzas's interpretation of Marx's ideas on Bonapartism.

The phenomenon of Bonapartism corresponds to the phase of expanded reproduction of capitalism. The concrete historical case of Bonapartism originates due to the contradictions of class and class fractions in power and inability of any one class or class fractions to become hegemonic enough to unite the power bloc. Poulantzas gives his own interpretations to Marx's analysis. When Marx talks of 'antagonism between state and society'. Poulantzas interprets it as dislocation and respective autonomy of political from the economic struggle. Similarly, Marx and Engels analysis of Bonaparte playing one class against the other means the autonomy of state from all classes including the dominant class. Bonaparte's dependence on the peasantry, the biggest class in France means the necessity of state to depend on the popular will to confront with individual interests of the bourgeoisie. Failure of the party of order signifies the inability of the bourgeoisie to rule itself. The emergence of Bonaparte coincides with the necessity of the state to constitute the unity of power bloc under the hegemony of the dominant class or class fraction. Basing himself on these grounds, Poulantzas studies how the capitalist state is related to class and class struggles.[39]

Capitalist State and Dominated Classes

According to Poulantzas, state is not a class instrument, it is dominant class's political power centre and the organising agent of their political struggle. It is not the state's responsibility to take care of the economic interests of the bourgeoisie. The flexibility of the state allows certain concessions to the dominated classes within the limits set by the system. The state sees that such concessions only help further extension of political hegemony of the dominant classes over the dominated. Relative autonomy of the state vis-a-vis the economic power centres makes extension of social policy for the benefit of the dominated classes and at the same time the curtailment of the economic power of the dominant class so as to protect their political interests. Stressing the difference between the economic and political struggles, he strikes a note caution not to misunderstand that the era of social policy changed the nature of the capitalist state.[40]

Capitalist State and Dominant Classes

In place of the notion that one class or class fraction acts as the ruling class, Poulantzas brings in the view that ruling class in all capitalist social formations consists of several classes and class fractions. To explain this Poulantzas coins the term, 'power bloc'. Power bloc constituted under the protection of the hegemonic classes or fractions of the bloc. Existence of so many classes and class fractions in the power bloc becomes possible due to (1) the very capitalist relations of production which gives birth to fractions; (2) the dominance of the C M P over other modes of production; (3) structure of the state which makes it possible for several fractions to present in the political scene.[41]

Though power bloc comes into existence, it faces numerous obstacles in realizing its own interests either due to the contradictory interests of different classes and fractions within it or due to the inability of the hegemonic class or fraction to extend its influence over all other classes and class fractions in the power bloc. This situation demands the state to intervence to act as the factor of political unity of power bloc under the protection of hegemonised class or class fraction. The state can play this role due to its intrinsic unity as against plurality of power blocs.

Poulantzas is opposed to the view that the state is a simple tool or an obedient clerk of the dominant class or fraction. It is because the power bloc does not consist of one politically homogeneous class that can guide the actions of the state. Moreover, as it is examined, the state as a structure is relatively autonomous of classes and class fractions which constitute the level of practices. As such the state instead of being a tool in the hands of the class, becomes an active unifier of the power bloc. Opposing the interpretation of the state monopoly capitalism as the state of monopolists, Poulantzas argues that the capitalist state while performing the function of constituting the unity of the power bloc, entertains special relationship with the hegemonic class or fractions in order to extend its hegeomony over other class and class fractions of the power bloc. By this, however, the state does not become a puppet of the hegemonic class or fraction. Rather, if necessary the state presents itself as guarantor of various classes against hegemonic classes and it may play one class against another. The state does all these things only as political organiser of the dominant class.

Capitalist State and Class Struggle :

It was stated that the separation of direct producer from means of production assigns of state a specific autonomy vis-a-vis relations of production. The autonomisation reflect in the field of class struggle as autonomy of economic class struggle from political class struggles. As a result the state has to confront in the field of social relations, two kinds of struggles viz. economic struggle and political struggle.

The development of capitalism and consequent socialisation of production brings into existence two kinds of threats of the systems, one in the form of growing unity of the Working class and the other in the form of mounting antagonistic contradiction within the power bloc which lead to its break up. In realty, it is the duty of the hegemonic class or fraction to protect the power bloc under its hegemony and project its interests as the interests of the people. It should be able to perpetuate the existing social relations by maintaining unstable equilibrium of social classes through a series of compromises. By using political and ideological organisation it should represent itself as the representative of people and embodiment of the unity of the nation.[42] But the (hegemonic class or fraction, in the wake of mounting obstacles, fails to fulfil its reponsibilities. Some of the difficulities, in the realisation of these necessities are (1) internal functioning of the bourgeois class, (2) continued existence of small scale producers and (3) growing threat of working class unity.

In such a situation the state is forced to act as the political organiser of the dominant classes. Accordingly the state acts as a factor of political organisation of dominant classes, and at the same time as a factor of political disorganisation of the dominated classes. The state reorganises the power bloc under the hegemony of dominant class or fractions. At the same time it attempts to disunite the working class, either by conceding certain economic demands of the workers or by extending the hegemony of dominant classes over the dominated class with the help of ideological state apparatuses.[43]

While acting as the political organiser of the dominant class, it acts in specific relation to the political parties of these classes. Sometimes, parties may be allowed, side by side with the state to act as political organiser, or at times it may substitute itself for the parties. But in critical conditions, it may take total control of the political interests of the classes.

As such in capitalism, relative atonomy depends on the characteristics peculiar to the economic and political class struggle in the capitalist social formation.[44] This relative autonomy has very little to do with the equilibrium of social forces. The state is always relatively autonomous of class struggles, though 'the variations and modalities of this relative autonomy depends upon the concrete relation between social forces in the field of the political class struggle, in particular, they depend on the political struggle of the dominated classes".[45]

Fascism and Fascist State :

The phenomenon of fascism, says Poulantzas, can be understood only when it is located within the era of imperialism characterised by the modification in the state's role. He thinks that though Lenin in his phamphlet on imperialism stresses, in the main, its economic aspect, imperialism is not to be considered as a simple economic phenomenon. According to Poulantzas "imperialism considered as a stage in the ensemble of capitalist process in not infact just a question of modification in the economic domain.....These economic factors actually determine a new articulation of the ensemble of capitalist system, thereby producting profound changes in politics and ideology".[46]

Poulantzas does not hold that all parliamentary democratic states necessarily tend to become fascist states. Fascism could rise its head in Germany and Italy because of the peculiar articulation of different levels of structures and practices during the period of transition to monopoly capitalism. During that period, Russia, Germany and Italy constituted the weakest links in the imperialist chain. Poulantzas argues that there were many obstacles in the path of development of monopoly capitalism. Some of them mentioned by Poulantzas include failure of bourgeois democratic revolutions, unaccomplished national unifications, war burden, economic crises, rise of the working class solidarity strength, and inability of the monopolists to extend their hegemony over other classes and class monopoly capitalism combind with sharpening class contradictions and consequent crises within the state apparatus, peculiar to the phase of transition moved Germany and Italy on the path of Fascism. It is precisely, due to the absence of similar contradictions in other countries like Britain and USA, they could escape fascism even though they also happened to be imperialist nations.

Poulantzas criticises the Comintern's economistic view of fascism. According to him, it is wrong to consider that the growth of fascism was the preconceived plan of the capitalists. In other words, it is wrong to suppose that the fascists were the paid agents of the monopolists. He also opposes the view that whereas the parliamentary republic is the instrument of the whole capitalist class, the fascist state is a puppet in the hands of the monpolists. Such a stand, according to Poulantzas, contradicts the fact that fascism represents the contradictory interests of various classes and thus denies the autonomy that the state enjoys.

Poulantzas maintains that throughout the period of fascism, the state was relatively autonomous of the dominant classes. It could exercise autonomy because of two factors: (1) inner contradictions within the power bloc which necessitated reorganisation of power bloc under the hegemony of the monopolist fraction and (2) contradiction between dominant and dominated classes which requires the state to mediate and reestablish political domination and hegemony of the power bloc.[47]

The relative autonomy of fascist state has nothing to do with equilibrium of class forces as Thalheimer interpreted. Also, it has nothing to do with Bonapartism as Miliband conceives. In fact, Poulantzas considers such interpretations to be unmarxian. Fascist state is relatively autonomous only to the extent that the dominant classes need reorganisation of power bloc under the protection of hegemonic fraction. Further identifying fascism with Bonapartism is not correct, for fascism is the product of specific contradictions in Germany and Italy, peculiar to the phase of transition to monopoly capitalism.

Finally one needs to know the role that Poulantzas assigns to the petty bourgeoisie. Thugh Poulantzas opposes the view that fascist state was the state of the petty bourgeoisie he gives considerable importance to this petty bourgeoisie, the class ignored by Comintern.[48] The rise of fascism corresponds to the ideological, political and economic crises of petty bourgeoisie. In fascism the petty bourgeoisie constituted itself into an authentic force through the fascist parties. In the first phase of fascism the fascist party acted like the representative of petty bourgeoisie and it voiced their grievances and aspirations. 'This position, however, changed once the fascist parties came to governmental power and then they become subservient to the interests of the state. In the phase, Poulantzas sees a peculiar and indirect alliance of the petty bourgeoisie with big monopoly capitalists. To quote Poulantzas, "In short, the historical role of fascism was to achieve an alliance between big capital and petty bourgeoisie, in the very conjucture in which their contradiction were being actually intensified".[49] Poulantzas cautions that such alliance however is not mechanical. It was never openly declared, it took the form of petty bourgeoisie support for a form of state whose ties with the interests of big capital it did not understand. In ideological sense, ideology of fascist state corresponds to the interests of big capital. But astonishingly, peculiar ideological position that petty bourgeoisie subscribed could only help the monopoly capital. The points of collusion between imperialist and petty bourgeois ideologies include: (1) statolatory aspect, cult of state, (2) elitist aspect with racist conception, (3) anti juridical aspect, blind acceptance of leaders, command or law. (4) nationalist jingoist aspect, (5) militarism, (6) anticlericalism, (7) role of family and education, (8) obscruantism and anti intellectualism and (9) corporatism. Practice of such ideology though satisfied at times the subjective intentions of the petty bourgeoisie, in reality, however, it only served the objective interests of the big capitalism.

Poulantzas argues that during the first phase of fascism in power, the petty bourgoisie became the ruling class. With the stabilisation step it fell back to the position in charge of the state apparatus.[50] Even in this role, the petty bourgeoisie continued to exercise considerable influence on the state apparatus and determine the particular forms that they took.

To conclude, according to Poulantzas, fascist state was an exceptional form of capitalist state and a specific form of regime. The fascist phase involved in reorganisation of the state repressive apparatus as well as the state ideological apparatuses ; the dominant role being assigned to the arbitrary will of the leaders of the state. Fascist state suspended popular elections. Executive prevailed over the legislature. The state was thoroughly bureaucratised. The state intervenes effectively in economy. Going farther from Althusser, Poulantzas accepts the role played by the state in reproduction of means of production, reproduction of labour power and also in reproduction of relations of production. But this so-called state regulation never went to jeopardise the traditional big capital, whose interests it constantly guaranteed.[51]

Poulantzas and His Critics

Poulantzas's theory of capitalist state was critically analysed by many a European American, and Latin American scholars. Some of them very effectively attemtped to expose the defects of the problematic he adopted and the interpretation he gave. In return Poulantzas tried to clarify his position by responding to the critics. A brief account of this debate is given here.

Perhaps, the first attack came from Ralph Miliband, whose work *The State in Capitalist Society* (1969) was criticised by Poulantzas. Miliband in his two articles, *Reply to Nicos Poulantzas* (1969) and *Poulantzas and the Capitalist State* (1973) attempts to point out what he considers to be the flaws in Poulantzas's formulations. According to Miliband, Poulantzas only substitutes the notion of structural constraints for the notion of ruling class. State is only compelled to be merest functionaries and executants of the policies determined by the system. But since within the system, the ruling class is the dominant class, Poulantzas is back at the point of subordination of the state elite to ruling class.[52] The relative autonomy of state, which Poulantzas wants to examine became impossible with this apporach of 'structural superdeterminism' which makes understanding of the dialectical relationship between the structure and system impossible. Though structural perspective is not without certain merits, Miliband cautions that it may lead to a hyper structuralist trap, which deprives agents of any freedom of choice and manoeuvre and turns them into the 'bearers' of objective forces which they are unable to effect. This perspective is but another form of determinism—which is alien to Marxism and in any case false. . ."[53]

This criticism is refuted by Poulantzas on the plea that he was never a structuralist, Poulantzas claims that in his subsequent books, for example, *Classes in Contemporary Capitalism*, he gives considerable importance to the role of classes and class struggles. He says that he tried to clear off the confusion created by his earlier works by eliminating the rigid separation between sturctures and practices and by giving primacy to the class practices and class struggles over the structures.[54] However, to the criticism that he did not give considerable importance to the role of individuals and creative persons, to human freedom and action, free will and human choice, Poulantzas refuses to answer, on the grounds that he answered them already in his books.

Laclau who intervenes in the debate considers that the relative autonomy and the structural constraints are not incompatible as Miliband thinks. According to Poulantzas, relative autonomy is a structural element, the product of particular articulation between instances of mode of proudction. Poulantzas insists that he examined relative autonomy of the state from two directions—first by separating the political from the economic within the CMP and secondly by analysing the specificity of constitution of classes and class struggles within it. To Miliband's question, how relative is relative autonomy and what makes it to be more or less, Poulantzas seems to have answered in his first book, *Political Power and Social Classes* itself when he says, "within limits imposed by the relation between the structures and the field of class struggles, this relative autonomy can vary according to (1) the modalities taken on by its function vis-a-vis the dominant classes and (2) the concrete relation between the forces present".[55]

Related to it is their conception of relation between class power and state power. Miliband who considers "that there is a basic distinction to be made between class power and state power" complains about "Poulantzas' failure to make the necessary distinction between class power and state power. State power is the main and ultimate—but not the only means whereby class power is assured and maintained... The blurring of the distinction between class power and state power by Poulantzas makes any such analysis (of relative autonomy of the state) impossible".[56] In his reply, criticising Miliband for lack of common sense, Poulantzas pleads that by comprehending relations of power as class relations, he in fact broke with structuralism which Miliband attributes to him. According to Poulantzas, viewing of class power and state power as different relations of externality necessarily leads to subordination of class to state power or state to class power, thus welcoming instrumentalist or revisionist theories of state. By locating relative autonomy at the level of separation of political from economic and by seeking the state as the resultant of class contradictions and as the structure "which is both shot through and constituted with and by these class contradictions", Poulantzas claims that he overcomes the defects of other approaches.[57]

Miliband who calls the approach of Poulantzas as 'structural superdeterminism' or 'structural abstractionism' aruges that such approach leads Poulantzas into the world of structures and levels which have very little to do with historical reality. Poulantzas according to Miliband fails to understand different forms of capitalist state. Further, "He seems... to have an absurdly exaggerated fear of empiricist contamination",[58] and hence never likes to supplement his theory with empirical proofs. Opposing this point Poulantzas reacts with an assertion that all his works provided sufficient historical data. Poulantzas aruges that he is for rigorous interpretation of data within a theoretical framework unlike empiricists or neopositivists who use facts without any problematic. On this Poulantzas was sensitive to historical data and that he was aware of the difference between constitutional and fascist forms of state is evident from his work, *Fascism and Dictatorship*.

However, one criticism of Miliband supported by Laclau, but not responded to by Poulantzas is the issue of Bonapartism. Miliband asserts that "Bonapartism is not the religion of the bourgeoisie at all—it is its last resort in the conditions of political instability so great as to present a threat to the mainteance of the exisitng social order, including of course the system of domination which is the central part of that order".[59] It is not known why Poulantzas who bases his theory of capitalist state mainly on his interpretation of Bonapartism does not react to this criticism.

In fact lack of mutual understanding unnecessarily prolonged Miliband-Poulantzas debate. Pointing out this Laclau clarifies, "In short Miliband is interested in determining concrete channels which in western Europe establish the link between fractions which hold power and dominant classes and in that emphasise that element of unity between the two. Poulantzas by contrast, is interested in determining at the theoretical level, the autonomouse character of political within the CMP and in that he emphasizes the element of separation between the dominant class and fractions holding power. They are in fact analysing different problems which they did not notice".[60]

Laclau goes farther than reviewing Miliband-Poulantzas debate and critically reflects on certain aspects of Poulantzas's theory. Commenting on the approach, Leclau says that Poulantzas does not try to demonstrate, the internal contradictions of the problematic which he rejects and the forms in which his own problematic supercedes the points of discrepancy. This defect was pointed out by Laclau from Poulantzas's treatment of historicist view of classes.[61] Secondly, Laclau says that though abstraction is necessary for scientific knowledge, this aspect reaches such heights that Poulantzas' analysis leads to formalism where descriptive categories and symbolic function of concepts predominate its theoretical substance.[62] Laclau considers the distinction made by structural Marxists between determinant in the last instance and dominant role as a series of metaphors which attempt to resolve through symbols of little theoretical content. Laclau calls it an artificial problem created by the metaphysic of instances.

Laclau reacting to their concept of mode of production, says: "We find ourselves with three instances established purely in descriptive ways... why only three? What has been the method of their deduction? Does there exist any logical link between them". Commenting on the crux of Balibar and Poulantzas analysis of the notion of 'extra economic coercion', Laclau argues that Marx uses the term 'economic' in two ways, understanding it at two different levels of abstraction to formulate two different theoretical structures. In one sense, it is used as synonymous with level of production and in another sense it is referred to the sphere of commodity and market.[63] Poulantzas who replies to other points of Laclau apologetically and that too unconvincingly, does not react to these important points of Laclau's criticism.

It is a debate among writers who accepted the specificity of politics. Another set of critics, who reject this idea, point out various other shortcomings of Poulantzas. Colin Crouch points out that what Poulantzas gives after abandoning instrumentalist view is the definition of state as one that is functionalist. According to Poulantzas the state automatically takes care of "the general interest of the capital because it is the role assigned to the State". Poulantzas discusses general theory in such a high level of abstraction that he fails to explain why "a particular fraction of British capital—the financial sector has been able to dominate state policies to the detriment of the long term insterests of capital as a whole".[64] Finally one may summarise the criticism of Holloway and Picciotto and other German derivativists in the following manner. According to them Poulantzas never considers it important to analyse Marxist doctrine that political forms can be understood only when it is related to the anatomy of civil society. Poulantzas's theory is not based of the historical meterialist concepts developed by Marx in his *Capital*. He approaches only the political works of Marx, that too in a fragmented fashion. Poulantzas's view of relative autonomy of the political and the economic "leads him to neglect the all-important question of the nature of separation of and relation between these instances" [65] His wrong approach makes Poulantzas identify economic with production relations and class struggle with the realm of the political. Bacause of these limitations in Poulantzas's theory of state, "There is not analysis of the development of capitalist society, of the changing forms of state-society relations and of the state itself... there is no systematic analysis of the relation between the capitalist state and its basis, capitalist exploitation of the working class in the process of accumulation, so too there is no analysis of the constraints and limitations which the nature of capitalist accumulation imposes upon state action".[66]

Estimate :

French structural Marxism was a timely response in the West to the problems created by the historicist, humanist and existentialist interpretations of Marxism. The structural Marxists exposed the inadequacy of empiricist approach and tried to study the structures hidden beneath the surface. Their uncompromising fight against economism and their recognition of important roles played by ideology and politics need to be appreciated.

In this regard, Althusser's contributions to the enrichment of Marxism are in deed significant. Though one may not agree with him Althusser's criticism of historicism and Hegelian dialectics is worth understanding. Althusser's idea of 'epistemological break' is an attack on all those intellectuals who sought to see true Marxism in the works of young Marx who was still under the influence of Hegelian idealism or Fuerbachean humanism. Accepting the contributions made by Lenin, Stalin and Mao, Althusser tries to further develop and enrich Marxian dialectics. In this attempt, he derives new concepts like 'displacement', 'condensation' and 'over determination' that perfect Marxian understanding of the nature of contradictions. Althusser attempts to show that Marx and Engels, unlike Hegel, understand the active and positive role played by the various components of the superstructure in social development. Althusser considers that all elements of the social structure—economy, politics and ideology are equally important and that each element relatively autonomous of another, has its own history, development trajectory and independent time scale.

Convinced by Althusser's argument many of his students undertook to study different aspects of society. Among them, Poulantzas is the first person, who attempted to develop a systematic regional theory of politics and state. He is a bitter critic of the instrumentalist view, which reduces the state to a mere tool in the hands of the dominant class. He fights out economistic interpretations of state, and shows that nature and dynamics of the bourgeois state cannot be reduced to the necessities of the economy. Poulantzas's analysis of Bonapartism, imperialism and fascism, where he sheds light on hitherto untouched aspects reveal a deep understanding. He considerably deviates from some Marxists, such as Laclau and Miliband in his method of determining one's class position. Though Poulantzas's works, in the main within strucutral Marxist problematic, he tries to overcome structuralist dogmas by assigning more importance to classes and class struggles over structures. Again, despite his opposition to Anglo-American empiricist approach, he does not fail to produce facts to substantiate his arguments.'

Though the contributions of the structural Marxists are somewhat novel, one should be cautious in evaluating each of their contributions.

Firstly, one may look at the structural marxist conception of the mode of production. Though Marx and Engels accept that superstructure plays an active and positive role, as is examined in the beginning of this chapter, they did not consider superstruture as a part of the mode of production. According to Marx and Engels, 'mode of production' is some thing which actually exists. In is not merely a theoretical tool devised by them to understand social dynamics, as the structural marxists conceive.

Further, as we have seen earlier, Engels's letter to Bloch in 1890 speaks of the important role played by the superstructure, but, this does not lead to the conclusion that the elements of superstructure, say politics or ideology, become part of the mode of production. Here one may look at structural Marxist's conceptions of dominant and determinant roles. Whereas Althusser seems to consider that economy plays a determinant role, Poulantzas maintains that the economy takes both the determinant and dominant roles. But in the actual course of social development, the element that plays dominant role is never constant. What element takes over the dominant role depends on the objective necessity of social development. At times, though not always, even, economy takes over the dominant role. For example, politics plays dominant role at the time of revolution. It even changes the economic base. But, once the new economic base is created, the economy takes over dominant role for a while, and gives birth to new political and ideological institutions.

Further, is it possible or even desirable, to study politics without relating it to other aspects of society? Can a comprehensive study of any particular phenomenon be achieved by such fragmented approach? At least, the dialectical materialist approach developed by the classical Marxists opposes such compartmentalised approach. Engels says-"Dialectics. . . comprehends things and their representations, ideas, in their essential connection, concatenation, motion, origin and ending."[67] In *Philosophical Notebooks*, Lenin notes, "Individual Being (an object, a phenomenon *etc*) is (only) one side of the Idea (of truth). Truth requires still other sides of reality, which likewise appear only as independent and individual. . . Only in their totality (zusammer) and in their relation (Bezietung) is truth realised".[68]

Then, coming to the concept of relative autonomy, Poulantzas seems to consider, that, this attribute is specific only to the state in the capitalist societies. But Marx and Engels do not entertain this view.

Engels in his mature work, *The Origins of the Family, Private Property and the State* says, "In order that these antagonisms; classes with conflicting economic interests might not consume themselves and society in fruitless struggles, it becomes necessary to have a power seemingly standing above society, that would alleviate the conflict and keep it within the bounds or order and this power arisen out of society, but placing itself above it, and alienating itself more and more from it, is the state."[69] Engels is referring here to the state in general, not to any particular state, say the capitalist state. Though it is true that the direct producers in capitalism are deprived of the means of production and instruments of production, one may question, how do these aspects lead to the separation of political from economic and hence to the conclusion that the cpaitalist sate is relatively autonomous of classes? Here one needs to remember Stalin's answer to the question of extra economic coercion in feudalism : "Of course, extra economic coercion did play a part in strengthening the economic power of the feudal landlords, however not it, but feudal owncrship of the land was the basis of feudalism".[70] So, also in capitalism, absence of extra economic ccercion is to be considered as a peculiar feature bearing some influence; and nothing more than that. It is not to be considered as the general law of capitalist social formation.

Poulantzas has a better understanding of the nature and role of the state officials and also of the dynamics of the different branches of the state machinery. He thinks that state uses ideology for consolidating the existing system. But the consideration by Althusser and Poulantzas, that, the ideology become a part of politics is subejct to criticism. As analysed in the beginning of the chapter, state and ideology are different components of the superstructure. It is true they influence each other, either to consolidate or to change the base. Just because state uses ideology, one should not make ideology a part of the state system. Seen in this light, the derivation of the concepts such as Ideological State Apparatus (ISA) or state ideological apparatuses seem to pose more problems than it can solve.

Poulantzas distinguishes Fascist state from the Bonapartist state. His criticism of the economic interpretations of the Comintern and his concentration on the importance of politics and ideology, as well as the roles played by different classes in bringing about fascism in Germany and Italy are indeed worth noting. However whereas it is wrong to attribute fascism only to the economic condition, it is equally wrong to underestimate, in a comprehensive analysis of fascism, economic factors such as sporadic development of capitalism, the problem of capital accumulation, the foundation of state monopoly capitalism, the need for colonial markets and hence the necessity of redivision of world market *etc*. Poulantzas does not totally ignore economic factors. But, as Holloway and Picciotto put it, "where he does so only in the context of the dominant classes—contradiction between big and medium capital, capitalists and landowners *etc*."[71] Further, his empirical analysis of the relations between various classes in Germany and Italy may be correct, but, if he argues that without similar class alliances there cannot be fascism in other countries, then he may not be right. Just as the class forces that allied themselves in bringing about bourgeoisie democracy or socialism, differ from one country to another, the class alliances, in case of fascism, can be different from one country to another. To say that fascism cannot come in countries where such class forces and class alliances (say between petty bourgeoisie and monopolists) do not exist is an unscientific argument.

Finally, one can discuss the role assigned to individuals. Althusser in his stress on structures seems to have neglected the conscious role of individuals or classes. Though Poulantzas does not neglect the significance of class practices, he underestimates the ability of class organisations of the bourgeoisie. He says, that, he sees individuals as supports or bearers of the structure. But what actually Poulantzas means by the words 'supports' or 'bearers' is not clear. Marx in his *Eighteenth Brumaire of Louis Bonaparte* says; "Men make their own history, but they do not make it just as they please, they do not make it under circumstances chosen by themselves, from the past".[72] Though structural constraints are noted, Marx clearly says in the passage that history is made by men, not by structures. Further, Third Thesis on Fuerbach reads, "The materialist doctrine that men are products of circumstances and upbringing and that therefore, changed men are products of other circumstnaces and changed upbringing, forgets that it is men that change circumstances and that educator himself needs educating".[73] Engels also cautions: "In one point the history of the development of society proves to be essentially different from that of nature. In nature. . . there are only blind unconscious agencies acting upon one another. In history of society, on the other hand, the actors are all endowed with consciousness, men are acting with deliberation or passion working towards definite goals, nothing happens without a conscious purpose, without an intended aim'.[74] One should not forget that the state, the relations of production *etc*. which influence people, are the structures that are brought into being and constantly influenced—even after they become relatively autonomous-- by the conscious role of the individuals.

Notes and References

1. Marx and Engels, *Selected Works vol.I* Progress Publishers, Moscow, 1976, p.503.
2. *Ibid*., p.20.
3. Engels, Frederick,*Anti Duhring*, Progress Publishers, Moscow, 1978, p.18.
4. Marx and Engels, *Selected Works Vol.I, op.cit*., p.20.
5. *Ibid*., p. 503.
6. Marx and Engels, *Selected Works Vol.III*, Progress Publishers, Moscow, 1977, p.487.
7. Marx and Engels, *Selected Works Vol.I, op.cit*., p. 503.
8 Marx and Engels, *Selected Works Vol.III, op.cit*., p. 49.
9. Refer Levi Strauss, Claude, *Structural Anthroplogy*, Harmondsworth, Penguin, 1978, Also *Elementary Structures of Kinship*, Boston, Bacon Press. 1969.
10. Harris, Marvin, *Cultural Materialism*, Random House, New York, 1979. p.167.
11. Levi Strauss, Claude, *Structural Anthropolgoy*, Harmondsworth, Penguin, 1978, p.279.
12. Godeliar, Maurice, in Blackburn Robin, *Ideology in Social Science*, Fontana/ Collins, 1971, p. 341.
13. Harris, Marvin *op.cit*., p.168.
14. Quoted in Bloch Maurice, *Marxism and Anthropolgoy*, Oxford, Clarendon Press, 1983, p. 153.
15. See Althusser and Balibar, *Reading Capital*, London, NLB, 1977, p.160. Also Godeliar in Blackburn, Robin, *op,cit*., p.343.
16. Blackbrun, *op.cit*. p.345.
17. Marx and Engels, *Selected Works Vol.III, op.cit*., 1977, p.98.
18. Glucksmann, Mariam, *Structuralist Analysis in Contemporary Socialist Thought*, London, Routledge, & Kegan Paul, 1974, p.108.
19. Althusser, Louis, *For Marx*, London, Penguin Press, 1972, p.206.
20. Blackburn, *op.cit*., p. 363.
21. Althusser,*For Marx*, *op.cit*., p.213.
22. Harris, Marvin, *op.cit*., p.229.
23. Poulantzas, Nicos, *Political Power and Social Classes, Verso,* 1982 p.13.
24. Althusser and Balibar, *Reading Capital*; *op.cit*., p.25.
25. Poulantzas, *Political Power and Social Classes*, *op.cit*., p.25,
26. Poulantzas, *op.cit*., p.32.
27. Marx Karl, *Capital Vol III,* Progress Publishers, Moscow 1977, p.790.
28. Poulantzas, *Political Power and Social Classes*, *op.cit*., p.78.
29. *Ibid*., p.69.
30. *Ibid*., p.88.
31. Poulantzas, *Fascism and Dictatorship*, London, verso, 1979, p.302.

32. Poulantzas, *Ibid.*, p.302. Also in *Political Power and Social Classes op.cit.*, p.44.
33. Althusser, Louis, *Lenin and Philosophy*, Monthly Review Press, 1971, p.142.
34. Poulantzas, *the Problem of Capitalist State,* in Blackburn, *op.cit.*, pp.251-52.
35. Poulantzas, *Fascism and Dictatorship*, *op.cit.*, p.304.
36. Poulantzas, *Political Power and Social Classes, op.cit.*, p.280.
37. *Ibid.*, p.289.
38. Poulantzas, *The Capitalist State :A Reply to Miliband and Leclau*, New Left Review, 95, 1976, p.71.
39. Poulantzas, *Political Power and Social Classes*, *op.cit.*, pp.281-82.
40. *Ibid.*, p.289.
41. *Ibid.*, p.296.
42. *Ibid.*, p.283.
43. Gold, Lo & Wright, E.O. *Recent Marxist Theories of State*, Monthly Review, vol. 27, Nos. 5 & 6.
44. Poulantzas, *The Capitalist State : A Reply to Miliband & Laclau, op.cit.*, p.74.
45. Poulantzas, *Political Powe and Social Classes*, *op.cit.*, p.289.
46 Poulantzas, *Fascims and Dictatorship*, *op.cit.*, p.19-20.
47. *Ibid.*, pp.85-86.
48. *Ibid.*, p. 237.
49. *Ibid.*, p.250.
50. *Ibid.*, pp.256-57.
51. *Ibid.*, p.258.
52. Miliband, *Reply to Nicos Poulantzas* in Blackburn, *op.cit.*, p.259.
53 Miliband, *Marxism and Politics*, Oxford University Press, 1979 edn, p.73.
54. Poulantzas, *The Capitalist State : A Reply to Miliband & Laclau, op.cit.*.
55. Poulantzas, *Political Power and Social Classes*, *op.cit.*, p.286.
56. Miliband, *Poulantzas and the Capitalist State*, New Left Review, 82, 1973, pp.87-88.
57 Poulantzas, *The Capitalist State: A Reply to Miliband and Laclau, op.cit.*, p.75.
58. Miliband, *The Capitalist State : A Reply to Nicos Poulantzas*, Blackburn, *op.cit.*. p.84.
59. *Ibid.*, p.91.
60. Laclau, Ernsto, *Politics and Ideology in Marxist Theory,* London, Verso, 1982, p.66.
61. *Ibid.*, p.63.
62. *Ibid*, p.70.
63. *Ibid.*, pp.74-75.
64. Crouch, Colin, *State and Economy in Contemporary Capitalism*, London, Croomhelm, 1979.pp. 25-26.
65. Holloway and Picciotto, *State and Capital*, London, Edward Arnold, 1978, p.6.
66. *Ibid*, p.7.
67. Engels, *Anti Duhring,* Progress Publishers, Moscow, 1978, p.66.
68. Lenin VI, *Collected Works 38*, Progress Publishers, Moscow, 1972, p.196.
69. Marx and Engels, *Selected Works Vol.III*, *op.cit.*, p.327.
70. Stalin, *Economic Problem of Socialism in th U.S.S.R.*, Foreign Languages Press, Peking, 1972, p.42.
71. Holloway and Picciotto, *op.cit.*, p.8.
72. Marx and Engels, *Selected Works Vol.I.* Progress Publishers, Moscow, 1976, p.398.
73. *Ibid.*, p.13.
74. Marx and Engels, *Selected Works Vol. III, op.cit.*, pp.365-66.

Chapter IV

WELFARE STATE AND SOCIAL REPRODUCTION
Myth and Reality

At a time, when large number of intellectuals in England, America, and France were involved deeply in Miliband-Poulantzas debate, an altogether new approach to the study of the capitalist state developed in West Germnay with the Free University in Berlin as its centre. This German Derivative school of thought which flourished especially between 1970 and 1975 is very critical of the approaches of Miliband and Poulantzas on the autonomy of the political. The Derivativists are opposed to the view that the capitalist state—its nature, and dynamics could be studied without referring to the economy as its starting point.[1]

In classical Marxist literature also there are a number of references that emphasizes the importance of studying the political economy to understand the nature of any state. Marx in his *Preface to the Critique of Political Economy* explains, "In the social production of their existence men inevitably enter into definite relations, which are independent of their will, namely relations of production appropriate to a given stage of their material forces of production. The totality of these relations of production constitutes the economic structure and to which correspond definite forms of consciousness".[2] In the same work he also says that "neither legal relations nor political forms could be comprehended whether by themselves or on the basis of a so-called general development of human mind, but on the contrary they originate in the material conditions of life, the totality of which embraces within the term 'Civil

The Derivative theorists claim to have been influenced by Pashukinas arguments as given in his masterly work, *The General Thoery of Law and Marxism,* where he discussed the form and content of law in bourgeois society and its relevance to the working class in its fight for socialism. He considers Engels analysis of the state as given in his work, *The Origins of the Family, Private Property and the State,* where the state is seen only in relation to the classes and class struggles, as insufficient. To Pashukinas the fundamental problems of the capitalist state are much more complicated than those of precapitalist states. While analysing the nature of the capitalist state, Pashukinas considers it necessary to trace the emergence of the separation of private and public as well state and society in the course of capitalist development. The important questions he poses are "Why does the dominance of a class not continue to be that which it is, the subordination of one part of the population to another part? Why does it take on the form of official state domination? Or which is the same thing, why is not the mechanism of state constraints created as the private mechanisms of the dominant class? Why is it dissociated from the dominant class taking the form of an impersonal mechanism of public authority isolated from society?"[13]

The German Derivative School attempting to answer these hitherto untouched questions, takes the debates to newer arena.

Method or Approach of the Derivativists

While analysing the Anglo-American empiricist approach and the structural Marxist method, it is observed that these theories are, either in the main related to the contribution of one important commentator or there may be some contributors who have built up their theories based on certain general agreements about the methodological problems. But this German School includes many Marxian intellectuals who have very little in common. Except for the fact that all of them agree, that the study of the process of capital accumulation and hence particularisation, forms, functions and limitations of the state should be derived form this angle, no general agreement as to what should be the starting point, what analysis is to be adopted, what are the different variables to be considered to determine the form and content of the state and how to categorise functions and limitations of the state can be discovered in the German debate. Hence, one has to study the views of each participant of the school, on the method they applied in their analyses.

Wolfgang Muller and Christel Neususs initiated the debate as a criticism against social democratic thinking, which created illusions among the workers about the real character of the interventionist state. In their understanding Marx's reading of the bourgeois state is that it is the product of a society of developed commodity production (capitalist society), and of contradictions which arose from this form of production. Muller and Neususs say, that they are not concerned with the formation of a general Marxist theory of the state, but with the investigation of the specific functions of the state in safeguarding the process of capital valorisation under advanced capitalism. They consider that the needs for and limits of the state arise from the contradictions of capitalist process of production as a labour process and valorisation process.[14]

Beginning with capitalist process of production, Elman Altvater intends to investigate the political expression of the relationship of classes in bourgeois society, and determine thereform the functions of the state. To him, the state is to be grasped as "a special form of establishments of the social existence of capital alongside and outside bourgeois society, as an essential movement in the social reporoduction process of capital.[15]

Blanke, Jurgens and Kastendiek adopt, what they call, form analysis along with historical analysis. The first important thing for them is to determine, whether the state is an essential form of the capitalist society, if so how it developed as such. From their analyses of capital in general they intend to see why genesis of the state become necessary, how this state form in this capitalist society is related to its other forms and how being outside the economic process, it helps capital accumulation. In this sense, they also intend to derive 'state' as standing alongside and outside bourgeois society as an essential form, necessary for the reproduction of captialist society itself.[16]

All the three approaches, observed hitherto concentrate on the dynamics of competing capitals and derive state as an institution to protect the general interest of the capital as a whole. A few other approaches which give importance to some other aspects may be studied.

Flatow and Huisken study the surface of bourgeois society on the basis of the derivation of the state forms. Quoting from *German Ideology* they contend that according to Marx[17] the common or general interest which finds its institutionalised expression in the state must be derived from the analysis of the surface of bourgeois society. They aim to construct a theoretical structure which will locate the class character of the state not in individual functions but in the form of particularisation as such. From this it follows that there is no need for a general derivation of the specific functions since what constitute itself as state function can only be analysed in relation to the process of accumulation and its barriers. Here constitutive function for the genesis of bourgeois state is attributed to ideology or surface consciousness.[18]

Heide Gerstenberger attempts to study the bourgeois state with the period of primitive accumulation as her starting point. In her concrete historical analysis of the general conditions of valorisation of capital, she analyses as to why and how changes in the form of the state necessitated. The contradiction between the form and content and also between form and function of the state are discussed. She then studies how the workers are made to accept the system something natural. To her, "concrete activity of the state is to be grasped as the result of social confrontation which are mediated through channels into the state apparatus".[19] Class struggles are brought in to explain the establishment of the connection at a given movement.

Claudia Von Braunmuhl introduces a new dimension altogether. She considers that the nation state should be analysed on the international market level. To her, it is wrong to consider that the national development and nation state activities are determined internally. Since it is the world market which mediates, in reality, national accumulation and productive forces, examination of the nation state should start from this point. Along with this influence of the world market and internationalisation of production on class relations within particular nations are to be examined. To quote her "the accumulation must be reconstructed conceptually in the world market context, vis-a-vis this totality, historical partitions, divisions, the political coming together of capitals in bourgeois nation state, nation state apparatuses are to the analytically determined as the particular". Her study is "turned to specifying the conditions under which capital. . . is particularised into national capital and their delinked political organisation in the national state".[20]

Joachim Hirsh thinks, that the starting point of the analyses of bourgeois state should be the capitalist mode of production, appropriation of surplus value and the laws of reproduction that continue within the system. State is to be seen as a particular form of social domination, not simply as a bearer of certain functions. The capitalist state has to be understood in all its relationship with the capitalist society. He considers that "an analysis of the concrete mode of appearance of the bourgeois state and its changing functions is only possible on the basis of a theory of the capitalist process of accumulation and crisis. Like the analysis of the form of the state, such a theory must start from the dual character of labour and the consequent determination of the capitalist process of production as the contradictory unity of labour process and process of valorisation".[21]

These being, in brief, the approaches adopted by different German analysts, one may examine their contributions to the study of the bourgeois state. It has already been observed that the aim of the debate is to determine at what point of the study of the capitalist mode of productions the derivation or the particularisation of the state as an independent entity outside and alongside bourgeois society becomes necessary. But given the method or approaches it is clearly evident that the participants of the German debate differ among themselves on many issues. This limitation also has a brighter side. Almost all of them throw light on a particular aspect of bourgeois state. Taken together, their contributions broaden the scope of the theory of the capitalist state.

Here, while discussing the German Derivativists one may refer to the analysis of Marxian writers of other countries who felt the necessity of relating the study of bourgeois state to the dynamics of capitalist economy. To enable one to have a comprehensive knowledge about the dialectical relationship between the bourgeois state and the capitalist economy.

The Problem of Welfare State :

The bourgeois theory of welfare state indeed posed a big challenge to the Marxist conception of the class state.[22] Marxists should be able to explain why the modern capitalist state undertakes so many social welfare measures benefiting workers and other weaker sections, that too against the wishes of the individual members of the capitalist class.

Poulantzas' explanation to this question is examined in the preceding chapter. His rigid distinction between economic and political struggles and his characterisation of the capitalist state as the political organising centre of the bourgeoisie make Poulantzas convinced that in order to protect the political interests of the bourgeoisie the state can force its members to concede the economic demands of the workers. But, as Mandel points out, the explanation advanced by Poulantzas that "in the present phase of capitalism the main function of the bourgeois state is political, while the main form of bourgeois ideology is economist, is a scholastic and artificial attempt to separate closely interdependent mechanisms".[23] Behind the economic concessions that the state makes, there are long term economic interests of the whole burgeoisie. This aspect is clearly brought out by the derivativists.

Muller and Neususs, attacking the belief as illusions created by the welfare state assert that the state's social policies are only a response in the face of growing threat to the very foundation of the capitalist society.[24] To them, it is the contradictory basis of the capitalist mode of production, which demands particularisation of the state. On the basis of Marx's analysis of factory laws, it is argued that the contradiction between individual and collective interests of the capital explains both the excessive exploitation of labour through the extension of the working day (absolute surplus value) and the consequent intervention by the state. Competition compels the individual capitalists to increase the working hours in order to increase the surplus value. If this is continued by consuming all the available labour power at one stroke, it will invite the resistance of the workers, posing a threat to the entire capitalist class. In order to avoid this danger, the collective interests of the capital demands reduction of the length of the working day. Since it cannot be achieved by voluntary action of the individual capitalist the need for forcible regulation of the individual capital arises. At this point comes the intervention of the institution of state, "external to capital, equipped with supervisory jurisdiction and effective sanctioning power, in short a giant and growing bureaucratic apparatus of coercion".[25] This is how many other social policies came into existence to contain the excesses committed by the individual capitalists.

The policy of nationalisation of industries or development of public sector in the developed capitalist countries falls into this category. Many Fabian-writers, social democrats, revisionists—claimed it as the gradual development of socialism within the bourgeois setups. However, explanation of this kind was given by Marx and Engels long ago. According to them State ownership of the means of production in capitalist societies does not bring socialism; rather it lays the foundation to state capitalism which further strengthens the capitalist system which may lead a state towards monopoly conditions. To withstand the recurring economic crisis and to control the anarchy in the system of production, the state takes-over weak and inefficient firms. Sometimes the inability of the private capitalists to undertake essential basic industries, forces the state to take the responsibility of starting the basic industries though they do not yield immediate profits because of their long gestation periods. Similarly, the modern state is taking up the job of creating infrastructural facilities such as transport, education, banking, research and health facilities. They have become inevitable because the welfare of the state has to be considered. Though other sections of the people may get temporary economic relief out of the state expenditure spent on them they become in reality "another fiscal burden on the state in the form of outlays required to meet the social cost of private production".[26] State ownership does not bring any structural changes to the capitalist system. Capital-labour relations remains. Extraction of surplus value continues. Workers continue as workers and do not have any effective right over the so-called public sectors. Engels says, "Then modern state, no matter what its form, is essentially a capitalist machine, the state of capitalist is the ideal personification of the total national capital. The more it proceeds to the taking workers remain wage workers-proletarians. The capitalist relation is not done away with. It is rather brought to a head".[27]

Let us discuss now, how, this welfare state is related to the working class. It should be kept in mind that social welfare policies are not implemented voluntarily by the state itself. Most of these rights are in fact won over by the united struggles of the working class on the whole. The direct threat of the working class unrest is one of the triggering factors in the taming of social policy and development. The state develops and utilises social welfare measures for defusing the discontent of the working class and, equally importantly, does so by developing policies which secure working class allegiance and their support for a better social order. Along with political necessity, there are certain practical economic compulsions forcing the state to undertake social policy which may bring in change in economic, political and class structures.

In course of time the capitalists had realised that labour is not a surplus commmodity that can be used up and then discarded. Capitalism has both an immediate and long term interest in healthy maintenance and reproduction of labour power in a state. Continuous extraction of the absolute surplus value by the capitalist endangers the reproduction of labour power in the long run. A worker can be more productive and efficient at work only if his basic requirements are met, is always realized and met-with. This realisation demands state intervention to ensure the reproduction of labour power through welfare policies such as bonus, pensions, medical care, insurance, minimum pay etc. which enhances the living condition. In the capitalist society there exists a vast number of non-wroking population—unemployed, children, students and socially and economically backward sections which can act as the industrial reserve force. Political and economic necessity demands that they do not get completely neglected by the system. The state in the long run interests of capitalism makes policies like unemployment relief, schooling, scholarships, housing and medical facilities benefiting these strata of people. Ian Gough considers the state as an institutional response to the two requirements of the capitalist society viz, reproduction of labour power and the maintenance of the non-working population.[28]

Here one may examine the question of exploitation of the workers in these so-called welfare states. It is a fact that the workers of the advanced capitalist states enjoy more monetary benefits than those of the underdeveloped countries. It is also a fact that this is made possible to an extent by the super profits that the capitalist earn ponticularly in the Third World countries. Emmanuel Arghiri stated that in imperialist states "the relative importance of national exploitation from which a working class suffers. . . diminishes continually as compared with that from which it benefits through belonging to a privileged nation....Therefore a de facto united front of workers and capitalists of the well-to-do countries, directed against the poor nations coexists with internal trade union struggles over the sharing of the loot".[29] If accepted, this amounts to concluding that proletarians of the rich countries are the exploiters of poor ones and that the labour of the workers in the imperialist nations ceases to be a source of surplus value.

The derivativists, however, realise the significance of the process of capital accumulation as well as the necessity of social reproduction and they avoid taking such a revisionist stand. They hold that the workers should continuously be exploited if the capitalist system is to reproduce itself. Hence the German writers observe that the state maintains labour as an object of exploitation by capital, it forces the working class to sell labour power at cheaper rates, and it regulates the conflict between the wage labour and capital by law or if necessary, by force.[30]

Charles Bettelheim, who takes issue with E. Arghiri, more effectively shows from Marx that although due to high level of intensity and productivity of labour in rich countries the wages and purchasing power of the workers of the advanced countries may be relatively more than that of the poor countries, they in reality get more exploited than the workers of the third world. In place of extraction of absolute surplus value the method of creating relative surplus value sets in making the exploitation "more refined, more civilised and more efficient and more intensive". Further Bettelheim points out that "domination by imperialism is based above all on the exploitation of proletarians in the imperialist countries".[31] Since getting superprofits in the third world itself requires the ability of the products of one country to compete with those of other nations, each state should intensify and devise more effective ways of exploitation of its own workers, so that it can produce good quality of goods at lower costs of production. Workers may not be conscious of these facts and they may become victims of bourgeois culture. This however, does not negate or at least minimise the exploitation of the workers in the advanced capitalist countries. However the third world countries are always subjected to labour exploitation.

Our discussion about the welfare state will be incomplete without analysing the contribution of Keynes. The growth of monopoly capitalism intensifies the tendency of overproduction leading to unemployment and other crises. Keynes "attributed the crisis to oversaving by rentiers and financial institutions; by proposing to remedy this through fiscal and monetary measures alone" and "he suggested a way of restoring profitability and full employment without sacrificing economic or political freedoms".[32] The simple solution put forward by him is to plug the growing gap between the investment and consumption by increasing the state expenditures. State spending on welfare measures will not be a waste, it only helps in further stabilising the capitalist relations by increasing the demand. Keynes suggested overall planning for the whole country to be undertaken by the clever and disinterested public servants and technocrats. Keynesianism came out as a deliverance to the advanced capitalist states which were than under crisis following the depression of 1930s and later the World War II. Implementation of Keynesian principles by the states strengthened the capitalist system and diffused the revolutionary forces. Many capitalist nations suffer due to inefficiency. The social reforms at times contain and modify some of the excesses of capitalist employers. By establishing a national uniformity the state compels the individual capitalists to follow certain standards and practices. The state forces manufacturers and industrialists to recognise 'the true interests of their own order' and to create a total social system which allows for a stable development. Through the provision of social policy the state relieves capital of a major part of the cost of maintaining and reproducing labour power and serves capital very effectively and efficiently. Thus anatomy to the social welfare policies shows that by implementing them, the so-called welfare state does not undermine capitalism rather it further strengthens the general viability of capitalism.

Limitations of the Welfare State :

The welfare state is a pragmatic response of the system to the day-to-day problems created by the caiptalist society. Though the welfare state to an extent mitigates the problems of the people, in reality, it does not create any new society based on justice as Gunnar Myrdal and others claimed. Similarly, in spite of the substantial increase in the authority and ability of the state, it amounts to overestimation, if one, like Offe and Habermas claims that in the present era market mechanisms are replaced by political decision making. These aspects are very clearly brought out by the Derivativists.

Pointing out the limitations of the welfare state, Muller and Neususs show that "social policy can never provide a conscious and planned care for the maintenance, renewal and improvement of the social working capacity of the collective workers, the associated producers themselves".[33] They expose the myth of welfare state by showing that the state does not redistribute income between labour and capital, at best it can do so within the various fractions of the same class. Altvater considers that the interventionist state is never 'a real material capitalist' but only an 'ideal fictitious capital'. Analysing the system limit imposed by capital, Blanke, Jurgens and Kastendiek show that the state shall be free to intervene in the face of its own barriers. But if at any time the state attempts to transcend the system by intervening at the source of production of surplus value, then the capital reacts in spectacular forms through inflation, withholding of investments, removal of production to other countries and withdrawal of capital.[34] Hirsh also concentrates on this aspect. He shows that the state neither creates money nor brings into existence the bourgeois relations and their foundations, private property. The state either Marxist or capitalist cannot change the system based on the process of extraction of surplus value and accumulations of capital. He says that under capitalist conditions, no unified interventionist strategy or political planning can be possible. The state intervenes only as heterogeneous conglomerate of individual bundles of measures.[35]

The stand of the Derivativists is reinforced in the writings of many other writers. For example, Larry Hirschhorn says that though social spending can play 'counter-cyclical' role in stabilizing the economy, the optimum level of social service spending is still determined by the immediate profit needs of the capitalists. "The size, scope and, with Keynesian amendments, the timing of social service spending are all determined by the existing conditions of production."[36] Michael Reich in his *Military Spending and Production for Profit* shows that social spending never had the blank cheque of the capitalists since "many kinds of social spending put the government in direct competition with particular industries and with the private sector as a whole. This goes against the logic of a capitalist economy".[37] Massive social spending also tends to upset the labour market and interferes with the market in consumer goods; thus bringing into question the necessity of private ownership and control over production. To avoid the displeasure of the capitalists arising out of these complications, Reich claims the capitalist state is resorting to militarisation of economy as an alternative to social policy.

O'Connor in his *The Fiscal Crisis of the State,* brings to light the contradictory functions that the interventionist state is forced to perform. He shows that mounting state expenditure (which includes social capital and social expenses) intended to fulfil accumulation and legitimation needs of the capitalist societies leads to big deficits in budgets. Though the state can overcome this problem by developing profit making state enterprise, politically such measures are not feasible. Such measures affect the profit making interests of private capitalists. "In capitalist societies, state investments are conferred to non profit making spheres. It is in the interests of the private capital to seize all possible profit making opportunities for itself and resist the encroachments of state capital on its own natural territory".[35] O'Connor further says that though there were periods when corporate capital used the state to develop and manage productive wealth in the interests of general economic efficiency, the state is rapidly stripped off its capital assets with the return to normalcy. Under such conditions, the only alternative left to the state to overcome the fiscal crisis, is to impose heavy taxes, thus affecting millions of people of different categories and different walks of life, depending directly or indirectly on the state for survival. Capitalist state fail in their welfare measures as for as taxing is concerned. Referring to the U.S.A. he says that during the recent years because of high taxation and inflation, real wages and salaries of the state workers declined. Welfare, education and health budgets are frozen or out across the entire country, though the state expenditure on social capital continue to increase. This shows the malhandling of capitalist state situations. Ramesh Mishra shows similar trend in Britain. Capital spending on social services rose rapidly in the early 1970s but was sharply cut back in 1974. The period 1973-75 might be termed Phase I of the cuts. Phase II began in 1976, when for the first time the rise in current spending was almost halted, even in the most labour intensive social services. By 1977-78, capital spending in education and the personal social services amounted to less than one half the level in 1973-74.

As such, whether capitalist or Marxist the myth of permanent welfare state is now at stake. The contradictions within the capitalist mode of production are now facing crises and they are likely to threaten the foundations of welfare state. Keynesian economics is now being replaced by Reaganomics or Thatcherism.[39] Disarray of international economy and structural constraints of domestic economics will not permit now to undertake many social welfare measures, as the state took in fifties and sixties. Hence Skidelsky points out, "If Keynes's attempt to establish the rule of philosopher kings failed when social authority was still relatively secure, it has even less chance today".[40]

Commodity Fetishism and Capitalist State :

One important question that German debate tries to solve is : why does the state in capitalist society appear to be netural or impartial authority, not the puppet of dominant class? Very few Marxist thinkers thought about this question. Most of the Marxists generally attributed the appearance of neutrality of the bourgeois state to ideology or legal relations. But the derivativists give importance to commodity fetishism peculiar to the capitalist's mode of production. Marx alleged that capitalism presents itself on the surface of life in distorted forms. What it is really like within its deep recesses is quite different from what its facial expressions suggest. Although in reality captialism is based on capital-labour relations, at the surface level the individuals appear to have relations not with one another, but only with the material commodities they possess. In other words, "Individuals exist to one another only in sofar as their individual commodities exist". The German thinker argue that the capitalist state being a form essential in the capitalist society, surface distortions of different aspects in the capitalist mode of production, reflect even in the state to make it appear as a neutral force. To quote Muller and Neususs: "The fact that it (state) is the particularisation of a specific mode of production is turned on its head. This reification or autonomisation of the state is a necessary illusion resulting from the bourgeois mode of production just as much as are the forms of money, capital, wage-labour, profit, factors of production or revenues. These illusions are forced up on the agents of production by the particular mechanism of this production, and it is these which really determine their activity".[41]

Gerstenberger and Hirsh claim that though the state uses force to bring capitalist relations of production, once the capitalist economy is established it can work without use of any force.[42] The economy automatically produces the general conditions necessary for the existence of social capital by assuring average condition of exploitation, equivalent rates of surplus value, average rates of profit etc. Since exploitation takes place by creating illusion that all labour is paid in the form of wages, no extra-economic coercion is needed. Moreover, state being an institution divorced from production process, hence form the duty of extraction of surplus value, it withdraws itself from society and takes an independent form in appearance.

Flatow and Huisken also take up the question; why is it that everyone-worker as well as capitalist -submits to the bourgeois state, and why does the state apparatus appear as the administrator of common interests? To answer them, Flatow and Huisken proceed from Volume III of *Capital* where Marx speaks of trinity formula—profit to capital, ground rent to land and wages to labour.[43] In bourgeois society all members get their income from one or the other source. All these members of the 'proud bourgeois' society always aim to protect and struggle to increase their income from their respective sources. Along with the capitalists and landlords, even the workers attempt to maintain and reproduce their labour power. Here the contradiction between labour and capital is subsumed under fetishised forms of surface. Dimension of false consciousness checks workers possible insight into the pursuit of their actual economic interests. In reality it helps in realizing the interests of capital. Social Darwinsitic tendencies are restricted to achieving dominance within their own spheres of activity.[44] However, in such a system where everyone is involved in the pursuit of their own interests, the need for regulating the particular interests and protecting the general interests of the whole community arises. Precisely at this juncture, the doubling of individual into private property owner and citizen takes place. It also presents, along side society, the state as an institution for general administration.[45]

Thus the derivativists attribute appearance of neutrality of the bourgeois state to the dynamics of commodity production. Recently David Wells also attempted to study the influence of commodity fetishism on the nature and appearance of capitalist state.[46] The derivativists almost completely neglect the role of ideology. The legal relations, though not neglected, are seen merely as the reflections in social relations of the law of value that operates within the capitalist mode of production as the basic general law.

Capitalist State and Social Reproduction

The German School looks at the capitalist State as arising out of the necessities of capital. Though all of them maintain that the state force is not necessary for extraction of surplus value, they argue that the institution of state become necessary to undertake certain functions necessary for the reproduction of capitalist society. Incapacity of the capital to create necessary conditions conducive to free operation of the law of value necessitates existence of an institution divorced from production process. Such institution is expected to remove all obstacles in the path of capital valorisation.

Altvater considers that all functions of the state will be aimed to secure the foundations for existence of society fragmented into individual interests. Different state functions, noted by him, include (1) maintenance of labour as an object of exploitation by capital, (2) regulation of the conflict between wage labour and capital by law or if necessary by force, (3) safe-guarding and expanding the national capital on the world market.[47] The state institutionalise the class conflict by legalising the trade unions. It follows different means to force the working class to sell labour power at cheaper rates.[48] The state regulates political and legal relationships between people in a bourgeois society. If situation demands it undertakes other economically determined actions.

Hirsch gives a more elaborate description of the role that the capitalist state plays in the social reproduction. According to him, the development of state functions depends on three moments ;

(1) The imposition of the capitalist structure, and the emergence of proletariat as a class and its dependence for its survival on capital accumulation. It requires welfare activities like creation of employment, social security from accident, illness, old age pensions, social assistance etc.

(2) Concentration and monopolisation of capital with the formation of the finance capital and the world imperialist market. It necessitates measures for redistributing revenues, taxation, regulation of credit system, budgeting, process etc. all for the benefit of the monopolists.

(3) Growing significance of technical reduction of labour process and process of circulation to counter the falling rate of profit. This phenomenon forces the state to mobilise capital in the sphere of technology organise labour process to suit technological development, revolutionise the technique of production—all these to create State-monopoly-science-technology complex.[49]

It was stated in the preceding chapters that both Miliband and Poulantzas consider the state to function in the main as political organiser. Autonomous status that they gave to politics and the state led them to minimise the growing responsibility that the capitalist state is undertaking to carry out economic functions. Though the derivativists did not ignore the functions related to the classes and class struggles, the importance they attributed to the economic functions performed by the state is so much that it makes one critic name this theoretical approach as 'economic functionalism', if not 'economic determinism'.[50]

Along with the German debate, one can also refer to O'Connor's *The Expanding Role of the State*,[51] where he gives a systematic account of the numerous functions that the modern state undertakes for the purpose of accumulation and legitimation. Some of the programmes that the state takes up to foster accumulation includes highway construction, basic research to develop new technologies, job training, subsidies to maintain essential rail service etc. O'Connor notes that larger part of the state expenditures is allocated to military forces, welfare and social security both at home and abroad.

Though the derivativists also reflect on such functions, important inadequacy seems to be their neglect of the role played by the state in militarising the economy, especially in a country like the U.S.A. Long back C.W. Mills observed,"The structural clue to the power elite today lies in the economic order, the clue is the fact that the economy is at once a permanent war economy and a private corporation economy. American capitalism is now in a considerable part a military capitalism...."[52] Since 1950 the U.S. government has spent over a million dollars or about one-tenth of total economic output on the military expenditure. Almost two-fifths of the federal budget feeds the 'military industrial complex'. Nearly one-tenth of the labour force is engaged in military related employment.[53] Militarisation of economy becomes the basic trend in all advanced capitalist countries, now witnessing the crisis in market due to the fall in demand. State spending on military gives stimulation to the sagging economy and serves the interests of monopolies by creating artificial demand in the market. Moreover, military spending unlike state expenditure on social policies is easily expandable without threatening the interests of the private capital. Military contracts are highly profitable. It is said that the North American Aviation Company realized profits of 612 per cent and 802 per cent on its investments in military contracts in two successive years.[54] Because of such high rate of profitablity, considerable percentage of the big business is involved in this particular field. Nathanson estimates that out of the 500 largest manufacturing corporations in 1964, at least 205 were significantly involved in military contracts, either in production or in research and development.[55] Among the top 100 firms, 65 are significantly involved in the military market. The military goods market usually has the decided advantage of supplying long term contracts, often accompanied by enough guarantees to reduce and even eliminate risks in building up additional plant and equipment and remove risky aspects of normal investment programmes.

In addition to benefiting the business community, the militarisation of economy has greater role to play in the reproduction of capitalist society as such. According to Harry Magdoff, state military activity is necessary to protect potential resources of raw materials, safe-guard foreign markets and foreign investments, conserve commercial sea and air routes, preserve spheres of influence, create new foreign customers and investment opportunities and maintain the structure of the world market.[56] For all these reasons, one can say that militarisation of economy became indispensable necessity for the reproduction of the domestic economies of all the advanced capitalist countries irrespective of their ideology, whether capitalist or communist.

Capitalist State and World Capitalism

Capitalism, which integrated the whole world for the first time is not merely a national system; it is a world system. Hence the study of capitalist state is to be related to the movement of capital in the world economy and not merely to the dynamics of domestic capital. However, here one should be very cautious in answering the questions viz., do changes in international capital necessarily to bring about change in political forms?; if, so, can any one conclude that since there is a tendency of internationalisation of capital, there is a probability of the development of international capitalist state? Criticising the oversimplified economistic view of Mandel's thesis that success and failure of European integration depends on the form taken by international centralisation of capital, Poulantzas points out that "the state is not a mere tool or instrument of the dominant classes, to be manipulated at will, so that every step that capital took towards internationalization would automatically induce a parallel 'supranationalisation of states. . .'. The problem we are dealing with cannot be reduced to a simple contradiction of mechanistic kind between the base (internationalisation of capital) and a superstructural cover (nation state) which no longer corresponds to it".[57] Though it may be a correct observation, Poulantzas fails to give an alternative to understand the dialectical relationship between the capitalist state and internationalisation of capital.

The national character of the state and cosmopolitan nature of the capitalist economy have not escaped the attention of Marx. In *The German Ideology* Marx writes, "The big industry created everywhere the same relations between the class and society and this destroyed the peculiar individualities of the various nationalities. And, finally while the bourgeois state still retained separate national interests, big industry created a class which in all nations has the same interests and with which nationality is already dead, a class which is really rid of all the old world and at the same time pitted against it".[58] Elsewhere, Marx says, "the class struggle is national not in substance, but in form". But the framework of the present day nation state is itself in its turn economically within the framework of the world market, politically within the framework of the system of states.[59] Refusal to study the state from this angle creates a great void in scientific study.

Claudia Von Braunmuhl attempts to reflect on his aspect. First she demands that the study of the capitalist state should no longer be taken as the level on which the movement of the capital is to be analysed, it should be world market as a totality. In course of analysing it, attempts should be made to know how capital is particularised into national capital and their delimited political organisation in the nation state.

The modern nation states are part of the capitalist mode of production. Capitalism first develops within the pre-existing boundaries where authority exists. Though in all capitalist countries economy dominates, it needs state for carrying out certain functions necessary for social reproduction. For this capital makes use of "the existing political apparatus of force to impose and safegauard itself, reforming and expanding it (state) for its own needs.[60] The first step in this attempt is transformation of feudal state to aboslutist state. Here the state's coalition with mercantile capital undermines feudal socio-economic foundations and acts as mid-wife to emerging capitalism. Notwithstanding its dependence on trade to amass wealth, it erects a tariff wall for the sake of ascending bourgeoisie by establishing state boundaries and by protecting its external borders. With further development, mercantile state integrates national economies within the world market. With the consequent development of international law each nation begins to recognise one another as political representatives of nation states. The industrial revolution that took place in England made the Great Britain a supreme power. In the wake of growing supremacy of England, threatened European states were also forced to undergo primitive accumulation and industrial revolution.

Analysis of Braunmuhl shows to an extent, the necessity of a national state to extend capitalist relations of production everywhere. State's role in reproduction of domestic economy consolidates and further strengthens the world capitalist order. Since there was no world state before, the question of the development of supranation state with the internationalisation of capital does not come into the picture. Though such analysis partially answers Poulantzas' questions, further calrifications may be made on the basis of E E C experience to show why the capitalist states continue to be nation states in spite of the growing internationalisation of capital.

The monopolists in the advanced capitalist nations achieved cosmopolitan character. For them the age of independent sovereign states indeed become obsolete. Surpassing the national barriers is necessary for them to squeeze, if possible, the whole world market. But their intentions cannot automatically bring into being, the supranation state. This is due to the existence of a number of contradictions within the capitalist system. Even the so-called internationalisation of capital refers only to the merging of monopoly capitals of different countries for certain benefits. The E E C which came into existence to check and prevent the growing influence and power of the U.S.A. and Japan in the European industry and market is a good example. Even within the E E C there are many contradictions. For, such an economic integration helps only the monopolist who have the ability and considerable resource to capture the markets for their goods and benefits. As such non-monopolists and small scale industrialists will not be benefited much by this integration, hence these sections may not support (at times even oppose) such economic integration. Consequently, even a country like Britain, was hesitant to enter the E E C in the beginning. Moreover the E E C confines its sphere of activity in the main to industrial field only. Considerable number of agricultural products still continue to have national markets. Even an advanced country like France, opposes complete integration of agricultural economy becuase of the existence of a number of small farmers within the country. They are infact unable to compete with big capitalist farmers in other countries.

Even if such economic integration is considered possible at European level, it will not extend beyond Western Europe to include even the U.S.A. and Japan. The U.S.A. —the biggest industrial power—itself is afraid of Japanese goods taking over American market. If so, countries like India, which are trying to achieve regional integration in the form of S A A R C, will be mortally afraid of joining the some such supranational organisation of advanced capitalist countries due to the fear of losing even the home market that they possess.

Along with them there is another contradiction. Even though the monopolists become cosmopolitan in character, the people are by and large nationalist in spirit, though the spirit has historically lost its progressive character. Any attempt to build supranation state will be opposed by the nationalist minded people. All these contradictions themselves explain why the capitalist state continues to be in the form of nation state though the capitalist economy became cosmopolitan in character.

Estimate

The German school's 'Neo-Orthodox Theory' has many remarkable features by which it can clearly distinguish itself from interpretations of other Marxist intellectuals and schools. It highlights the defects of Miliband and Poulantzas whose intentions to construct a regional theory of politics makes them turn blind eye to its base, economy. Relating the state to economy, by itself does not lead to instrumentalism or even to economic determinism. Infact, the German derivativists take a firm stand against instrumentalism which sees the state as a mechanical tool that can be used by the members of the dominant class to promote their personal interests. Their taking of this stand, even though they attempt to start the analysis by relating it to the process of capital accumulation, shows that it is not necessary to build up autonomous theory of politics to establish the relative autonomy of the capitalist state vis-a-vis the classes, more particularly the ruling class. This school presents a new method of posing the problems.

The way Pashukinas raises questions about the nature of the state is indeed worth noting. Though no one theory accepted by all could come out of this debate, the derivativists widened the dimension of scientific analysis of the state by pointing out different angles from which the state can be studied. Opposing the wrong conception that the state is a political organizer; looks after only the political interests of the class and hence even compels the capitalists to forgo their economic interests,[61] the German analysis shows that there are economic interests of the entire class hidden behind the so-called concessions that individual capitalists are forced to make due to the state intervention. Their awareness of the limitations of the state activity and acceptance of the role of class struggles protect them from the evil of economic determinism.

However, it should be noted that the German debate is not without certain drawbacks. At times their attempt to solve certain problems itself gives birth to many more questions. Though no attempt is made to point out the defects of the participants individually, certain generalisations about their drawbacks can be made.

First, one can examine their stress on relating the state to the problems and process of capital accumulating. To say that captalist state does not have any kind of relationship with the capitalist economy is indeed wrong. Yet the arguments that the derivation of forms, functions and limitations of the state, should be done only by relating it to the necessity of capital seems to be an exaggeration. It is true that the capitalist state creates the conditions. "But this relationship", as Mandel says "should not be exaggerated. The state is older than capital and its function cannot be immediately derived from those of commodity production and circulation".[62] Here, although one need not go along with the structural Marxist stand, it is worth noting what Domine Strinati is saying; "The economy is composed of different structures and the state consists of, to varying degrees, distinct apparatuses which may be differentially related to each other in terms of the specific functions performed. It is not the state as a whole, as it were, which performs the functions of capital accumulation but specific state apparatuses charged with differing and specific functions".[63]

Further, John Urry argues that the capitalist state is not directly related to the economy. For further illumination one may note again Marx's words "neither legal relations nor political forms could be comprehended whether by themselves or on the basis of a so-called general development of human mind, but that on the contrary—they originate in the material conditions of life, the totality of which embraces within the term 'civil society', that the anatomy of this civil society, however has to be sought in political economy".[64] This quotation shows that the political forms are firstly to be related to the civil society since it is in it that the state originates. But to understand the civil society, not the state, one needs to know the political economy. The German Derivativists, ignore the existence of civil society which actually mediates state and economy and they attempt to formulate a theory of capitalist state by directly relating it to capital.[65]

Further, one can observe, most of the contributors considering that the capitalist mode of production is based on the operation of law of value. Based on this, they also conclude that the state is a form essential in commodity production and that its appearance as a class neutral force is due to reflection of commodity fetishism. Here it may be observed that though law of value operates in the fullest form in capitalism it is not merely the law of capitalism, the law of value is the general law of commodity production. Though "capitalism is the most developed form of commodity production, where labour power becomes commodity",[66] commodity as such existed even before the advent of capitalism and it continues to exist in restricted sense, even in the early stages of socialism. When this is accepted, the state should in some sense appear as a class neutral force in pre-capitalist and even socialist societies, and this appearance is to be attributed to the commodity fetishism. This explanation does not appear to be a satisfactory answer. Further as Stalin points out, the basic law of capitalism is the law of surplus value, not the law of value.[67]

History shows that in the early stages of the development of capitalism, the state indeed acted as a coercive power in the interests of the emerging capitalist relations. (This is noted by Gerstenberger and Hirsch also). Even, the revolution of 1848 and Paris commune of 1871 show that commodity production which got consolidated by that time, could not create illusions among the workers of the class neutrality of the state in bourgeois society. It is only after the state started to regulate individual capitalisits, assure economic concessions to the workers and grant them political rights by conceding the universal adult franchiese and conferre legal status to trade unions and workers parties, that these illusions about the nature of the state started getting strengthened. Here one should not forget the role of law and ideology. Insufficient attention to the political works of Marx and Engels has caused some confusions among the German thinkers.

Though the Derivativists assign a role to the class struggles, they seem to look at classes as mere economic categories, the resultants of the given economic base, the relations of production. As such no importance is given to the role of class consciousness and class organisations. Likewise no role is assigned to the conscious role of individuals. Men are seen as the bearers of some form of commodity relations and hence are to get influenced in the main by the capital varisation proces.

The state is not analysed as the concrete structure, and so the dialectical relationship among the various organs of the state apparatus and between the state and ideology has not been clearly brought out. The origin of the state is attributed to the necessity of carrying out certain Functions. Even here state's function as a coercive power has not been highlighted.

Finally, while seeing the state as protector of the general insterest of the whole bourgeoisie most of them do not pay much attention to the special status of the monopolist fraction. Altvater and others discuss the dynamics and limitations of individual capitals. Here one should keep in mind the fact that the individual capital are not homogenous in their nature, form and functions. Situation does not change even after the advent of monopoly capitalism. Though monopolies and pure sectors exist side by side, in this era of imperialism, monopolies attained dominance over other sectors. Due to its superior economic position and organisational capabilities to manoeuvre others in their favour, monopoly becomes the order of all the advanced capitalist states. The pure firms are not to be (or cannot be) swallowed completely by the monopolies. Their existence and influence in the economy will be of little significance; at best the competitive firms can effectively play subrodinate roles to monopolies.[68] This trend influence even the class nature of the bourgeoisie. Within the capitalist class the monopolist fraction achieves dominance over other fractions of the capitalist class because of its affiliation to the system of monopoly. Under such circumstance, the form and functions of the state which runs 'along side and outside bourgeois society', necessarily undergoes certain changes. As the economic and political necessities and hence the survival of the bourgeois society demand, the state while attempting to look after the interests of the whole bourgeoisie, is forced to give more importance to the interests of monopolies, as well the monopolist fraction which is in reality supporting the system of monopoly capitalism. Under normal conditions the state tries to accommodate all fractions of capital. But if at any time the contradictions among the different fractions of capitalists become antagonistic, then the state necessarily stand benind the monopolist fraction and guards its interests.

Notes and Reference

1. Holloway, Johan and Picciotto. *State and Capital*, Edward Arnold, London, 1978, pp 5-6.
2. Marx and Engels, *Selected Works, Vol. I*, Progress Publishers, Moscow 1976, p. 503.
3. Marx and Engels, *Ibid.*, p.503.
4. Marx, Karl, *Capital Vol. III*, Progress Publishers, Moscow, p. 791.
5. Marx, Karl, *Economic Manuscripts of 1857-59* Progress Publishers, Moscow, 1970, p.273.
6. Engels, Frederick, *On Marx's Capital*, Progress Publishers, Moscow, 1975. p.18.
7. Lenin V.I, *The State* (Sverdlov University Lecture 1919) Progress Publishers, Moscow, 1973, pp. 20 and 23.
8. Lenin, *Imperialism the Highest Stage of Capitalism*, Progress Publishers, Moscow, 1978, p.77.
9. Lenin, *Ibid*, p.80.
10. Holloway and Picciotto, *op.cit* p. 15.
11. For Offe's conception of capitalist state, see his "Structural Problem of the Capitalist State", in *German Political Studies vol.I*, Sage, London, 1974. Also *The Theory of Capitalist State and the Problems of Policy Formation*, in L. Kindberg, R. Alford, C. Crouch, C. Offe (edited), '*Stress and Contradiction in Modern Capitalism*, Lexington Books, 1975.
12. Dyson, Kenneth, *State Tradition in Western Europe*, Oxford, Martin Robertson, London, 1980. p.237.
13. Holloway and Picciotto, *op.cit.*, pp. 19 and 58.
14. Muller, Wolfgang & Neuss, Christel, *The Welfare State Illusion and the Contradiction between Wage Labour and Capital*, in Holloway and Picciotto, *op,cit.*, pp.33-34.
15. Altvater, Elmar, *Some Problems of state Intervention*, in Hollway & Picciotto, p. 47.
16. Blanke, Bernhard, Jurgens, Ulrich, Kastendick, *Form and Function of the Bourgeois State*, in Holloway & Picciotto, *op,cit.*, pp. 118-119.

17. Marx, Karl, *the German Ideology in Selected Works Vol,I*, Moscow, Progress Publishers, 1976, p.35. Marx says-"Out of the very contradiction between the interests of the individual and that of the community the latter takes an independent form as the state, divorced from the real interests of individual and community and at the same time as an illusory communal life".
18. Reicheld Helnut, "On the Problem of the Derivation of the Bourgeois State". In Holloway and Picciotto, *op,cit.*, p. 45.
19. Gerstenberger, Heide, "Class Conflict, Competition and the State Functions' in-Holloway and Picciotto, *Ibid.*, p. 158.
20. Braunmuhl, Claudia, "Bourgeois Nation State Within the World Market Context", in Holloway and Picciotto, *Ibid.*, p.66.
21. Hirsch, Joachin. "The State Apparatus and Social Reproduction", in Holloway and icciotto, *Ibid.*, p.66.
22. This aspect has been examined in the first Chapter.
23. Mandel, Ernst, "The State in the Age of the Capitalism", C.G.Shaw Memorial Trust Publiation, Bombay, 1976, p. 18.
24. Holloway and Picciotto, *op.cit..*, p.37.
24. Holloway and Picciotto, *ibid.*, p. 37.
26. O'Connor James, "The Expanding Role of the State". In C. Edwards, M. Reich, M. E. Weisskopf. E.s *The Capitalist System*, New Jersey, Prentice Hall, 1978, p.238.
27. Engels, Frederick, *Anti Duhring*, Progress Publishers, Moscow, 1978, p. 338.
28. Gough, Ian, *Political Economy of the Welfare State*, Macmillan, 1979., pp 48-49.
29. Arghiri, Emmanuuel, *Unequal Exchange*, Monthly Review press, 1972, pp 180-182.
30. Holloway and Picciotto, *op.cit.* pp. 42, 138.
31. Bettelheim, Charles in Arghiri, *op.cit.*, pp. 303-04.
32. Skidelsky, Robert, *The Decline of Keynesian Politics.* In Crouch, Colin, London, Croomhelm, 1979, p.79.
33. Holloway and Picciotto, *op,cit.*, p. 39.
34. Holloway and Picciotto, *op.cit.*, p.140.
35. Holloway and Picciotto, *op.cit.*, p. 101.
36. Hirschham, Larry, *Contemporary Crisis*, The Netherlands, 1978. Reproduced in Quinney, Richard, *Capitalist Society*, Illinois, The Dorsey Press, 1979, p. 154.
37. Reich, Michael, *Military Spending and Production for Profit.* In C. Edwards, Reich, Weisskopf, E. *The Capitalist System*, *op.cit.*, p. 416.
38. O'Connor, James, *The Fiscal Crisis of the State.* In Quinney, Richard, *Capitalist Society*, *op.cit.*, pp. 287-288.
39. Mishra, Ramesh, *The Welfare State in Crisis*, Brighton, Wheatsheaf Books, 1984, p. 19.
40. Skidelsky, *op.cit.*, p. 81.
41. Holloway and Picciotto, *op.cit.*, p. 41.
42. Holloway and Picciotto, *ibid.*, p. 155.
43. Marx, Karl, *Capital Vol. III*, Progress Publishers, Moscow, 1977, p. 814.
44. Bhattacharya, Sisir, *Social Darwinism in India's Welfare State*, MVF, Hyderabad, 1984, p. 19.
45. Holloway and Picciotto, *op.cit.*, p. 52.
46. See Wells, David, *Marxism and the Modern State*, New Delhi, Select Book Syndicate, 1983.
47. Holloway and Picciotto, *op.cit.*, p. 42.

48. Holloway and Picciotto, *op.cit.*, p. 143.
49. Holloway and Picciotto, *op.cit.*, pp. 95-97.
50. Huge, Mosley,"Capital and the State : West German Neo-orthodox state Theory" in *The Review of Radical Political Economics*, Spring, 1982, p. 27.
51. O'Connor, "The Expanding Role of the State", R.C. Edwards, Reich, M, Weisskopf E. *op.cit.*, p. 242.
52. Mills, C.W., *The Power Elite*, Oxford University Press, 1977, pp. 276-77.
53. Reich, Michael, "Military Spending and Production for Profit". In R.C. Edwards, Reich, M. Weisskopf E., ed. *op. cit.*, p. 410.
54. Reich, Michael, *op.cit.*, p. 413.
55. Nathanson, C. "The Militarisation of the American Economy'. In Horowitz ed. *Corporations and the Cold War*, Monthly Review Press, 1969, p. 231.
56. Magdoff, Harry. "American Empire and the U.S. Economy". In Rhoden R I, *Imperialism and Underdevelopment a reader*, London Monthly Review Press, 1970. pp. 28-29.
57. Poulantzas, Nicos. *Classes in Contemporary Capitalism* N.L.B. London, p. 78.
58. Marx and Engels. *Selected Works vol. I*, Progress Publishers Moscow 1976. p.62.
59. Marx, *Critique of the Gotha Programme* Progress Publishers, Moscow, 1978. p. 29.
60. Holloway and Picciotto, *op.cit.* p. 173.
61. Polulantzas, Nicos. *Political Power and Social Classes*. Verso, 1982, pp. 190-94.
62. Mandel, Ernst, *The state in the Age of the Late Capitalism*, C.G, Shaw Memorial Trust, Bombay, 1976, p. 8.
63. Strinati, Dominie. In Crouch Colin, *op.cit.*, p. 194.
64. Marx and Engels, *Selected Works Vol.I* Progress Publishers, Moscow, 1976, . 503.
65. Urry, John, *The Anatomy of Capitalist Societies*, Macmillan, 1981, pp. 84-85.
66. Lenin, *Imperialism the Highest Stage of Capitalism*, Progress Publishers, Moscow, 1978. p. 59.
67 Stalin, *Economic Problems of Socialism in the U.S.S.R*, Peking, Foreign Language Press, 1972, pp 37-38.
68. O'Connor, James, *Competitive Capital and Monopoly Capital*. In R.C. Edwards, Reich, M. Weisskopf E. ed. *op.cit.* p.159.

Chapter V

STATE AND RULING CLASS IN THE THIRD WORLD

Dependency or Self-reliance

Emergence of the Third World, now covering more than half of the world territory and about two-thirds of the world population is a significant event in the post-war world. Behind their appearance as new actors in the international system, there lies a history of about 100 years of anti-imperialist struggles. With the weakening of the imperialist chains during the World War II these freedom movements gained momentum in most of the colonies and semi-colonies. The birth of socialist block as a powerful anit-imperalist force and the growing strength of the patriotic forces in colonies and semi-colonies made it difficult for the imperialists to stick on to their policy of colonialism. Taking advantage of the weakness of the imperialist forces, many countries in Asia and Africa attained political independence. Along with them, a few other countries like Iran, Maldiaves and some of the Arab States which were never colonies of any imperialist power also identified their interests with the developing societies.

Ever since the Third World countries made their presence felt in the international politics, their dynamics began to attract the attention of the intellectual world. In the initial years, the intellectuals concentrated mainly on the problems of development and modernisation in the Third World. However after the mid-sixties, many scholars have started coming forward to understand the nature of state in the UDCs. Apart from liberal thinkers there are many Marxist and other radical schools which attempted to theorise the dynamics of the underdeveloped countries. But the social formation in the Third World is so specific that it has become difficult to arrive at consensus about the character of the state in these developing nations. Since each nation in the developing world exhibits so many specific features, a comprehensive knowledge of the nature of the state in the Third World requires concrete analyses of the dynamics of class struggles, structure of civil societies and stages of development study is not possible unless a theoretical discourse is built by perfecting the existing Marxist analytical categories. Keeping this necessity in mind, an attempt is made in this chapter to evaluate different Marxist and other radical schools of thought, especially on questions relating to the state, classes and economic development in the Third World. Since such evaluation presupposes a fair knowledge of the Third World, one may first try to grasp the specificities of the social formations in the developing societies.

Multi-structural Societies

All the underdeveloped countries (UDCs) are multi-structural and multi-stratified societies exhibiting considerable variations in the levels of economic development. Many countries including those with the highest population are among the low income countries with highest percentage of people living below the poverty line. According to an estimate, 75% of people in Bangladesh, 51% in Indonesia and 34% in Pakistan live in poverty. On the other side one can see some of the oil rich countries like Saudi Arabia, United Arab Emirates and Kuwait whose per capita income is equal to or in some cases more than many of the western capitalist countries. In addition there are newly industrialising countries like Singapore and South Korea whose per capita incomes remain around $3,000.[1] Despite these variations in the levels of economic development, in almost all countries capitalist and pre-capitalist structures exist side by side for a long time. Unlike 'pure' economic formations of the advanced capitalist societies, the developing nations are characterised by the existence of different modes of production. Even within the Third World, nature of multi-structural economy differs from one country to another. The multi-structural socio-economic systems of Saudi Arabia and Bhutan cannot be reduced to those of India and Sri Lanka. Yet it should be admitted that in all countries social forces having their roots in precapitalist social formations dominate the internal politics. Mention may be made here of castes in India, tribes in Africa and religions in countries like Iran, Bhutan, Nepal and Pakistan. The roles that these structures and their corresponding social forces play are so dominant in certain countries that they even overshadow the role of the classes and class struggles. Even in these countries where they play subordinate role, they succeed in giving specific orientation to the class politics of these states.

Specificity of Classes in the UDCs

As far as the question of the nature of classes is concerned, the developing societies show certain distinct features which cannot be seen in the West. Though in certain countries of Africa classes are still in formative stages, one can see well developed classes in many of the nations of Asia and Latin America. But correlation of social forces is not alike in all these countries. In certain countries such as India, Pakistan, Malaysia, and Singapore, capitalist growth reached the stage of monopoly. Taking advantage of the state control over production sector, in many African states a class of bureaucratic bourgeoisie developed. In Pakistan, Jordan, Morocco and in many countries of Latin America land lords who still inherit hundreds of acres of land reign as influential classes. But in countries where communal ownership dominates, say as in Tropical Africa and Oceania class of land lords is completely absent. Numerically dominant classes in the developing societies seem to be the peasantry and the petty bourgeoisie. Peasants constitute 60% to 80% of the population of certain countries. Petty-bourgeoisie including the professional and urban middle class and semi-proletarian strata constitutes sometimes about 65% of the population. As far as the working class is concerned, one can notice uneven development. In countries like India, South Korea and Egypt the working class is numerically a well developed class. But in countries like Kenya and Fiji the workers are yet to emerge as a class. In countries like Swaziland, Tonga and Western Sahara the working class is almost absent.[2]

Question of Ruling Class

What constitutes the ruling class of such countries? This is another controversial question. As is mentioned earlier, most of the scholars tend to generalise the issue by basing on the experiences of one or a few countries. During Mao's regime, the official circles in China used to argue that the ruling class in the Third World countries is composed of feudal lords and comprador bourgeoisie.[3] Hamza Alavi who based his arguments on his study of Pakistan, Bangladesh and Indonesia concluded that in the post-colonial societies the ruling class is constituted by "three propertied classes, namely the metropolitan bourgeoisie, the indigenous bourgeoisie and the landed classes".[4] Followers of A.G. Frank would argue that the underdeveloped countries are led by the lumpen bourgeoisie. On the other extreme, we have Michael Kalecki who says that most of the liberated countries have intermediate regimes where the petty-bourgeoisie and the rich peasantry form the ruling coalition.[5] However, such wide generalisations seem to go against the dialectical method which demands study of the particularities of each phenomenon before giving a general theory of it. Since classes and social forces which attained power after independence differed from one country to another, it is not appropriate to say that the class character of all countries in the Third World exhibit uniformity. Due to differences in correlation of class forces that led to the anti-imperialist struggles, the class character of the state also differ from one to another. In fact the questions related to the nature of liberation struggles and the classes or groups which attained state power are so complex that even those who claim themselves Marxists find it difficult to identify the nature of dominant classes in most of the countries of the Third World. For example, referring to Africa where indigenous bourgeois class is weak, Markovitz, Joel Samhoff and J.S. Saul argued that the bureaucratic bourgeoisie or 'the organisational bourgeoisie' became the ruling class.[6] But the communist activists like Babu consider that all the African states are dominated by the petty bourgeoisie or proto-bourgeoisie who act as lackeys of foreign imperialism.[7] In India also, even after forty years of independence the communists find it difficult to arrive at consensus about the class character of the state.[8] Such kinds of conflicting characterisations are unknown in the advanced western societies. Since the classes which attained state power after independence differ from one country to another, one can see different kinds of states viz., national bourgeois states, bourgeoisified feudal states, bureaucratic or comprador states and also countries where state power is jointly shared by the capitalists and the land lords.

Government and Political Regimes

Now one may have a look at the specificities of the nature of government and political regimes in the Third World. The Third World is a laboratory which is experimenting different forms of government and testing all kinds of political regimes. At the beginning, most of those colonies tried to experiment with parliamentary forms of government implanted on their soil by their colonial masters. But due to lack of essential conditions necessary for successful experimentation with bourgeois parliamentary superstructure the limitations of the experiment came to light within a short span of time. Contradictions between political superstructure and the actual dynamics of internal socio-economic structure led to modification of the role of parliaments in the Third World. Most of the countries opted for military-bureaucratic rule where parliaments became subordinate to the executive. In some other countries authoritarianism developed within the context of parliamentary forms of government. In countries like India legislatures became political power centres to reconcile the conflicting interests of different classes, castes, tribes, regions and religious communities. In some other countries like Bhutan, Nepal and many Arab countries the parliaments remained as only consultative organisations without any real powers.

Certain amount of democratic freedoms are guaranteed in countries where the national bourgeoisie dominates other classes. But in most of the countries with monarchical, and bureaucratic forms of government, the rights of the people are restricted. Status of political parties may be taken as an instance. In countries like Saudi-Arabia and Bhutan even the ruling classes do not have parties of their own. The political parties are generally banned in countries where military takes over governmental power. In certain countries communist parties are not generally allowed to function legally. In many of the African countries like Tanzania, Mozambique and Zaire there exists only one official party. But certain countries like Sri Lanka and India have multi-party system. However, it should be made clear that the nature and content of the single party system or multi-party system in the Third World are qualitatively different from those of the West.[10]

Another feature of the Third World is the transitory nature of its regimes. Generally no government or political regimes remain stable for a longer period. Among the UDCs there will be a very few states which did not experience any forms of the authoritarian government from the beginning. Such changing nature of the political regimes can be attributed to the changing correlation of class and other social forces within the Third World. International economic crises, external intervention, attitudes of the local elites and the dynamics of military officials, religious leaders and tribal chiefs—all these factors play important roles in giving particular colour to the government and the political regimes. If necessary, responding to the objective necessity to overcome the immediate problems, these political regimes mobilise one section of people against other. In the context of Latin America the roles that different regimes--populist, democratic, military and revolutionary regimes—could play in response to the necessity of managing different crises; the class or social forces that they could rally and the overall success and failures of all these regimes were well accounted in Gary.W. Wynia's book, *The Politics of Latin American Development*.[11]

Autonomy of the State in the Third World

Whatever be the forms of government or political regime, the states in all underdeveloped countries enjoy certian amount of autonomy vis-a-vis the dominant classes and their economic base. Levkovsky argues that this relative autonomy is "objectively caused by the very socio-economic and class-political structure of the transitional societies". Though all states enjoy some amount of autonomy, the forms of independence differ from one country to another. As Levkovsky puts it, "This increased relative autonomy of the state superstructure at various stages of revolution and under the impact of dissimilar objective and subjective factors, is realised in different forms".[12] In another sense, intellectuals like Hamza Alavi see it as the consequence of the weakness of the dominant classes within the post-colonial societies. To quote Alavi, "the state in the post-colonial society is not the instrument of a single class. It is relatively autonomous and it mediates between the competing interests of the three propertied classes namely the metropolitan bourgeoisie, the indigenous bourgeoisie and the landed classes, while at the same time acting on behalf of them all to preserve the social order in which their interests are embedded, namely the institution of private property and the capitalist mode as the dominant mode of production".[13] In the cases of certain Asian and African states sudden disappearance of colonial masters left a vacuum which could not be filled by the indigenous classes. Since none of the indigenous classes achieved the status or strength to be able to use the state power to its own advantage, the military-bureaucratic apparatus aquires relative independence. The scope of such autonomy is however restricted in countries like India where the bourgeoisie is fairly developed even before independence and it was and is conscious of its economic and political interests. But even in such countries the key role that the state plays in economy gives enough strength to the state to withstand any kind of pressure from the monopolist groups. Almost in all developing countries the state imposes many rules and restrictions to regulate the activities of the individual capitalists. While initiating the process of development in these multi-structural societies, the state creates conditions for the development of certain classes and social forces. For example, by providing irrigation, banking and marketing facilities the state facilitates conditions for the transformation of individual land lords into the rich peasants. If the conditions demand, to legitimise its own authority and to give credibility to the whole system, the state in the developing societies use nationalist ideology, religious dogmas or even pseudo-socialist slogans.

Compulsions of Economic Development : Imperialism and Third World

Political instability in the Third World is, in one sense, the result of the contradictions created by the low level of economic development. Except OPEC nations and the Western show pieces like Singapore, South Korea and Hongkong, all other countries are backward—most of them with lowest per capita income in the world. The economic crises in turn aggravates the already existing political and cultural problem thereby posing danger to the stabilty and integrity of those new nations. The pressure on states to play ideological and repressive roles will be relieved only when these countries can achieve economic self-sufficiency. Awarensess of this fact forces the states in the developing societies to play a complex role in economy.

With the achievement of political independence, one important phase of the history of imperialism came to an end. Political independence could keep the alien powers away from direct control of the affairs of the state and allow the newly liberated nations to decide their future. However, while setting up priorities conducive for their economic progress no native rulers can overlook the power of imperialism that indirectly continue to influence the economy and politics of the post-colonial societies. Domination of foreign capital and unequal status that the Third World occupies in the world capitalist system force the UDCs to depend on the West. It only shows that political independence is not sufficient for total liberation. Unless full economic independence is achieved political separation from the colonial powers becomes meaningless. At the same time it should be remembered that economic independence can't be achieved without prior political independence. As such achieving and maintaining political independence is a precondition for the attainment of economic self-reliance in these newly emergent nation states.

Once it is concluded that the countries in the Third World are formally independent, then a discussion of efforts that these countries made in developing their economy becomes logical. In developing countries, the weakness the indigenous ruling classes and the necessity of responding to the aspirations of the people for a decent living forces the states to take active roles in economic development. The tasks ahead of these countries are many. The anomalies perpetrated by the imperialists for their colonial exploitation should be overcome gradually. The precapitalist socio-economic structures that stand in the way of development need to be eliminated. The countries should develop the forces of production and achieve technological independence. They should limit the role of foreign capital in the native economy and carry on radical reforms in the agrarian structure of these countries. The whole economy must be systematically planned and utmost care should be taken to see that the plans are implemented properly by keeping in check the vested interests interested in preserving the status quo. In addition, instead of limiting its role to supervision and regulation of economic activities, the state should intervene in the priority areas by setting up basic industries wherever necessary. If all these tasks are carried out to their logical ends, one can expect true economic independence.

In practice fulfilment of these tasks is not easy. To an extent, the success depends on internal structural constraints and the attitude of the imperialists who still exercise considerable influence over the native economies. As far as the role of state is concerned, it has to be said that in almost all developing societies the states made attempt to develop their economies. In fact almost in all these countries the state became a leading actor in economy. The state took over the responsibility of establishing and managing the priority sectors. The share of the contribution of state sector in the national economy increased gradually in all countries. For example, in Algeria, Mozambique, Angola and People's Democratic Republic of Yemen the state sector accounts for 70 to 90 per cent of industrial output. In Tanzania 75% of the mining and manufacturing industries and 75% of the country's foreign and domestic trade are taken over by the state.[14] In Sri Lanka and Bangladesh the state sector controls about 40 and 70 per cent of the assets of the industries respectively. Most of the capital investment in the developing countries is maintained by the state themselves. In Syria, Burma and Guinea Bissau its share is about 75 to 90 per cent. Even in Latin American countries like Brazil, Chile, Columbia, Peru, Mexico and Venezucla, the public sector contributes more than 50% to the annual formation of capital. In 1975, 56 out to the 100 largest Brazilian enterprises are state owned.[15] In all those countries state took the responsibility of planning and supervising all sectors of economy. Many laws are enacted to regulate the private sector. In India the government enacted number of acts such as Companies Act, FERA, MRTPA to regulate the activities of the capitalists. Land reforms were initiated in many countries and ceilings on land holdings were imposed.

The developing societies tried to overcome the adverse impact of foreign imperialism. New laws were enacted to regulate the role of foreign capital. Vigorous attempts have been made to take possession of the natural resources of their country. Many foreign firms were nationalised. At the international level all the developing countries came together through forums such as UNCTAD and GATT to pressurise the West for a just and mutually beneficial international economic order. Sincere efforts were made to change the existing unequal and one sided trade practices by gaining many concessions from the West.[16] Similarly pressure was built around the developed countries to democratise the existing financial organisations such as IMF and IBRD and to divert more funds to the economc development of the Third World.[17] More over, to overcome their dependence on the metropolis the Third World countries began to initiate South-South cooperation by forming regional organisations like OAU, OPEC, ECLA, SAARC and ASEAN. By following nonaligned policy many of the Third World states took the financial and technical assistance from both capitalist and socialist blocks. That the UDCs maintained their political independence vis-a-vis the imperialism is evident from the fact that they all voted against the western powers in the UNO, especially on question concerning neo-colonialism, militarism and racism. These facts indicate that the attempts are made in most of the UDCs to bring about economic development without giving up political independence.

But how far such attempts have been successful? It is not correct to say that there is no development in the Third World countries since their independence. However, the development seems to be so uneven that it could not extricate most of the countries from underdevelopment. Implementation of the plans could not bring solace to the people of the Third World. The so-called state-sponsored industrialisation did not bring any expected changes in the lives of the poorest of the poor. The countries continued to the exploited by the mulitnationals. Dependence on foreign capital and foreign technology increased. For example, the US investment in Latin America which was $ 22,100 million in 1975 increased to about $ 39,000 million dollars in 1987. Between 1973-79 direct investments of the US banks increased by sixfold.[18] Foreign trade debt position in the Third World reached on alarming stage. The aggregate external debt of developing countries zoomed from 755 billion dollars in 1981 to a whopping 1,190 billion dollars in 1987. Thier debt to GNP ratios rose up from 18% to 28% during this present decade. Interest payments brcame an important problem. According to Deutsche Bank, the interest expenditure of the 15 highly indebted countries came to about 200 billion dollars in the past five years.[19] In Latin America, between 1960 and 1979, the interest payments swelled over 30 times *i.e.*, from $ 282 millions to $ 8,994 million.[20] The reaction of the Third World to this crisis is interesting. Some countries sought loans from the IMF to pay back the interest. Countries like Guyana, Trinidad and Tobago and Surinam started searching for foreign investors.[21]

Such state of affairs calls for a scientific explanation. What went wrong with the system? Why is it that the states in the Third World fail to achieve the much needed self-reliance in the economy? How come so many decades of planning could not bring any qualitative change in the lives of the masses? What are the obstacles that need to be overcome to initiate uninterrupted process of economic development? Is such a process ever possible in the Third World? These are some of the questions which require answers from social scientists trying to understand the problem of development in the developing societies. But for us, these questions became important to the extent, that they throw light on the nature of the state, its class character, its dynamics and limitations.

Here it should be mentioned that with the failure of western Modernisation theories, the problems of development in the underdeveloped countries received the attentions of many radical scholars of the world. Several schools of radical developmental theorists came out with systematic theories for underdevelopment which while trying to locate the causes of underdevelopment, presented alternatives for bringing about development. Since the scope of present enquiry does not permit us to explain the view-points of all scholars, with a stress on their understanding of the role of the state in the Third World.

Soft State : Radical Liberal View of Gunnar Myrdal

Gunnar Myrdal was perhaps the first liberal to make sincere efforts to understand the Third World by breaking the self-imposed limitations of liberal frame-work. By opting for the historical-institutional perspective—the method which the bourgeois theorists generally refrain, Myrdal tried to analyse the specificity of the new world. He studied the dynamics of different institutions and social forces within the specific institutional settings that they inherited from their predecessors.

Myrdal considers that halt in the growth of the indigenous industry and commerce, which is the consequence of the effects of colonial hangovers is one of the determinant factors responsible for the continued underdevelopment of the developing societies. Economic stagnation, severe population problem and existence of precapitalist social and economic structures are cited as the causes for the poverty of the people of the Third World. In his book, *Beyond Welfare State* he expresses great faith in planned economy. If plans are implemented with nationalist fervour, the UDCs are bound to see the economic development. However in his later works, *Asian Drama* and *Challenges of the World Poverty*... he observes that despite national planning the fate of the developing countries did not change. His search for underlying causes lead him to development of the concept called 'soft state'.

Myrdal opines that in varying degrees all UDCs are 'soft states'. Among other causes, this specific feature of the Third World constitute an important cause for their underdevelopment. What does the terms 'soft state' signify? To him the soft state is understood to have comprised" all types of social indiscipline which manifest themselves by : deficiencies in legislation and in particular, law observance and enforcement, a widespread disobedience by public officials on various levels to rules and directives handed down to them, and often their collusion with powerful persons and groups of persons whose conduct they should regulate".[22]

In the UDCs, keeping in view the aspirations of the masses, the policy makers at times enact various policies aiming at bringing radical transformation of the traditional society. But at the time of implementation, the policies become so diluted that they fail to bring about even moderate changes in society. Within Asian context, he studies different policies such as land reforms, population policies and acts aimed at improving the status of women and Dalits. But in all countries, the author finds betrayal of the accepted goals that they themselves set to achieve. For example, deliberate delay in legislation and collusion of the bureaucrats with the landlords are pointed out as causes for the failure of land reforms in Asian countries like India, Indonesia and Pakistan. Lack of social discipline, structural linkages between the bureaucrats and the economic elites and rampant corruption that prevails in all branches of government result in social and economic stagnation.

Why do things go this way in the underdeveloped countries? Myrdal sees the answer in the class character of the state. To him "political power in UDCs is held nearly everywhere by privileged groups, the first rank including big landowners, industrialists, bankers, merchants and higher military and civil officials".[23] In this ruling oligarchy he also places the 'middle class' which is composed of the professionals and intellectuals. These privileged sections are in unchallengeable position to prevent implementation of any policies that would upset their inherited pattern of social relations. Even officials and politicians entertain vested interests in preserving the status quo. They assume greater powers in such society where controls are not integrated into plans and the directives for their use tend to be vague and application becomes merely a matter of administrative judgment.

Myrdal unhesitatingly asserts that in such 'soft state', the political, legal and administrative system is systematically and heavily weighted against the poor masses of these countries. The states are ruled by compromises, accommodation and sometimes by infighting among various groups that constitute the upper class. As far as the masses are concerned, in all UDCs, there are merely the objects of politics—not its subjects. According to Myrdal, the so-called democracy in the Third World failed to organise the majority of people for utilising the political power to advance its own interests. Naturally, "when that pressure from below is almost totally absent, as in most underdeveloped countries, we should not be surprised that the inequalitarian social and economic stratification from colonial times is preserved and that development moves in the direction of greater inequality".[24]

What is the way out of this impasse? Myrdal's solution would be reversing the present trend—by widening the scope for popular participation, education and organisation of the masses, overcoming the values that preach status quo and ending all kinds of indiscipline and corrupt practices in the society. To sum up, Myrdal expects 'soft states' to become 'hard states'—as in the Western welfare societies.

Myrdal does not see underdevelopment as a product of the crises of capitalist system or of continued exploitation of the imperialist power. Of, course, he points out in his studies the disadvantageous position in which the UDCs are placed vis-a-vis the Western powers and criticises the short sighted policies of the Western World that go against the interests of the developing societies. He even expresses his sympathy for the Third World nationalism. However, Myrdal strongly feels that the interests of the developed countries and the developing countries are complementary and not contradictory. To him, there are two alternatives open to the world—the first being the international class conflict that could be permitted to grow to catastrophic dimensions, ending our civilisation in calamity. The other would be to resolve the conflict by a series of gradual accommodation with an aim to establish a democratic welfare world. His belief in innate good of humanity makes him think that western powers can be pressurised to initiate economic policies that would enable rapid economic development of the Third World states. He considers such a policy to be advantageous even to the developed countries. He says. "The stronger they become the more the attainment of a new situation of the world stability made possible. The stronger they become the more they will be in a position to abstain from policy measures which build up resentment against them".[25]

Semi Feudal State : Paul Baran's Enquiry Into Political Economy of Backwardness

Among the Western scholars, Paul Baran belongs to the first generation of Marxist intellectuals who tried to account for the backwardnesses of the post-colonial societies. He looks at the problem of underdevelopment from the point of view of the impact of imperialism on its erstwhile colonies and semi-colonies. In one sense, he is the founder of Dependency School. However, Baran needs a separate study since he differs from other dependency theorists in his analyses of the problems of the Third World and in his characterisation of the class character of the state.

Karl Marx expected that colonialism would work as a blessing in disguise, in the sense that by shattering the traditional stagnant societies, colonialism would create a progressive momentum in the colonies and semi-colonies by sowing the seeds of capitalist development.[26] But Paul Baran observes that Western capitalism, far from being a catalyst in the right direction, affected adversely the social and economic conditions in the UDCs by introducting all the economic and social tensions inherent in the capitalist order. The ultimate result was not transplantation of Western capitalist social and economic structures on backward areas. What actually happened was super-imposition of business mores over ancient oppression by landed gentries resulting in compound exploitation.[27] For Baran, integration of the backward countries into the international capitalist network of exploitation leads to a partial disintegration of precapitalist modes of production and imcomplete development of capitalist economic and class structures making the countries 'semi-feudal'.

Baran attributes the continuing reproduction of semi-feudal status of the developing societies to the weakness of the 'middle classes' *i.e.*, the indigenous bourgeoisie. Having grown up in countries that inherited backwardness and poverty the middle classes could not acquire the necessary self-confidence to play a leading role in society. What is worse, instead of fighting the feudal rule, as in the West they themselves started assimilating political, cultural and moral values of the feudal class. Such a class cannot play its historic role of accomplishing anti-imperialist and antifeudal tasks to its logical ends. Rise of labour radicalism and imminent danger of a social revolution destroyed the chances of capitalist classes joining the democratic forces. Apparent or real threat of working class unity forced the middle classes to compromise with the Church, landed gentry and foreign interests. This led to the formation of counter revolutionary coalition in which "whatever differences or antgonisms existed between the monopolistic and competitive business, between liberal bourgeoisie and reactionary feudal lords, between domestic and foregin interests, were largely submerged on all important occasions by the overriding common interests in staving off socialism".[28] As the popular pressure mounts up the middle class cements a new alliance of all conservative elements which decries all attempts at reform as assaults on the very foundations of society.

In a country dominated by such reactionary coalition all possibilities of economic development would be thwarted. Compromise with landed classes will not allow any radical transformation of agrarian structure. Extreme economic inequalities limit the market potentialities in the Third World. Lavish consumption pattern of the middle classes and their blind imitation of the life-styles of feudal classes drastically limit the savings that could be invested is productive activities. Parasitic economic stratum depending on the service sector and the vested interests obstructing the productive utilisation of landed resources hinder the possibility of uninterrupted industrialisation. In industrial sector, the industrial entrepreneur responding to the monopolistic structure of market involved in production of luxury goods which results in import of foreign capital and technology. As far as the establishment of basic industries is concerned, their responsibility will be vested with foreign multi-nationals who in turn exploit huge amounts in the form of royalties, interests and profits. Their relationship breeds mercantile bourgeoisie whose interests are linked with those of foreign imperialism. In such societies, Baran feels that the establishment of state sector also proves tremendous waste since it only involves squandering of large sums for the maintenance of sprawling bureaucracies and power of the 'comprador bourgeoisie'.[29]

Baran thinks that there are possibilities of reversing such trends if the state askes up certain necessary responsibilities. If it can impose progressive tax system to check the inflationary tendencies by limiting non-essential consumption, create the infrastructure necessary for the development of industry, provide technical education to the people, impose rigorous controls over speculation in scarce goods, excessive profiteering and then prevent capital flight, then it will bring radical changes in the structure of effective demand in the UDCs. However, Baran understands that the state machinery manned by incompetent and corrupt officials cannot take up this task. Even if policy-makers announce blue-prints of progressive measures such as agrarian reforms, equitable tax legislation, their structural linkages with the dominant classes will sabotage the strict enforcement of the policies. As Baran puts it,"set up to guard and to abet the existing property rights and privileges, it cannot become the architect of a policy calculated to destroy the privileges standing in way of economic progress, and to place the property and incomes derived from it at the service of society as a whole."[30]

Given the circumstances how can these countries come out of backwardness ? Baran sees very little possibilities of capitalist development in the UDCs. Yet he attributes important role to the national bourgeoisie in deciding the fate of their states. To him, the possibilities of bringing about an indigenous capitalism under conditions of underdevelopment depends "on the economic and political strength of the national bourgeoisie, on the quality of its leadership, on its determination to disolodge the feudal and comprador elements from the position of dominance, on the intensity of the resistance on their part and on the extent to which the international constellation permits the elimination or considerable weakening of the support given to those strata by the world's imperialist powers".[31] In other words, "which way the historical wheel turn and in which way the crises in the backward countries will find its final solution will depend, in the main, on whether the capitalist middle classes in the backward areas and the rulers of the advanced industrial nations of the world, overcome their real fears or myopia. Or are they too spell bound by their narrowly conceived selfish interests, too blinded by their hatred of progress, grown so senile in these latter days of the capitalist ages as to commit suicide out of fear of death?"[32]

Lumpen Bouregois State : Analyses of Frankean School of dependency

Though Paul Baran is considered as the father of the Dependency school, it was actually in the hands of Andre Gunder Frank that the Dependency theory blossomed into a theoretical framework—which could subsequently attract many intellectuals in and around Latin America. Frank and Baran do not have dispute on the question of dependency. But Frank differs from Baran in his analyses of internal economic structure of the UDCs. Wherever Baran considers that backwardness of those countries is to be attributed to semi-feudal character of the state, A.G. Frank believes that once the metropolis-satellite relationship is established, then the internal structure of the periphery also tend to acquire capitalist features. Baran locate the cause of underdevelopment the difficulties involved in transition to independent capitalist development in the pheriphery. On the contrary Frank asserts that there is no escape from underdevelopment within the framework of world capitalism.[33]

Frank's theory of underdevelopment is based on three hypotheses

1. "Underdevelopment is not due to the survival of archaic institutions and the existence of capital shortage in regions that have remained isolated from the stream of world history. On the contrary, underdevelopment was and still is generated by the very simple historical process which also generated economic development; the development of capitalism itself".
2. "The satellites experience their greatest economic development. . . if and when their ties with their metropolis are weakest".
3. "The regions which are most underdeveloped and feudal-seeming today are the ones which had the closest ties to the metropolis in the past."[34]

According to Frank the same process which brought development in the metropolis is also responsible for the development of underdevelopment in the satellites. On the question of reproduction of dependence, Frank like Baran argues that centuries of close association with the metropolis leaves the satellites with economic and class structure which is characterised by differentiation in income distribution. The market structure formed as a consequence of this forces the native industrialists to opt for the production of luxurious goods leaving the basic industries to foreign entrepreneur. This leads to greater dependence on foreign capital and technology and throws the country into the vortex of a host of economic problems such as severe balance of payment, obsolescence in production, under utilisation of productive capacity and high foreign remittances in the form of profits and royalities all these leading to further dependence on the metropolis. Such dependence makes the UDCs subservient to the desires and preferences of the industrially advanced nations. The result is that each tortured inch of industrial advance become a giant step backward. These ideas of Frank are developed by intellectuals like Dos Santos, F.H. Cordoso and E. Faletto.

Dos Santos point out that the historical form of dependence are conditioned by (1) the basic forms of the world economy which has its own laws of development, (2) the type of economic relations dominant in the capitalist centres and the ways in which the latter expand outward and (3) the types of relations existing inside the peripheral countries which coerce them to the status of dependent nations within the world capitalist order.[35] Dos Santos distinugishes different types of relations of dependency—colonial, industrial-financial and industrial technological. Like Santos, Cordoso and Faletto also emphasise the differences and discontinuities between different types of dependency and between the internal structures which result from them.[36]

Though there are some difference among the Dependency theorists on certain aspects, all of them stress the role of local elites in the transfer of economic surplus from periphery to the metropolis. All these classes sharing the state power in such countries are called by Frank as 'lumpen bourgeoisie'. His definition of capitalism as production for profit leads him to consider that even latifundum, economienda, catequil and hacienda as different forms of capitalist proudction and exploitation. According to him both the developed and underdeveloped parts of the world are equally capitalist and both of them are part and parcel of the same worldwide capitalist system. This understanding drives him to include all groups—land lords, merchants, financiers, industrialists and all those involved in service and other sectors which act as passive instruments of foreign domination by perpetuating dependency as "lumpen bourgeoisie". When he calls them 'lumpen' he does not mean that in the UDCs there can be bourgeoisie which can be national but not lumpen. He considers the entire national bourgeoisie in the Third World as 'lumpen', since none of them can disentangle the national economic good from their own interests. In fact all these sections are benefited by perpetuation of such lumpen development.

The Dependency theorists see that the structure and composition of the ruling coalition are determined by the particular forms that dependency relations take place in course of economic development. According to Cordoso and Faletto, in all developing but dependent countries "social structures reflect the double edge of the economic system "its external interests and pressures, those that derive from external economic influence and those that are national."[37] In Latin America, almost from independence to the beginning of 20th century merchants, financiers and groups such as latifundistas, agricultural cpaitalists, traders and mine-owners constituted as ruling coalition under one or the other hegemonic class. It was in the first three decades of the 20th century that the industrial bourgeoisie made their appearance felt. Even during the transitional period the ruling coalition remained tied to the export sector. However, between depression and the end of the World War II, when the ties with the metropolis were weakened and the necessity to import-substituties arose, attempts have been made by the populist regimes of different Latin American countries in bringing about rapid industrialisation. During this period as a consequence of the development and consolidation of the state sector, the industrial bourgeoisie has strengthened its position. By 1950s it became a strong faction of the ruling coalition, at times even dominating the landed aristocracy and export enclaves.[38]

The Dependency theorists gave considerable importance to the role the state plays in such countries in mediating the interests of different classes or class fractions of the ruling coalition. With the advancement of bureaucracy, Military and technocracy, the dynamics of the state become more complicated. The state plays a major role in perpetuating the dependency. Different policies of the government such as liberalisation of controls for capital and intermediate goods, repeated currency devaluation and a halt to agrarian reforms are cited to point out how the state is held responsible in promoting the lumpen development.[39] Though the role played by the sector is recognised the Dependency theorists argue, in the post-war world the public sector had been subservient to the interests of the multinationals. They, however, accept that dependent development does not take place in a smooth way. It occurs through frictions, accords and alliances between the state and business enterprises. The contradictions between the state and the big business sectors are not as antagonistic as the contradictions between the state and the vast sections of the people, worst affected by this development. Cordoso and Faletto point out that in order to counter the popular opposition, now becoming more and more popular in Latin American countries, the states are expanding and fortifying themselves by having recourse to repressive and anti-people policies. Under the given conditions authoritarian forms of the state became the only alternative for the national bourgeoisie to continue its domination.[40]

In such conditions, where the state and the national bourgeoisie are involved in fostering dependency and underdevelopment, the Dependency theorists do not find any scope for independent capitalist development in the Third World. The only alternative that Frank suggests is a radical break with the imperialism and immediate transition to socialism through anticapitalist socialist revolution. While attempting to find out the principal enemy, Frank asserts that, "the immediate tactical enemy is the bourgeoisie itself.....in spite of the fact that, strategically principal enemy is imperialism".[41]

Anti-Imperialist State : Expectations of the Soviet Marxists

During Stalin's period, Soviet theoreticians believed, the independence gained by countries like India under the bourgeois or petty bourgeois leadership would only be formal and such countries could only be puppets of their colonial rulers. However the Soviets gradually realised that the dynamics of the Third World cannot be seen in such simplistic terms. The first Asian Conference of 1947, Korean and Indonesian crises and Bandung conference of 1955, showed that the developing societies can play a positive and independent role in the world, though they may not be ruled out by the proletariat. After realising all these events the Russian Marxists who earlier characterised the newly independent states as lackeys of imperialism gradually portrayed them as "potential anti-imperialist forces in the world". The dynamic role of the countries like India, Egypt and Indonesia made their party ideologues realise that it would be a great mistake to minimise the world-historical significance of the process of decomposition of the colonial system only because it has brought in its wake non-socialist states... Whatever the form of national liberation of the colonies and semicolonies might be.. this liberation is a great blow to imperialism and consequently, necessarily does not strengthen, but weakens the world capitalist system".[42]

In the wake of development of this new paradigm, many Soviet scholars began to concentrate and comprehend the role of the state and classes in developing societies. Unlike their Chinese counterparts, the Soviet scholars undertook strenuous surveys to understand the reality and specificity of states in the UDCs. They argue that due to differences in correlation of class forces in developing societies, ruling classes may differ from state to state. The Soviet scholars indentified that there are national bourgeois states, bureaucratic bourgeois states, bourgeoisified feudal states and states where the state power is jointly shared by the bourgeoisie and landlords.[43]

Like many other developmental theorists, the Russian Marxists are aware of the impact of imperialist exploitation and the consequences of unequal status that the UDCs enjoy within the world imperalist system. In addition, internal factors such as the existence of outmoded production relations, lower development of productive capacities, lack of adequate capital and shrinking internal market as causes for the backwardness of the developing societies. In short, foreign imperialism, internal precapitalist elements and the local elites (big bourgeoisie/feudal lords/tribal chiefs) allied to foreign imperialism are generally cited as obstacles to the path of development of states in the Third World. Russians believe that there are possibilities of considerable economic development in the UDCs, if the state power is used to sub-plant the outmoded production relations and the economy from the control of the foreign monopolies and broadening of the internal market by generating industrialisation and agrarian reforms. Soviet theoreticians attribute positive role to the public sector. As V.V. Rymalov puts it, "state sector in industry and other branches of the national economy of the former colonies and semi-colonies is the decisive instrument for attaining the economic aims of the liberation revolution. Its all-round development is designed to create the strongest possible progress'.[44] Development of state sector and nationalisation of private industries are considered as progressive steps having anti-imperialist and anit-monopoly characteristics. Further Soviet scholars recognise that it is not possible to undertake such massive development programme without necessary technological development and financial help. So they see the necessity of dependence of the UDCs on foreign capital and technology. Though such dependency gives an opportunity of us Socialist bloc, they can utilise foreign capital and technology for the neo-colonialist exploitation, the Soviet Marxists argue that by taking advantage of the presence of the Socialist bloc, they can utilise foreign capital and technology for their own advantage without sacrificing its political independence. Close ties with the socialist bloc and mutual economic interdependence of the countries belonging to the South are cited as external prerequisites for economic development. Hence the Soviet theoreticians place non aligned movement on a high pedestal and claim themselves as its natural allies.[45]

Depending on the attitudes that different states take on question relating to the implementation of the tasks ahead of them, the countries are designated as progressive or reactionary. Based on the path of development that they opted, and the foreign policy they adopt, the Third World is classified into "the capitalist oriented and socialist oriented countries". All countries which have taken the capitalist path of development are included under the category named, 'capitalist oriented countries'. State power in these countries may be with the national bourgeoisie or bourgeoisie and landlords or bourgeoisified feudal lords or the protobourgeoisie sections. Soviet theoreticians argue that in countries where national bourgeoisie is in power, radical reforms necessary for economic self-reliance cannot be implemented properly. In these countries land reforms fail owing to opposition from the landlords and bureaucrats. Potentialities of state capitalism cannot be realised properly. In most of these countries (other than the progressive national bourgeois states like India) the state sector bows down to pressures exercised by the private capitalist and foreign imperialists.[46] Due to weak industrial base and lack of diversification in production and exchange. The process of development initiated in such countries became susceptible to the pressures of unjust international economic order.

Parallel to the capitalist oriented countries, the Soviet Marxists believe that there are socialist oriented countries which follow non-capitalist path of development and declare socialism as their ultimate goal. Such countries include Algeria, Tanzania, Mozambique, Guinea Bissau, People's Democratic Republic of Yemen, Angola and Afghanistan. In these agrarian countries where peasants constitute a dominant class, the state power is claimed to be in the hands of working class of people and peasants.[47] In these countries where the bourgeoisie is weak, the state sector dominates the industrial sector. In many of these countries 70 to 90% of total industrial produce is attributed to the public sector. In the main the land reforms are strictly implemented and many foreign firms are nationalised. The state here gives considerable importance to the welfare activities such as education, housing and health care *etc*. In spite of these progressive attributes, the Soviet theoreticians themselves observe that there are forces capturing the state power and reversing the process of development.[48] However Russians argue that if the states adhere to the same path, these countries could sustain uninterrupted development without becoming victims of all those economic crises that impede the development of capitalist states.

Finally it should be mentioned that the Russians consider all Third World countries—whether socialist oriented or capitalist oriented—as unconscious vehicles in achieving world socialism. As N.V. Simoniya puts it, "Given this situation the development and certain degrees of captalists relations in some countries does not at all imply "rejuvenation" or strengthening of world cpaitalism. The liberated countries are not only a potential source of exploitation systems, marxist and capitalist, but bring new contradictions into capitalism and complicate and aggravate the old contradictions. . . (All) these contradictions heighten the possibilities of the revolutionary alternative"[49] *i.e.* Socialism.

In Search of a Theoretical Frame-work

In the context of peculiarities of socio-economic conditions in the Third World, we have so far reviewed different interpretations of the role of the state in the economic development of these backward societies. Different authors threw light on different aspects related to state, classes and economic prospects in the Third World. Though there are certain points of similarities here and there, the authors seem to entertain competing and at times, even conflicting views about the nature of the state and ruling classes in the developing societies. In one sense, these differences are the products of the paradigms within which they happen to see the problems of the UDCs. Critical evaluation of these paradigms become necessary to develop a more meaningful and comprehensive Marxist Leninist framework for the study of the nature and dynamics of the states in developing countries.

Gunnar Myrdal offers an 'institutional theory' that analyses the economic structure and living standards, agriculture and industry, social stratification and ideology, not as separate problems but in their totality and interconnection. He even recognises the reactionary role of the dominant classes whithin countries and the impact of centuries of imperialist exploitation. However the solutions he offers are not uncompromising struggle against imperialism and the vested interests within these nations. Like all humanists, he believes in the possibility of reconciling the interests of different classes within the countries and also the conflicts between the UDCs and imperialists, through a gradual process of mutual understanding, reconciliations and accommodation. But the logic of historical process of development makes it difficult to make Myrdal's myth of 'welfare world' a reality.

Paul Baran correctly understands the historic limitations of the bourgeoisie of the developing societies. He understands that in an era of imperialism and proletarian revolution, the bourgeoisie cannot but compromise with foreign imperialism and local feudalism. However, his attempts to generalise the causes for underdevelopment as joint exploitation of capitalism and feudalism, his innate belief in progressive character of capitalism even in this era and the decisive role that he assigns to the national bourgeoisie in directing the course of development need a second look. He prefers socialist alternative. But what is the course of revolution he proposes—anti-capitalist socialist revolution or people's democratic revolution where even the national bourgeoisie becomes allies in the revolution? It seems, he considers, that at this stage of development, semi-feudalism and imperialism are the main enemies-not the national bourgeoisie. He comes to this conclusion by his analysis of the stage of development of economy in the UDCs—and not the class character of the state power.

A.G. Frank, by defining capitalism as production for profit, goes to another extreme of characterising all dependent relations in the Third World as capitalist relations. He thinks that the national bourgeoisie of the Third World (he calls it 'lumpen-bourgeoisie') can never escape dependent relationship because of its specific relationship with the world imperialist system. Like Trotskites, he sees anti-capitalist socialist revolutions as the only solution left for all developing societies. It may be true in case of Latin American countries where the state power lies basically with the capitalists. But this solution does not hold good in countries where in spite of considerable capitalist development, the state power lies with the feudal lords or comprador bourgeoisie. He makes the same mistake as his counterpart, Baran in determining the present stage of revolution in different countries of the Third World.

The Soviet scholars are better informed, in the sense that they understood the pluralities of the developing societies and did not generalise the class character of the state and the stage of development of economy. Through systematic empirical work, they argued that the classes which came to state power in the Third World differed from one country to another and hence the path of development varied from one state to another. The Soviets see the prospects of development only in two sets of countries—progressive national bourgeois states and states with socialist orientation. However, complete economic independence is possible only in socialism—a goal which will be accepted by all developing countries sooner or later by following non-capitalist approach in development. It is surprising to note however that in spite of their recognition of differences in class character of the state belonging to the Third World the Russians point out imperialism as the main enemy and prescribed national or people's democratic revolution as the present stage of revolution of all developing countries.

Though all the analyses reviewed so far give us an understanding of states, classes and economic development in the Third World, the dialectical interaction between these categories are not properly established. There seems to be a tendency of reducing one structure to another—without comprehending the relative autonomy that each structure or social force has vis-a-vis other structures or social forces. Ignorance of pluralities of the socio-economic structures of these societies make the scholars generalise their experience of a group of countries to the whole Third World. Attempts to comprehend the complexities of the social formation in the Third World within the rigid framework of concepts developed in the context of Western societies cannot make any headway. Take the instance of classes in the Third World. In some countries, the classes are still in formative stages. In some other states, though classes as such are well developed, their members are much influenced by other precapitalist struetures (like castes, tribes and religion) that it becomes very difficult to judge one's class character by the apparent ideology. To put it other way, a bourgeois in the Third World behaves not only as a capitalist but also as a man belonging to a particular caste, tribe or religion. How to characterise the role of these precapitalist structures is again a problem. Wherever these structures are obstructing the captalist path of development in certain countries, in many others, they are coopted in such a way that they play a complementary role in development. For example, religion as institution might have become an obstacle to development in countries like Bhutan and Nepal, but in countries like Iran, religious nationalisation led to implementation of many radical reforms. Finally, one need to say that there is no eye to eye relationship between the class character of the state and the economic role that it plays. There are semifedual or bourgeoisified feudal states such as Nepal and Saudi Arabia where the ruling feudal elite itself attempts to bring capitalist development. On the other hand one can find predominantly capitalist states like Brazil and Pakistan, compromising with feudal and semi-feudal elements in their countries.

In view of these multiple complex relationship between the classes and the state, classes and other social forces, and the base and superstructure in the Third World, one should stop generalising about the nature of the state in the developing societies. It however does not mean that one should totally ignore the features common to all developing countries. What is to be stressed is the study of the States of the Third World, in all its specificities and its inter-relationship in general. Developing and perfecting the concepts such as classes, class interests and ruling classes become necessary. In addition, a meaningful political discourse on the nature of the state requires arriving at consensus about meanings assigned to terms such as 'comprador states'. 'semi-feudal states' or 'independent national bourgeois states'. Keeping this necessity in mind, attempts may be made to develop as analytical framework on the nature of the state in the Third World.

In developing such a theoretical framework, the following points may be considered :

1) Though one may take note of the economic status of the people, classes should not be seen merely as economic categories. Homogeneous classes which may be defined as "groups of people having similar status in production relations, followed by corresponding ideological outlook and political practice", are rarely found in the developing societies. In the Third World we come across a wider strata of people who cannot be grouped under any class. Hence in addition to taking into consideration one's position in relations of production, identification of one's class or status should stress on the need to understand as to whose class interests one is promoting 'consciously' in his or her day-to-day praxis. The term 'consciously' is important, for, we should ignore here the unconscious victims of ideologies and praxis of other classes. Seen in this sense, even if a member is not a capitalist, if he or she consciously acquires bourgeois

ideology and practices bourgeois politics he or she should be called a bourgeois. In case of mixed categories,[50] dominant ideological position and political praxis may be taken into consideration. Such criteria are needed to identify class status of certain social categories such as politicians, intellectuals and professionals—who may not have any particular status in the relations of production.

2) By the term 'class interests' we should not mean what individual members of the class consider to be in their interests. Class interests refer to the objective possibility of a class to realise under given conditions, its basic urge to hold or ensure that which they posses or to aspire for that they need to posses.[51] Since, along with economic interests each class shall have certain political and ideological interests. By the term, 'possession' we mean both material production and the realm of ideas corresponding to it.

3) Wide generalisations about the role of the classes—without taking into consideration the given context need to be avoided. For example, while trying to understand the dynamics of the bourgeoise in the Third World, we should first see, whether they are imitating policies that lead to widest and speediest development of capitalism under the given national and international conditions. To expect the bourgeoisie in the post colonial societies to behave like the bourgeoisie of the Western Europe is not a dialectical way of looking at reality.

4) The word 'comprador' should not be misused. All economically dependent states need not be 'semi-colonies' or 'comprador states'. Some measure of dependent relationship become inevitable for all the Third World countries. Though some of them may be semi-colonies, possibility of existence of independent national bourgeois states among those economically dependent nations need not be ruled out. The basic issues to be considered here are as follows : whether one willingly accepted dependent status or not; whether all activities of the bourgeoisie only promoted the interests of foreign imperialism or it also contributed to indigenous capitalist development; and whether or not the class used all its potentialities to fight foreign imperialism to the extent its own national interests are involved. All these points need to be examined to judge the nature of indigenous bourgeoisie.

5) The other aspect is related to pre-capitalist socio-economic structures. It is true that the UDCs are multistructural and multistratified societies. But it should be noted that all structures and strata in the social formation may not be evenly developed. Indentification of the dominant structures and social strata is necessary to know the direction of economic development. If any state is to be characterised as feudal or semi-feudal, one should firstly identify the structures and strata that can be named as semi-feudal or feudal. Then one should examine whether they acquire dominant status or play subordinate role to the dominant capitalist mode of production. The third aspect to be observed is whether the state policies are perpetuating those feudal or semi-feudal relations or trying to change them gradually into capitalist or socialist relations.

6) It may be noted that many times such indentified categories may not be in essence semi-feudal or feudal. Traditional structures like castes, tribes and religious communities may modify their roles in such a way that they may not be in conflict with development process. Hence it is necessary to know whether such relations are obstructing the capitalist path of development or whether they themselves started changing their roles in the wake of new opportunities thrown open to these sections in course of development of the economy.

7) So is the question of Ancient tradition or culture. In most of the countries—developed as well as underdeveloped—traditions play a very important part in shaping the psychological makeup and value preferences of the people as well as the policy makers. Political and economic structures are also influenced by them. Though old traditions are considered as impediments to capitalist development, under certain circumstances the bourgeoisie itself may use feudal or precapitalist structures. It may be due to their compromise with the feudal elements in the society. But sometimes the bourgeoisie may use them for their own interest. Even if the economic interests suffer for a short period, if their political necessities so demand, the traditions will be used to consolidate the positions of the bourgeoisie. There is nothing feudal or semi-feudal in the usage of traditional slogans if they ultimately serve the interests of the capitalist class. In view of the different possibilities, one should examine the following aspects :(1) Do the feudal and semi-feudal traditions remain as remnants of old society or are there any semifeudal or feudal structures exists at the base, reproducing, the old traditions at the superstructural

level ? (2) Does such a traditional culture promote the interests of any group which can be clearly identified as feudal or semi-feudal or whether these are only used by the bourgeoisie for promoting its own interests? Finally, what is the role that the state plays in dealing with these kinds of traditional and cultural values?

8) In the light of all these guidelines, the dynamics of the state is to be studied of all relating variations in the forms of government and political regimes to the changing correlation of class and social forces inside each country. All these dimensions should be examined within the context of the status that the ruling classes and the state occupy in the world capitalist system in general and the Third World in particular.

Notes and References

1. Simoniya, N.V. *Destiny of Capitalist in the Orient*, Progress Publishers, Moscow, 1985, pp. 223-224.
2. Chirkin, Veniamin, *Constitutional Law and Political Institutions*, Progress Publishers, Moscow, 1985, pp. 153-54.
3. See passages from Lin Biao's writings in Dhanapala J. *China and Third World*, Vikas, Delhi, 1985, pp. 40-42.
4. Alavi, Hamza, 'The State in Post-Colonial Societies: Pakistan and Bangladesh' in Goulbourne H. ed., *Politics and State in the Third World*, Macmillan, London, 1979, pp. 38-69.
5. Kalecki, Michael, *Selected Essays on the Growth of the Socialist and Mixed Economies*, Cambridge University Press, London, 1972, pp. 162-167.
6. Saul J.S., 'The State in Post-colonial Societies : Tanzania' in Goulbourne ed., 36. *Politics and State in the Third World*, *op.cit.*, pp,. 70-88; Samhoff. J., 'Class, Class conflict and the State in Africa', *Political Science Quarterly*, Vol., 97, No, 1 Spring 82 pp. 124-130 and Smith, Anthony D, *Stae and Nation in the Third World*, Wheat Sheaf Books, Sussex, 1983, pp. 59-90.
7. Babu, A. M. *African Socialism or Socialist Africa*, Zed Press, London, 1981, pp. 2-5
8 Srikanth. H. 'Reflections on Dominant Marxist Conceptions of Indian State' in *Teaching Politics*, Vol. XIV, No. 1., 1988.
9. Simoniya, *op.cit.*, pp. 90-115.
10 Chirkin, *op.cit.*, pp. 158-159.
11. Wynia, Gary W., *The Politics of Latin American Development*. Cambridge University Press, New York, 1985, pp. 135-303.
12. Levkovsky, Alexei, *The Developing Countries Social Structure*, Progress Publishers, Moscow, 1987, p. 151.
13. Alavi, Hamza, *op.cit.*, pp. 41-42.
14. Stanis, V.F., Khromushin G.B. ed.,, *The Role of the State in Socio-economic reforms in Developing Countries*, Progress Publishers, Moscow, 1976, p.51.
15. Cordoso, F.H. & Felletto, E, *Dependency and Development in Latin America*, University of California Press, London, 1979, pp. 203-204.

16. · See Primakov, M.Ye. *The East after the collapse of the colonial System*, Progress Publishers, Moscow,1983, pp. 161-168; Kovalenko ed., *The Nonaligned Movement*, Progess Publishers, Moscow, 1985, pp. 97-110.
17. William, G., *Third World Political Organisations,* Macmillan, London, 1987; Ferguson T, *The Third World and Decision Making in the IMF*, Pinter Publishers, London, 1988, pp. 88-116.
18. Klochovsky, L:L., *The Economy of the Countries of Latin America,* Progress Publishers, Moscow, 1974, pp. 22-23.
19. PTI, *Economic Service*, May 1, 1988, pp. 78-84.
20. Klochovsky, *op.cit.*, p. 30.
21. PTI, *Economic Service,* July 15, 1988.
22. Myrdal, Gunnar, *Challengẽs of World Poverty*, Vintage Books, New York, pp. 219-220.
23. Myrdal, *Ibid*, p. 61.
24. Myrdal, *Ibid*, p. 76.
25. Myrdal, *Beyond the Welfare State,* Yale University Press, 1960.
26 Marx and Engels, *Selected Works Vol.I*, Progress Publishers, Moscow, 1976, pp. 488-493.
27. Baran, Paul, 'On the Political Economy of Backwardness' in Rhodes, Rober I, *Imperialism and Underdevelopment : a reader*, M.R.P. New York, 1970, p. 288.
28. Baran, *Ibid.*, p. 289.
29. Baran, *Political Economy of Growth*, New York, M.R.P., 1957,p. 215,
30. Baran, "On the Political Economy of Backwardness' *op.cit.*, 297.
31. Baran, *Political Economy of Growth, op.cit.*, pp. 300-301.
32. Baran, 'On the Political Economy of Backwardness' *op.cit.*, pp.300-301.
33. Barone, Charles A, *Marxist Thought on Imperialism*, Macmillan, Michigan, 1985, p. 100.
34. Frank. A.G., 'Development of Underdevelopment' in Rhodes, Rober I, '*Imperialism and Underdevelopment : a reader*, M.R.P. 1970. pp. 9, 10, 13.
35. Dos Sontos, Theotonio, 'Structure of Dependence', *American Economic Review* 60, No. 2, May 1970, pp. 231-233.
36. Cordoso and Faletto, *Dependency and Development in Latin America*, University of California Press, London, 1979.
37. Cordoso and Faletto, *Ibid*, p. 25.
38. Cordoso and Faletto, *Ibid*, p. 77-78.
39. Hoogevelt, a, *Third World in Global Development*, Macmillan, London, 1982, pp. 169-170.
40. Cordoso and Faletto, *op.cit.*, pp. 204-210.
41. Frank, *Lumpen Bourgeoisie and Lumpen Development*, M.R.F. New York, 1972, p. 145.
42. Quoted in Kanet Roger E, *Soviet Union and the Developing Nations*, John Hopkin University Press, London, 1975, pp. 169-170.
43. Chirkin, *op.cit.*, p. 153.
44. Quoted in Clarkson, Stephen, *The Soviet Theory of Development : India and the Third World*, Macmillan, London, p. 39.
45. Alimov, Yuri, *The Rise and Growth of the Nonaligned Movement*, Progress Publishers, Moscow, 1987, pp. 174-191 & Kovalenko and Tuzmukanedov ed., *The Nonaligned Movement*, Progress, 1985, pp. 219-234.
46. Simoniya, N.A., *op.cit.*, pp. 233-239.
47. Chirkin, *op.cit.*, pp. 206-207.

48. Stanis & Kromushin ed., *op.cit.*, p. 38.
49. Simoniya *op. cit.*, p. 251.
50. Here we refer to those persons who earn livelihood by different means at the same time.
51. Srikanth, H., 'Nature of Indian State', in Chaubey N.P., ed., *Indian Society at the Turn of the Century*, Allahabad. 1988, p. 209.

Perestroika : Gorbachev's version

What provoked the citizens of U.S.S.R. to think of 'Perestroika' and 'Glasnost' after 70 years of socialist experiment? Do they think that what was constructed so far in the name of socialism is not really socialism which Marx, Engels and Lenin dreamt of ? Or did the people of U.S.S.R. decide to abandon the path of Marxism-Leninism? Answers to these and other related questions need to be sought by all those who are interested in understanding the nature and dynamics of the state in socialist society.

Before evaluating the recent scenario in the U.S.S.R. one should first examine the official version. In U.S.S.R., none other than the party's General Secretary himself, Mikhail Gorbachev came out in favour of 'Perestroika'. Since he argues that perestroika is not based on the subjective perception of the present leadership, but has its roots in the objective conditions with in the Soviet Union, looking at Gorbachev's description of the present Soviet society becomes indispensable. To begin, in his book *Perestroika* Gorbachev writes, "At some stage this became very clear in the latter half of the70's — some thing happened that was at first sight inexplicable. The country began to lose momentum. Economic failures became more frequent. Difficulties began to accumulate and deteriorate and unresolved problems to multiply. Elements of what we call stagnation and other phenomena alien to socialism began to appear in the life of society... we discovered a slowing economic growth. In the last 15 years the income growth rates had declined by more than half and by the beginning of the 80's had fallen to a level close to economic stagnation. A country that was quickly closing on the world's advanced nations began to lose one position after another".[1] In this report to the nineteenth All Union Conference of the C.P.S.U. Gorbachev observed, "In the period of stagnation the machinery of management began to decide its will in both the economic and political fields. It was those agencies and other administrative structures that handled the execution of the decisions... The soviet and, in many respects, the party bodies as well, proved unable to control this pressure from departmental interests".[2] What is worse, many of those who remained in leading posts for years got a false idea of being infallible and irreplaceable. Responsibility declined among a large number of elected persons and in the party apparatus. They lost contact with the party masses and working people which often ended, as we know, in the political and moral degradation.[3]

If such is the status of economy and administration, what about the people of socialist Russia? See the confessions of Gorbachev, "Decay began in public morals; the great feeling of solidarity with each other that was forged during the heroic times of the Revolution, the first five year plans, the great patriotic war and the post-war rehabilitation was weakening; alcoholism, drug addiction and crime were growing; and the penetration of the stereotypes of mass culture alien to us which bred vulgarity and low tastes and brought about ideological barrenness increased... People were losing interest in social affairs, that labour no longer had its respectable status, that people, especially the young, were after profit at all costs".[4] In addition to the above mentioned social, political and economic phenomena, Gorbachev also talks of technological stagnation, scarcity of consumer goods, wastage of resources and of rampant corruption and bribery in the bureaucratic apparatus in the U.S.S.R. If such is the present status of the first socialist country which showed to the world the unknown potentialities of the rule of the proletariat, then all those who sympathise with the cause of socialism feel the necessity of 'Perestroika' in all aspects of Soviet society. But what is the real content of 'Perestroika' which Gorbachev talks of? Does implementation of the reforms he prescribes really set the things in the right direction? To be able to answer these questions, a brief study of the official version of the reforms is desirable.

Programme of Perestroika : Gorbachev's plan

In order to overcome the malaise in U.S.S.R., Gorbachev proposes 'revolutionary' changes in all aspects of Soviet society. His programme includes many changes in economic, political, scientific, technological, educational and cultural fields. The scope of this book does not permit a comprehensive analysis of all the so-called radical reforms prescribed by the present political leadership. Yet, keeping in view the necessity of understanding the nature and dynamics of the state, classes and economy in the socialist setup a brief sketch of the fundamental economic and political changes initiated by the Gorbachev's 'Perestroika' may be given.

Gorbachev considers the inability of the economy to meet the ever growing demands of the people of the U.S.S.R. society for more consumer and other goods as a serious economic problem. Hence he lays stress on increasing the productive capacity of the socialist economy by the educational, scientific and technological innovations, Gorbachev stresses on fundamental changes in agriculture and industry. "By intensifying these processes" Gorbachev avers, "We intend to switch over to an economy having higher level of organization and effectiveness, with comprehensively developed productive forces, mature socialist relations of production and a smoothly functioning economic mechanism".[5]

He considers drastic changes in laws relating to agro-industrial complex system as a means to achieve the proposed goals. They include re-introduction of cooperatives in manufacturing and processing of products in gardening and housing construction and also in the sphere of services and trade. To facilitate the changes a law on cooperatives was enacted recently. The present leadership claims that cooperatives did not exhaust their utilities and that they are essential in meeting the ever growing needs of the Russian people. Gorbachev indirectly criticises Stalin for switching over to collective farms at a time when cooperatives did not exhaust their potentialities in contributing to socialist production. As he opines as "a result of departing from Leninist principles of the co-operative movement, the country and its economy have suffered substantial setbacks in political, moral and social terms".[6] To 'rectify' those mistakes, Gorbachev proclaims that the promotion of "the cooperative movement will open up extensive opportunities for resolving many of society's vitally important problems. *We have imparted to cooperatives the very meaning and the very role which Lenin ascribed them'*."[7] (emphasis mine — author).

Though in his book, *Perestroika*, Gorbachev appreciates the result of collectivisation except for the so-called 'excesses' in his address to the 4th All union congress of collective farmers, he argued that collectivisation did "harm to the agricultural sector". "The ill effects", he cites, include "slow progress in the solution of the food problem, the shortages in and narrow choices of many consumer goods and the limited range of daily services".[8] To do away with this state of affairs the new law on cooperatives suggests that the structure of the collective farms should be modified to facilitate the rebirth of cooperatives of independent primary work collectives. Gorbachev considered it justified to use all restrictions on their auxiliary business. From now on collective farms will be able to rent out part of the land assigned to them and part of their fixed assets both to other enterprises and to industrial citizens; to set up all kinds of agricultural cooperatives and to conduct foreign economic operation".[9]

In this new system, stress will be given to small farms. The farmer will be made sovereign master. Now the law is so changed that the farmer cannot only rent the land for any number of years, he can also inherit the land to his children. It is contended that such private ownership would inculcate a sense of possessiveness which is essential for augmenting production. In other words, "the reform will not yield the results we expect, if it does not affect the personal interests of literally every person, if it fails to become very person's vital affairs".[10]

It is claimed that the cooperative movement would encourage public initiative, supplement the supply of consumer goods and make self management methods possible. Besides, Gorbachev locates an extra argument in favour of cooperative movement. In his words, cooperative movement "is one of the more important levers for broadening the democratic process as a whole, for the struggle against administrative methods and bureaucracy".[11] In view of all these practical advantages he considers it as the immediate duty of the soviets and the party organs to lend every support to people interested in joining cooperative movement.

In addition to these reforms pertaining to cooperatives, perestroika entails drastic changes in the structure of industrial sector and labour relations in the state enterprises. To that effect a new 'law on the state enterprises' is enacted. The present regime now stresses on advantages of having small plants and pleads for complete operational autonomy and self-financing methods in all state enterprises. These reforms are justified on the grounds of preventing the production of useless goods combating the command style administration of central government and of creating a sense of responsibility among the workers. Under the new laws, central ministers will be endowed with the responsibility of giving only limited directions . Enterprises and organisations are given autonomy in production of consumer goods and services. They will hereafter enjoy the right to sell in the markets after meeting the contractual agreements. Some of the enterprises are given the rights to establish foreign economic ties directly. One official source says that over 70 enterprises and more than 20 ministries are allowed to have direct outlets to the foreign markets.[12] To facilitate these change laws regarding internal and external trade are changed.

Hereafter the criterion for the existence of state enterprises would be the profits they make and the demand they would meet. Enterprises producing goods not demanded in the market and thus incurring losses will be curtailed.No state subsidies are going to be provided to the enterprises not running profitably. It is the responsibility of the enterprises to operate without losses. Logic behind such move is ; "You cannot be a master of your country if you are not a real master in your factory or collective farm, in your shop or your livestock farm. It is the duty of the work collectives to answer for everything, to multiply the social wealth."[13]

Related to these changes is the Soviet government's land-lease or contractual agreements in the agro-industrial complexes. Instead of collective farms the emphasis is now on small farms run by groups of people or individual farms on contract basis for a term extending from 25 to 50 years. The owners of small units can rent the machinery or other inputs from collective farms or from organisations outside. The government is now in favour of dissolving all inefficient farms and transferring of their land and assets not only to socialised farms and enterprises but also to collective individual tenants. In his 29th July, 1988 speech Gorbachev argued, "We should open widely the ways for autonomy and responsibility of the producers in every ways and extend an agricultural market. And let no one of us be confounded, if the usage of production means in the long term remains in the disposition of peasant on the basis of a contract with the farm enterprises. There is nothing unsocialist in this."[14] It is necessary that podryard, and in particular the rent forms of farming, spread out widely in the country.

All these changes necessitate extension of commodity production and introduction of market mechanisms in the country, though such measures will have adverse impact on prices of the commodities. Gorbachev considers that there is nothing wrong in widening the scope of commodity production. He argues that it is "high time to overcome prejudices regarding commodity-money relations and underestimations of those relations in planned economic guidance. Refusal to recognise the importance of their active influence on people's interest in working better and on production efficiency leads to a weakening of the cost-accounting system and other undesirable consequences. Conversely, sound commodity-money relations on a socialist basis can create a situation under which the results depend entirely on the standards of the work done by the collectives and on the ability and initiative."[15]

Corollary of these changes is introduction of a new wage policy which claims to bring socialist society in conformity with Marx's principle of "from each according to his ability and each according to his work". It is claimed that wage levelling did undue harm to development of productive forces. The Soviet authorities claim that at times unnecessary bonuses were paid to inefficient and idle workers employed in one or the other jobs, in the name of sticking on to the ideal of full employment. The workers were paid wages though the industries incured losses due to production of inefficient and useless goods. This kind of policy is said to have affected productive capacity of the socialist economy and discouraged the initiative among the efficient and active members of the working class. Hence 'perestroika' thinks of introducing a new wage policy which would "link wages and salaries more closly to the productivity of labour and labour's quality indicators." Wage levelling must be firmly eliminated and payment of unearned money and unmerited bonus must be stopped; it is essential to combat uncompromisingly unearned incomes and to root out other deviations from the basic principles of socialism.[16] As such, from now on descrimination will be made between' good and bad workers' and the managers will be given the right to "hire" and "fire" the workers. Workers will not be given salaries if their goods are not sold in the market. Wages will hereafter be decided according to the profits it secures. Monetary incentives will be given to the able and hard working labourers so as to encourage them to work harder to put national riches to the best possible use.

To sum up, the economic reforms initiated by the new regime, "provides for fundamental changes in every area, including the transfer of enterprises to complete cost accounting, a radical transformation of the centralised management of economy, fundamental changes in planning, a reform of the price formation system and of the financial crediting mechanism and the restructuring foreign economic ties. It also provides for the creation of the new organisational structures of management and for the all round development of the democratic foundations of managements, and for the broad introduction of self management principles".[17]

Gorbachev's perestroika does not merely stop at economic reforms. As a precondition for effective implementation of perestroika Gorbachev considers it necessary to bring about radical changes even in the political sphere. His political reforms aim at many modifications in the structure and functions of the government, party, soviets, trade unions, Young Communist Leagues and local administrative bodies. The purpose of all these reforms is the development of the 'socialist democracy' or 'people's socialist government' where the people will have ultimate say in policy making and policy implementation. Of the many reforms, Gorbachev's appeal to end bureaucratisation, his appeal for decentralisation and assignment of new roles to the soviets and party bodies are important for understanding the dynamics of state in socialist society.

In all his books and speeches, Gorbachev makes explicit his contempt of the process of bureaucratisation in the USSR. Though he accepts that the bureaucracy has objective roots in the Russian society, Gorbachev indirectly argues that Stalin's role in the '30s and '40s was also an important factor in the development of command style method of administration. This bureaucratisation began to exert its influence on all political institutions viz., state, party, trade unions and administrative affairs and became a hindrance to economic progress. Managers virtually took all decisions from top to bottom, many a time ignoring the suggestions of the party and soviets. People's participation and their initiative were greatly hindered by this process.

The magnitude of the problem should naturally force the socialist regime to search for the methods to end bureaucratic centralism. To achieve this purpose Gorbachev proposes restructuring of managerial system, abolition of some of the redundant elements, reduction of the size of its apparatus, demarcation and delineation of the functions and responsibilities of each managerial unit. Accordingly 27th Congress demanded the simplification of administrative procedures and elimination of delays, formalistic attitudes, petty fogging and red tapism in the administration. It also laid stress on improving cultural standard and use of mass media and public platform to attack bureaucratic forms of working. The struggle "must be conducted through a tireless effort to promote democracy, extensively develop forms of socialist self-government, enhance and strengthen the powers of the soviets, ensure direct involvement of people in taking and implementing government decisions, make the public better informed about the state of affairs in various spheres of the country's life and enhance people's control over the activities of the government bodies."[18] He claims that the "radical economic reforms, the reforms of the political system, democratisation of the party and of society, glasnost, the promotion of criticism and self-criticism, and the genuine involvement of the people in running the country are seriously undermining the position of bureaucracy".[19]

Marxists may not have any serious objections to the above proposals to combat the evils of bureaucracy. However Gorbachev becomes controversial when he claims decentralisation in economic and political spheres as one of the effective methods of combating bureaucratisation. He firmly believes that the new law on state enterprises, widening of the scope of cooperative movement increasing the powers of work collective councils, promotion of khozraschot relations, autonomy and accountability and lease contract system would combat command style system prevailing in the economic field. To put in Gorbachev's words, "given the existing scale of our national economy and the diversity of our social problems, a single control authority cannot resolve all issues promptly and adequately. Hence the need to transfer many powers to the local level—to republics, territories, regionals, districts and work collectives."[20] Gorbachev is not ignorant of the dangers of decentralisation and significance of central authority in socialist state. So what he really wants appear to be decentralisation which does not contradict the legitimate power of the centre. That's why Gorbachev who at one level accepts the possibilities of decentralisation degenerating into self serving communalism, makes a contradictory statement at another place where he says that those who believe that the decentralisation which he proposes would lead to self serving communalism are making a grave mistake. To quote him, what is required now is "decentralisation that retains those functions of the central authorities without which one cannot assert the advantages of socialism or ensure the interests of the people—is the principal trend consonant with the demands of social development."[21]

The other aspect of Gorbachev's concern is the need to charge the existing relations between the party and the soviets. He is primarily interested in enhancing power and prestige of the soviets—the elected bodies. To Gorbachev, it is not merely the bureaucratic-managerial interference which is responsible for deprivation of the real powers of the present state of affairs. As such, the party General Secretary's favourite term 'command style administration' refers to both bureaucracy as well as the party. Gorbachev tries to justify this understanding by quoting Lenin. According to him, "Lenin repeatedly pointed to the harmful nature of the notions that a governing party must directly administer, ignoring or replacing other organisations of working people. He insisted on the need to "delimit much more precisely the functions of the Party (and of its central committee) from those of Soviet government". Lenin strongly criticised attempts to saddle the party with the responsibility for solving every specific problem and censured the practice whereby "minor matters are dragged before the political bureau."[22] Hence Gorbachev insists that "there must be a strict demarcation of the functions of the party and state bodies in conformity with Lenin's conception of party as a political vanguard of society and soviet state as an instrument of the government by the people".[23] Accordingly, the All Union Conference expressed its desire to enhance the executive, legislative, financial and supervisory powers of the soviets. New laws are enacted to entrust the soviets the necessary legal authority over legal enterprises, collective farms and the work collectives. Hereafter the party should not 'dictate' or 'command' the soviets to do this or that. Party should get its economic, social, ethnic policies implemented primarily via the bodies of people's representatives. In addition to all these changes, Gorbachev, keeping in view the necessity of implementing perestroika, suggested many modifications in the structure, functions and responsibilities of the party bodies at all levels.

Along with party reforms, perestroika's scope embraces even the higher governmental bodies like the Presidium and the Supreme Soviet. Recent conference advocates some kind of presidential form of government where the president would be charged with many responsibilities which are hitherto exercised by the Supreme Soviet. Such president, to quote Gorbachev, "should be granted sufficiently broad state authority powers. Specifically, its president could exercise overall guidance in the drafting of the legislation and of major socio-economic programmes, decides on the key issues of foreign policies, defence and national security, chair the defence council, submit proposals on nominating the chairman of the USSR's Council of Ministers, and discharge several other duties traditionally connected with presidency."[24]

Is Gorbachev a Leninist ?

Once a brief summary of the official version of the various political and economic reforms introduced in the name of 'perestroika' is made, it becomes essential to know whether the changes initiated by Gorbachev are consistent with the fundamentals of Marxism Leninism and whether the reforms will strengthen the possibilities of taking the advanced socialist states towards the classless and stateless communist society.

As far as Gorbachev is concerned, he always tries to project himself as a true Leninist. Not a single book or speech of Gorbachev is without references to Lenin. Whenever he talks of any reforms—either in cooperative farming or in the soviet and the party, he does not forget to quote from Lenin's works. What is more, he claims that his perestroika was inspired by Lenin's teachings. In his own words, "turning to Lenin has greatly stimulated the party and society in their search to find explanations and answers to the questions that have arisen'. Gorbachev considers that all his predecessors deviated from Leninist understanding of socialist development. Hence Gorbachev takes upon himself the responsibility of restoring Lenin to his earlier glory, for, "today we have a better understanding of Lenin's last works which were in essence his political bequest and we more clearly understood why these works appeared".[24a] However Gorbachev is very well aware of the criticism that many of his reforms do not have any sanction in classical Marxist writings. Hence he justifies perestroika as creative interpretation of Leninism to deal with the problems of advanced socialist society. To quote him, "the classics of Marxism Leninism left us with a definition of the essential charactersticis of socialism. They did not give us a detailed picture of socialism They spoke of its theoretically predictable stages. It is our job to show that what the present stage should be like... for, the classics teach us the approach, not the techniques".[25]

To know how far Gorbachev's claims are true to the essence of Marxism, it is essential to study them by relating it to what Lenin and Stalin said at given historical junctures in Russian socialist development. Since the main purpose of the book is to comprehend the nature and dynamics of state, classes and economy under socialism, the chapter briefly touches various aspects of Soviet society to the extent they become necessary to theorise the nature of the socialist state in general.

New Economic Policy : Cooperatives as a form of state capitalism

Gorbachev's stress on promotion of cooperative movement to resolve many of the vital problems of socialist Russia is already highlighted. To him development of cooperatives is synonymous with the development of socialism. He argues that according to Lenin, "when state power is in the hands of the working people when the socialist state is the owner of the land and the basic means of production and when it directs the work of cooperatives, the growth of cooperatives in these conditions is identical with the growth of socialism".[25a] In order to evaluate Gorbachev's claims, one may examine the circumstances which led Lenin to formulate cooperative policy and the status that Lenin assigned to cooperative movement in the building up of socialist setup in Russia.

Cooperative movement was initiated by Lenin as a part of the 'New Economic Policy'. Though the workers and peasants captured the state power in 1917 itself, for about three years after revolution, the Russia got entangled in civil war which was further complicated by the interference of the external forces. For that reason almost upto 1920 the Bolsheviks directed their whole attention in consolidating the revolution by diverting huge funds for strengthening the defence system. Strict controls were imposed on the economic activities and freedom for private trade was completely denied. Large amounts were extracted from agriculture to strengthen the power of the workers and soldier deputies. Some of the extremist elements in the Bolshevik party started attacking even the ordinary peasants. Ths situation caused extreme inconveniences to the peasantry and the much needed alliance between the workers and peasants was about to collapse. So, once the objective compulsions imposed by war-communism were overcome, it became the duty of the Bolshevik party to reestablish the relationship between the peasantry and the working class by taking appropriate steps.

In addition, the Soviet government had to make an objective assessment of the conditions in Russia in order to pave the way for socialist economy. It needs to be mentioned that at the time of revolution Russia was the most backward capitalist state in Europe. Though after February revolution, Lenin gave call far anti-capitalist socialist revolution on the basis of his analysis of the classes which attained power, he was fully aware of unaccomplished tasks of bourgeois democratic revolution, especially in social and economic spheres. Even though the dictatorship of the proletariat was established, Soviet Russia remained economically a backward capitalist society with ramnants of many precapitalist structures. Building up socialist economy in such society requires accumulation of capital, development of productive forces, and increase of production of all commodities. Since the socialist sector was not in a position to meet all the material requirements necessary for improving the conditions of the peasants and workers, as a necessary retreat, Lenin introduced the New Economic Policy. Under the NEP the Soviet state permitted freedom of trade, capitalism and hired labour under overall guidance and supervision of the dictatorship of the proletariat. Stalin was right when he said that the "NEP is a policy of the proletarian state aimed at permitting capitalism while commanding positions are held by the proletariat state, aimed at increasing the role of socialist elements to the detriment of the capitalist elements, aimed at the victory of the socialist elements over the capitalist elements, *aimed at the abolition of classes and the building of the foundation of a socialist economy*".[26] (italics mine - author)

As such the NEP Russia is not capitalist Russia. Though the capitalist and the kulaks took advantage of the concessions given by the state, the main purpose of the NEP was to strengthen the bonds with the peasants by assuring them the right to trade. Because of the weakness of socialist sector trade became a condition indispensable then for the survival of peasant community.

While it is true that the NEP Russia was not capitalist Russia, it should also be mentioned that the NEP Russia was also not socialist Russia. Look at Lenin's words, "socialism is no longer a matter of distant future, or an abstract picture, or an icon... *NEP Russia will become socialist Russia*".[27] It can be understood from the quotation that the NEP Russia is not a socialist Russia but it was a precondition for the development of socialist Russia. As Stalin points out, Lenin never says that NEP would give us socialism ready made. There is great difference between the possibility of building socialism an the actual building of socialism. Correct understanding of this dual character of the NEP is essential for evalutating the status assigned to cooperatives.

Lenin pointed out that at the time of implementing the NEP Soviet Russia had multistructural economy with different modes of production viz. the patriarchal, small-commodity production, private capitalism, state capitalism and socialism all existing side by side. Among them, small-commodity production which included the majority of the peasants was a dominant mode of production. Lenin understood that one of the reason for the backwardness of Russia lies in small production. Since direct transition to the socialist form of agriculture was not possible, Lenin saw in the development of state capitalism, a possibility of transition to socialism. To quote him, "although it is not a socialist form, state capitalism, would be for us, and for Russia, more favourable form in a country whose economic system was and is to this day very backward."[28] At a time when there was no large scale industrial base and adequate trading and transport facilities state capitalism was seen as necessary conditions for linking peasant economy with industry; for amalgamating the small production and for augmenting capital accumulation. To achieve this end, many concessions were given to foreign firms, local industrialists and traders. But this state capitalism is to be differentiated from the state capitalism that exists in the advanced capitalist countries. By implanting state capitalism what the soviet government wanted was to "strengthen large scale production against petty production, advanced production against backward production and machine production against hand production... It also obtains a large quantity of products of large scale industry and strengthens state regulated economic relations as against the anarchy of petty bourgeois relations. The moderate and the cautious application of the concession policy will undoubtedly help us quickly to improve (to a modest extent) the state of industry and the conditions of the workers and peasants".[29] Such state capitalism obtained different forms in different fields. In agriculture it took the form of cooperatives.

Lenin was aware of the fact that transition to socialism is not possible by keeping the small farming intact. He firmly believed that "the small farming system under commodity production can not save the mankind form the poverty and oppression of the masses". In his opinion, "if we continue... on our small farms, even as free citizens on free land we shall be faced with inevitable ruin".[30] The only way out of poverty and backwardness was switching over to common cultivation in large model farms through application of modern techniques. As a step towards that Lenin appealed to the small peasants to organise the cooperative societies. The party and the government were advised to attract the peasants towards cooperative farming by patiently explaining to them of its practical advantages. Cooperatives are seen as practical solution to strengthening the bonds between the working class and the mass of peasantry. In addition to agricultural cooperatives the NEP encouraged promotion of cooperatives in trade and other services. Since the state cannot provide the peasants all necessary goods from the socialised factories in exchange for his surplus, freedom to trade with surplus was legally guaranteed. Public initiative and competition were encouraged and different forms of exchange among the people and between agriculture and industry were developed.

Here one may attempt to know the status that Lenin assigned to the cooperatives. Does promotion of cooperatives synonymous with the growth of socialism as Gorbachev claims it? Lenin who argues that "exchange is freedom to trade; it is capitalism" contradicts Gorbachev when he clearly says "the cooperatives are also a form of state capitalism... The small commodity producers, cooperatives inevitably give rise to petty bourgeois, capitalist relations, facilitate their development, push the small capitalists into the foreground and benefit them most. . . In Russia's present conditions, freedom and right for the cooperative societies mean freedom and rights for capitalism. It would be stupid or criminal to close our eyes to this obvious truth".[31] For Lenin cooperatives are necessary under the given conditions just as any other forms of state capitalism. They are considered as preconditions for large scale farming i.e., socialism. Gorbachev clearly misquoted Lenin when he wrote that, "*When the state power is in the hands of the working people*" growth of cooperatives is indentical with the growth of socialism. For clarification let us look at Lenin's quotation, "Indeed the power of the state over all large scale means of production, political power in the hands of the proletariat, the alliance of this proletariat with the many millions of small and very small peasants, the assured proletarian leadership of the peasantry etc., — *is this not all that is necessary to bring complete socialist society out of cooperatives, out of cooperatives alone... It is not still the building of socialist society, but it is all that is necessary and sufficient for it.*"[32] [italics mine-author] In the same work, Lenin also says that under our present system cooperative enterprises "do not differ from socialist enterprises *if the land on which they are situated and the means of production belong to the state i.e. the working class.*" [italics mine-author] What do these passages imply? Lenin clearly says that co-operatives are only essential conditions for the development of socialism. It can be called socialism if only the land and the means of production belong to the working class. Gorbachev wrongly uses the term "working people" when he should have used the word,"working class". At the time of initiating the cooperative movement, every one knows that the land and means of production belonged to the peasants and not to the workers. Only when the cooperatives develop to the stage of state farms where all would be workers, one can say that cooperatives are like state industrial enterprises.

From the above discussion it is clear that the cooperative movement was initiated as a part of the NEP at a time when there was the necessity of amalgamating small production into the larger ones. Cooperatives are not seen as socialist forms of production which are to be retained even after seven decades of socialist experiment. Cooperative movement is only a transition phase towards the development of large scale socialist production. With the development of strong socialist industrial base that could link the agriculture and industry the need for concessions to state capitalism disappeared. At this stage of Soviet economic development Gorbachev thinks of promoting or to put it more clearly, reverting back to cooperatives which are considered by Lenin as different forms of state capitalism. As such promotion of cooperative farming and widening exchange relations at this advanced stage of socialist development is against the spirit of Leninism.

Stalin and collective farm movement

Like Bukharin, Mikhael Gorbachev argues that Stalin's policy of collectivisation overlooked the significance that Lenin attributed to cooperative movement as "high road" to socialism. Gorbachev is critical of the collectivisation movement for introducing the command style method of administration; for ignoring the interests of the working peasantry and for making the middle peasants the target of collectivisation. Criticising the "excesses' committed during the period of collectivisation he asserts, "if there had been more considerations for the objective economic laws and if more attention had been given to the social processes taking place in the country-side, if in general the attitude to this vast mass of the working peasantry, most of whom have taken part in the revolution and had defended it from the white guards and the forces of intervention, had been politically more judicious, if there had been a consistent line to promote the alliance with the middle peasant against the kulak, then there would not have been all those excesses that occurred in carrying out collectivisation".[33] Though in his book, *Perestroika*, he was full of appreciation for the success story of collectivisation movement, in his speech at the 4th All Union Congress of Collective Farmers Gorbachev argued that collective farm movement did more harm to the agricultural sector. Examples he cites are "repeated amalgamations and the appointment of poorly trained personnel, at times, as executives....The consequences of this kind of attitude are the slow progress in the solution of the food problem, the shortages in and narrow choice of many consumer goods and the limited range of daily services. . . As a result of departing from the Leninist principle of the cooperative movement the country and its economy have suffered substantial setbacks in political, moral and social terms".[34]

To know how far such criticism is valid and is consistent with the real facts, one should look at the history of collectivisation in the USSR. At the outset, it may be made clear that the idea of collectivisation was not the brain child of Stalin. It had its basis in teachings of Lenin who insisted that, "We must pass to common cultivation in large model farms; otherwise there will be no escape from the truly desperate situation in which Russia finds itself".[35] As such, Lenin did not consider cooperatives of small peasants as an end in itself; they are only means to be utilised, only to transform them to large scale production at appropriate time.

It is seen that Gorbachev accuses Stalin of ignoring the basic knowledge of the laws governing economic development and that he hastily implemented the policy of collectivisation when the cooperatives did not completely exaust their capabilities. Before examining these assertions, it needs to be made clear that the criterion for switching over to large collective farms was not whether the cooperatives exhausted their capabilities or not. The question under consideration is whether the cooperatives created the necessary conditions where collectivisation becomes possible and desirable. A keen study of Stalin's literature shows that almost upto the end of 1930 Stalin did not speak of collectivisation. Even in 1927 also he opposes fomenting any class struggle in the country-side.[36] But what forced Stalin initiate collective farm movement at the time when the first Five Year Plan was implemented? Stalin answers the question on the basis of development of the productive forces and relative strengths of the collective farm and of the kulak class. During the period of the NEP, the kulaks took advantage of the state concessions and amassed considerable wealth. Their share in total agricultural production and exchange was still significant. So long the productivity of collective and state farms did not out weigh that of the kulaks, it is not possible to eliminate the kulaks. It is this understanding which made Stalin wait upto 1929, when the total production and marketable surplus of the collective and state farms increased substantially.[37] The moment this position is achieved the process of collectivisation was initiated.

What was the substance of collectivisation movement? In essence collectivisation means passing over to large scale mechanised production by eliminating the class of kulaks from the agrarian sector. It presupposes fulfilment of a few conditions. At first, it needs liberation of the small peasants from the slavish attachment to his little plot of land and combining small peasant plots into large scale collective farms. Secondly, it requires attracting the middle peasants towards collective farms by demonstrating to them of the gains of inroducing highly mechanised methods of farming. Finally the collectivisation should initiate class struggle to deprive the kulaks of their products, instruments and means of production.

The Soviet state under Stalin's leadership formulated a new agrarian policy aiming at achievement of these conditions. Soviet agrarian laws accordingly demanded nationalisation of land and abolition of the absolute rent and private ownership of land. They attacked property of the kulaks and took possession of grain reserves totalling tens of millions of poods. Attempts were made to supply adequate tractors and other material support of the farmers who joined the collective farms in large numbers. In the main, contrary to the expectations of Bukharinites there was good response from the peasants to the collective farm movement. Between 1929 and 1933, number of collective farms increased from 57 thousands to 224.5 thousands and the number of households in collective farms raised from 1 million to 15.2 millions. By 1933, 65% of the peasant farms were collectivised.[37a] Despite opposition from the kulaks and the initial technical difficulties of reorganisation the production of agricultural products showed a moderate increase. Before Stalin's death, Russia could increase the production of consumer and other productive goods to a considerable extent. Though Soviet economy was almost shattered during the second World War, within a decade Russia could reconstruct its economy. Industrial output in 1950 stood at 73% above 1940. Production of capital goods doubled and the consumer goods increased by 23% per cent. Labour productivity in industry increased by 50% between 1940 and 1951.[38] Concentrating on production of capital goods was then a historic necessity. However during this period production of consumer goods also increased considerably. Between 1930 and 1953 production of fabrics increased from 1,947 millions square metres to 4,582 million square metres; paper from 495 thousands tonnes to 1,611 thousand tonnes; that of leather shoes from 75 to 331 million pairs and clocks and watches from 0.23 million units to 12.8 million units. Production of refrigerators increased from 3,500 in 1940 to 49,200 in 1953 and that of TVs from 300 to 34,000 during the same period. Supply of radios and radiogrammes increased from 29,300 in 1932 to 1.64 million units in 1953.[38a] Fifth Plan gave considerable importance to increase the consumer goods. Now one may have a look at agriculture. In spite of the crop failures that followed the war, grain output increased to 100 million tonnes in 1955. Between 1940 and 1950 the total heads of productive livestock, sharply reduced during the war, restored and in 1950 increased by 4 per cent. It was true that production in agriculture did not increase considerably. But attributing this slow growth only to collectivisation and ignoring the factors such as the opposition of the kulaks, second World War and the periodic famines that hit Russia during this period, is not a dialectical way of evaluating the given phenomenon. If the objective limitations imposed by the national and international conditions are taken into consideration, one has to agree that the economic progress achieved during Stalin's period was indeed remarkable. It is not difficult to understand that such spectacular achievements could not be achieved with command style method of administration. No amount of bureaucratic oppression could succeed without the absence of active participation of the masses.

The achievements however need not make one ignore the mistakes or the so-called 'excesses" committed during the period of collectivisation. Gorbachev accuses the party of its ignorance of the necessity to maintain alliance with the middle peasants. But reading of Stalin's works shows that the truth was contrary to what Gorbachev asserts. One can find number of references in Stalin's writings[39] where he stressed the necessity of aligning with the middle peasants against the kulaks. The official policy was to attract the peasants towards collective farms by convincing them of the practical advantages of the mechanised production. During the initial years of collectivisation the principle was strictly followed. As a result, lakhs of middle peasants voluntarily joined the collective farms.

However, in their over enthusiasm to meet the plan targets certain local party men and government officials began to attack the property of the middle peasants also. It created illfeeling among the affected middle peasants. Moreover, it was found out that Lenin's principle of taking into consideration the diversity of conditions in various regions of the USSR was violated in building collective farms. The moment such incidents were brought to the notice of Stalin, he reviewed the situation and directed the party and government to put and end to such "excesses". He was highly critical of the bureaucratic attitude of those conceited representatives of the party whose belief in the omnipotence of the decrees, resolutions and orders diluted the party's revolutionary measures.[40]

It is known that once the causes of "excesses" are detected the state took appropriate measures to rebuild the confidence among the middle peasants. An unbiased analysis shows that the "excesses" are not the result of party's official policy. Accepting that there are some excesses, one should question oneself whether the historic necessity of collectivisation be overlooked just because certain excesses were committed in implementation of a correct policy. That was precisely the question Stalin poses to Bukharin and his friends who were magnifying the mistakes committed during that period. Stalin, then rightly observed, "the conclusion to be drawn from this is that we must combat the excesses. But can one on those grounds decry the line itself, which is the only correct line".[41]

Centralisation vs Decentralised Economic Planning

In decentralisation Gorbachev finds solutions to problems of bureaucratisation, inadequacy of consumer goods, poor quality of industrial products and lack of initiative among the workers. His ideas on 'co-operative', 'lease contract agreements', 'khozraschots', 'cost accounting system' and stoppage of state subsidies are all different aspects of his policy of economic decentralisation. Since he justifies all these things by referring to Lenin it becomes essential to examine Lenin's view on centralisation and decentralisation.

Lenin was always in favour of large scale industry. He considers heavy industries as foundations for future communist society. Hence in spite of all difficulties he stood for the development of socialist sector at any cost. In his report to the 4th Congress of Communist International he clearly stated : "The salvation of Russia lies not only in good harvest on the peasant farms — that is not enough; we also need heavy industry. And to put it in good condition we will require several years of work... Heavy industry needs state subsidies. If we are not able to provide them, we shall be doomed as a civilised state, let alone as a socialist state".[42] Lenin was not unaware of the fact that there may be losses in certain heavy industries, yet he never thought of abandoning them merely for the losses they incurred. Further one may see that in contrast to Gorbachev's argument, Lenin demanded greatest possible centralisation of large scale production throughout the country. "The All Russia centre therefore should definitely be given the right of direct control over all the enterprises of the given branch of industry. The regional centres define their functions depending on local conditions of life etc., in accordance with the general production directions and decisions of the centres. To deprive the All Russia centre of the right of direct control over all the enterprises of the given industry throughout the industry would be a regional anarcho-syndicalism and not communism"[43].

Centralism which Lenin speaks of is centralism created on the foundations of proletarian democracy. Gorbachev does not understand that it is not the existence of democratic centralism but its degeneration into mechanical centralism, which was the basis of so many problems affecting the Russian society. It is this ignorance which makes Gorbachev talk of autonomy to the production units and self-management. But Lenin was clear in his ideas when he says "any direct or indirect legalisations of the rights of any given factory or any given trade on their particular production, or of their right to weaken or impede orders of the state authority, is a flagrant distortion of the basic principles of Soviet power and a complete rejection of socialism".[44] He clearly says at another instance that, "we suggest nothing like ridiculous transfer of the railways to railway men or tanneries for the tanners."[45] When Kautsky alleged that Lenin gave such anarcho-syndicalist slogans at the time of revolutions, Lenin retorted, "Just think: on August 5, when numerous decrees on the nationalisation of factories in Russia had been issued. . . not a single factory had been "appropriated" by the workers, but had all been converted into the property of the republic. . . Kautsky on the strength of obviously crooked interpretation of one sentence in my speech, tries to make the German readers believe that in Russia the factories are turned over to the individual groups of workers !"[46]

Now let us examine Gorbachev's idea of making farmers the sovereigns of their lands. It is already observed in our discussion on cooperatives and collective farms that Lenin's preference was in favour of converting small units into large agricultural farms based on advanced technology. In pleading for large scale production in agriculture, Lenin was not concentrating merely on the problems of increasing the volume of production. In reality Lenin was more particular about overcoming the roots of capitalism which lie hidden in the small commodity production. Though commodity production in itself is not capitalism, its very presence presupposes existence of private property and exchange. And there lies the possibility of engendering capitalism and there exists the danger of restoration of bourgeois system. As Lenin clearly points out in his work, *Left Wing Communism and an Infantile Disorder*, the burgeois elements arising on the basis of small production, "surround the proletariat on every side with a petty bourgeois atmosphere which permeates and corrupts the proletariat, and constantly causes among the proletariat relapses into petty bourgeois spinelessness, disunity, individualism and altering moods of exaltation and dejection".[47] It injects vacillation and wavering mentality among the ranks of the proletariat and its party. Hence Lenin stressed the need for overcoming the small production.

Considering the specificity of Russia, Lenin clearly understood that it is not possible to do away with commodity production at once. Commodity production exists so long the socialist sector is not developed to a stage where it can satisfy all the national needs of the society. This is a process which can only be overcome gradually. During the period of NEP, it is true that, Lenin stressed the necessity of proletarian state utilising the commodity relations to increase the productive forces and to combat bureaucratic evils. Considering the then objective situation, what Lenin did at that time was indced a correct step. But to argue that the scope of commodity relations should never be restricted amounts to negation of Leninism. In course of the development of higher and higher forms of social production, the operation of law of value should be restricted gradually by curtailing the scope of small commodity production· This was what Stalin did while initiating the process of collectivisation. However Stalin was not unaware of the fact that the commodity production would continue to exist for a long time to come. So long collective farms and socialist industry exist side by side, exchange between town and country becomes inevitable. Only when the collective farms are elevated to the status of state farms and one single integrated economic relations comes to stay in the economy, then the necessity of commodity relations disappears. Until this stage is reached, commodity relations are to be regulated by the proletariat with the ultimate aim of establishing the communist society.[48] But what Gorbachev's government is doing is the reversal of this trend. In the name of increasing production somehow, the present regime created conditions for widening the scope of small commodity production. Though it may solve temporarily the problem of scarcity in production this negative process creates many hurdles by engendering the seeds of capitalism in social, economic and political spheres. All these will further complicate the things as in East European countries.

Monetary incentives and the law of socialist production

Gorbachev thinks it necessary to reform the wage system. This reform is a part of his overall policy to increase the production in the U.S.S.R. He demands that the perestroika should strictly implement the Marx's principle of "from each according to his work and each according to his abilities". Through such reforms Gorbachev wants to "fire" the incompetent and idle workers and "reward" the hard working people with monetary incentives. He believes that the incentives would encourage them to produce more and more. Hence he extends this scope of incentives even to the farmers in collective farms. It is also seen that Gorbachev's idea of making farmers the real sovereigns is primarily based on his belief that sense of posessiveness and the possibility of earning more would encourage the peasants to work hard. All his ideas on 'cooperatives', 'agrarian market' and 'socialist competition' are precisely directed towards that end.

To be frank, Gorbachev's plan of increasing the production is not his original contribution.. It is merely a continuation of the same process which Khrushchev initiated in the early sixties. To Khrushchev, socialism was synonymous with abundance in production. On the plea that the production in the socialist Russia was lower when compared to that of the U.S.A. Khrushchev took upon himself the responsibility of drawing the programme for creating abundance in production. It was then that monetary incentives were introduced in the name of encouraging the workers to produce more. Here, Khrushchev failed to understand how Russia, a backward capitalist country before the revolution was transformed within 35 years into a powerful socialist society that could compete with the U.S.A. and other capitalist countries both in the economic and military fields. No material incentives were given to the Russian masses for making great sacrifices to build up the socialist system. Without understanding how this could happen, Khrushchev and his disciple Gorbachev think of giving monetary incentives as in the capitalist countries to make the people produce more.

Another mistake that Gorbachev does is to see monetary incentives in contrast to wage equalisation. Gorbachev criticises that the wage policies that his predecessors adopted were based on the idea of wage equalisation. But Stalin's literature shows that he was very much opposed to the practice of wage equalisation. He understood that since the society did not reach the second stage of communism, the principle of "from each according to his work and each according to his ability" should be continued. In such society where the difference between the skilled and unskilled labour continues to exist, wage differences are bound to be there. Those differences in wages are necessary to encourage the unskilled workers to become skilled so that the differences between the mental labour and the manual labour can gradually be eliminated from the society. This understanding is opposed to that of Gorbachev who considers that the wage differences are necessary to reward the talented and punish the idle and insincere workers and also those workers whose products are not sold in the markets. Undue stress Gorbachev gives to monetary incentives will have adverse impact on the minds of the workers. As a result hereafter the workers would start working if only they get personal benefits for the work they do. Consequently the workers would become individualistic and forget their social responsibilities. All this would only amount to negating the socialist consciousness which is very essential for building up of a communist society.

In the capitalist society, where due to exploitation of surplus value the real incomes of the workers continue to fall, the capitalists use the tactics of incentives only to exploit the workers more and more. Such a necessity does not exist in socialism. Here the basic aim of production is not extraction of surplus value but maximum satisfaction of the material and cultural needs of the people. In socialism where there is no exploitation, the real incomes of the people continue to increase. As a consequence of the rise in purchasing power the demand for the goods always exceed the actual production capacities. It is in contrast to capitalism where the demand always falls short of the actual production capacities. That production falls short of the demand, is not the defect of socialist society, as Gorbachev seems to consider; in fact that is an asset. It is this feature which gives impetus to the continuous development of the productive forces in socialist society. What is actually needed in such system is the organisation of production relations in conformity with the growing productive forces. It necessiates opting for higher forms of social production keeping in pace with the process of economic development.

Ignoring the basic principles of Marxism, Deng Xiao Peng and Gorbachev opted two diverse interpretations of socialist law of production. The present leadership in China argues that the relations of production in their country are ahead of the productive forces to bring them in conformity with the relations of production. On the contrary, Gorbachev started arguing that in Russia the previous regimes hastily ran after higher forms of production relations when the lower forms had not yet exhausted their capabilities. The result in both the cases is the same. Both China and Russia started stressing the application of modern technology and ignored the necessity of upgrading the relations of production. In the case of the USSR, encouraging the cooperatives and individual farming at this advanced stage of socialism amounts to reversing back the course of socialist proudction.

The criterion for socialist production is not how much one produces but how one produces. Socialist production is to be organised by elevating continuously the cultural standard of the people. Higher forms of socialist production require that individualism among the workers, slavish attatchment of the peasants to their lands and "it is not my business" psychology of the petty bourgeois elements should be attacked from all sides. They cannot be overcome by mere technological advancement. What is needed is a proletarian cultural revolution that eliminates all anti-working class ideas that obstruct the socialist path of development. In spite of the stress that Lenin gave to improve the educational and the cultural standard of the people,[49] from the beginning the Bolsheviks failed to initiate ideological and cultural struggle. What is now initiated in Russia in the name of 'glasnost' is not a proletarian cultural revolution, but a counter-revolution which started injecting burgeois ideas, values and habits—all in the name of socialist consciousness. If these trends in the mass thinking remain unchecked, the chances of restoration of the capitalist mode of production becomes all the more strong.

Transition from Dictatorship of the Proletariat to Communism :

In the light of far reaching economic changes taking place in the USSR, can the political system remain true to what the classical Marxists thought of? How does the present leadership characterise the nature of the state and society in the Soviet Union ? To know answers to these questions let us turn to Gorbachev once again. According to him, "established as a result of the socialist revolution, the dictatorship of the proletariat played a decisive role in creating the new society and in the process it too underwent changes. With the abolition of the exploiter classes the function of the suppressing the resistance of the overthrown exploiters gradually faded away and full scope was given to accomplishing its foremost constructive tasks. *Having fulfilled its historic mission the dictatorship of the proletariat has evolved into a political power of all working people, while the proletarian state has become the state of the whole people*".[50] The statement implies that the present state should no longer be considered as the dictatorship of the proletariat. Historic mission of the dictatorship was to eliminate the exploiting classes was accomplished successfully and with that Russian society entered the new stage of socialist development i.e. the state of all people. All the prevailing classes namely, the workers, peasants and the intelligentsia are non-antagonistic in nature and they are the allies in favour of building up of communist society. Hence present Russian state is the state of all people and the Communist Party of Russia is the party of all people.

Here it may be mentioned that this interpretation is not Gorbachev's innovation. It has its roots in Khrushchev who for the first time introduced such ideas in the 21st and 22nd Congress of the CPSU. With little modifications Brezhnev introduced the concepts of "developed socialism" and "state and party of all people" in the Russian constitution of 1977. The Russian intellectuals like Antoly Yegerov and E. Chekharin tried to project his ideas as a further creative innovation in the theory of Marxism and Leninism and a mile stone on the road to communist self-government and the withering away of the state. To justify this E. Chekharin quotes from Mikhail Kalinin who in 1926 said, "as the building of socialism goes ahead, capitalist relations are uprooted and the capitalists disappear, the proletarian state gradually turn into a state of the whole people, full of new significance and substance."[51] Thus starting from Khrushchev to Gorbachev all of them made attempts to justify the idea of "state of all people" by citing quotations from different classical sources. Hence critical evaluation of their interpretation of the present Russian state presupposes a comprehensive understanding of the role of the dictatorship of the proletariat.

Marx considers that between capitalism and communism there is a transitory phase where revolutionary transformation of one to another takes place. During this period, Marx insists that the state cannot be anything but the revolutionary dictatorship of the proletariat. Unlike the anarchists who plead for abolition of all forms of state, the Marxists argue that after overthrowing the political rule of the exploiters, the victorious proletariat should establish its own state after destroying the old bourgeois state machinery. Establishment of the state of the proletariat is considered essential to eliminate the exploiting classes completely from the political and economic spheres. Applying this theme to the concrete conditions of Russia, Lenin called the Russian state after November Revolution as the state of workers and peasants. The Dictatorship of the Proletariat under the concrete conditions of a backward include within its system the semi-proletarian strata and the poor peasants as its supporting base and the middle peasants as its allies. But this ruling coalition is to be led by the revolutionary proletariat whose ultimate aim is to establish classless and stateless communist society.[52]

Such a system of the dictatorship of the proletariat is essential to overcome the challenges of the capitalists and the Kulaks who remain powerful for many more years after revolution owing to their material possessions, organisational abilities, professional skills, administrative and military contacts and their links with the international bourgeoisie. The overthrown burgeoisie use all its energies to restore the rule of capital. Hence Lenin said that the strength of the bourgeoisie would grow ten fold after the revolution.[53] To overcome and eliminate the resistance of such enemy a protracted struggle against the kulaks and the capitalists become essential. In Russia the task was fulfilled in the 1930s with the successful implementation of the policies of industrialisation and collectivisation. Recognising this change, in his speech delivered at the time of introducing the constitution of the USSR in 1936, Stalin claimed that the exploiting classes were completely eliminated from the Russian society.[54]

If the aim of the dictatorship of the proletariat is only to eliminate exploiting classes from political and economic spheres, the task was accomplished in Russia in mid-1930s itself. Hence one tempts to argue—like Gorbachev—that the dictatorship is now no more essential in the USSR where the existing classes are only allies of the proletariat. However, reading of the Marxist classics would show that the dictatorship of proletariat is necessary not only to eliminate the exploiting classes but also to put an end to the existence of all classes. The dictatorship of the proletariat should exist as long as the classes exist; no matter whether they are antagonistic or non-antagonistic. One may find numerous references about this aspect in Marx's and Lenin's writings. As early as 1852, Marx wrote to J. Weydemeyer that what he actually found out was "that the existence of classes is merely linked to particular historical phases in the development of production, that class struggles necessarily lead to the dictatorship of the proletariat, that this dictatorship only constitutes the transition to abolition of all classes and to a classless society.'[55] Lenin developed this idea of Marx into a systematic theory. In the Third Congress of the Communist International he said, "The dictatorship of the proletariat does not signify a cessation of class struggle, but its continuation in new forms, and with new weapons. This dictatorship of the proletariat is *essential as long as classes exist*, as long as the bourgeoisie overthrown in one country intensifies ten fold its attack on socialism on an international scale".[56] In his *Greetinges to the Hungarian workers* he further clarifies, "the abolition of classes requires a long, difficult and stubborn struggle which after the overthrow of the capitalist rule, after the destruction of the burgeoisie, after the establishment of the proletariat does not disappear but merely changes its forms and in many respects becomes fiercer". In the same article Lenin writes " in order to abolish classes a period of the dictatorship of one class is needed, the class, precisely that oppressed class which is capable of not only overthrowing the exploiters, not only ruthlessly crushing their resistance, but also breaking ideologically with the entire bourgeois democratic outlook, with all the philistine mongering about the liberty and equality in general".[57] When can one expect to abolish the classes completely? Lenin answers, "... in order to abolish the classes completely, it is not enough to overthrow the exploiters, the landowners and the capitalists, not only to abolish their rights of onwership, it is necessary also to *abolish all private ownership of the means of production, it is necessary to abolish the distinction between the manual workers and brain workers. This requires a long period of time. In order to achieve this an enormous step forward must be taken in developing the productive forces; it is necessary to overcome the resistance of the numerous survivals of the small scale production, it is necessary to overcome the enormous force of habit and conservatism which are connected with the survivals*.[58]

The essence of all these passages may be summarised as follows:-

1. The dictatorship of the proletariat does not merely mean the use of force. It does not exist only to eliminate the exploiting classes.

2. Proletariat dictatorship exists as long as classes exist. It is the job of the proletariat to create conditions for elimination of classes.

3. The historic mission of such dictatorship is not fulfilled merely by eliminating exploiters from the economic scene. It has to fight out bourgeois thinking which continues to persist even after the elimination of classes as economic categories.

4. The dictatorship of the proletariat continues so long as small commodity production and petty bourgeoisie thrive in the towns and countryside.

5. Under the dictatorship of the proletariat, the state should organise the labour and production with ultimate aim of elevating the economy to a stage where the principle "from each according to his work and each according to his needs" can be implemented.

6. The state of the working class has the responsibility of organising the workers on higher moral and ethical grounds. Unless the workers get out of bourgeois and petty bourgeois cultures, they will not be able to administer themselves. Thus the dictatorship is seen as a stage where the proletariat state becomes a teacher, guide and mentor of the working class.

In view of such complex role that the proletariat state plays, Lenin defined the dictatorship of the proletariat as "a stubborn struggle—bloody and bloodless, violent and peaceful, military and economic, educational and administrative—against forces of tradition of the old society".[59]

Now one may look at the present state of affairs in Russia to judge whether all the historic tasks of the dictatorship of the proletariat are accomplished or not. Gorbachev himself accepts that in Russian society along with workers there exists peasant community which is to speak in Lenin's language nothing but a petty-bourgeois class. In addition, Gorbachev himself talks of moral degradation in Russia, of "penetration of stereotypes of mass culture alien to us" and of young generation who are "after profit at all costs".[60] Here one may also take note of the rebirth of nationalist feelings within the Soviet Republics, in spite of the fact that economic exploitation of one national by another disappeared long ago. In 'class terms' none of them exhibits revolutionary proletarian culture and ethics. The so-called 'radical' demands for freedom and multi-party system gaining momentum in the name of 'glasnost' is nothing but infiltration of bourgeois democratic thinking. Again it needs to be remembered that the USSR is now only in the first stage of communism where the possibility of infiltration of powerful international bourgeoisie still remains. In such conditions it is wrong to claim that the historic mission of the dictatorship of the proletariat is already accomplished. The proletarian dictatorship continues to have relevance so long the unaccomplished tasks in political, economic and cultural spheres remain unfulfilled.

To speak of a different stage in the development of socialist state, when its old stage is still relevant, is a negation of Marxism Leninism. At no place Marx and Lenin spoke of another stage called 'state of all people' in between the dictatorship of the proletariat and communism. When Lenin stated that in socialism "state" is no longer a state in the proper sense, he said that to make it explicit that the proletarian state is the state of majority of the people against the exploiters which is an insignificant minority. Hence it is not necessary to shed so much blood as in the cases of all other regimes led by the exploiting minorities.[61] Lenin long back made it clear: "The class which took power into its hands, did so knowing that it took power alone. That is a part of the concept of the dictatorship of the proletariat. The concept has meaning only when one class knows that it alone is taking political power in its hands and does not deceive itself or others with the talk about 'popular' government elected by all, sanctified by the whole people".[62] Even if the existing peasant community in Russia is not exploitative in nature, on its own, it will not choose communism unless it is led by the revolutionary proletariat. If the leading role of the proletariat is accepted, it only means that even if there is absence of violence or external threat, there still exists the dictatorship of the proletariat.

Question of Bureaucracy In Socialist Society

Marx, Engels and Lenin thought that after the overthrow of the bourgeoisie, the proletariat would break the bureaucratic machinery of the state and replace it by a new proletariat state devoid of all bureaucratic distortions. But it should be admitted that in the case of Russia, notwithstanding its socialist development under the dictatorship of the proletariat, bureaucratic institutions could not be eliminated. On the contrary, as Gorbachev would point out, bureaucracy become a powerful institution that could affect the working of all administrative and economic bodies. Since such command-management system is responsible for the weakening of the role of peoples' bodies like the soviets and trade unions, Gorbachev's perestroika expresses its desire to fight out bureaucratisation.

What is the root cause of such bureaucratic distortions in the socialist set ups? At least in his book, *Perestroika*, Gorbachev accepts that the problems related to bureaucracy have objective base. However, Gorbachev indirectly argues that some subjective factors are also responsible for command management system.[63] He becomes more explicit in his speeach at the 19th All Union Congress where he blames Stalin and his associates for initiating the process of bureaucratisation. According to Gorbachev, "at a certain stage the political system established as a result of the October Revolution underwent serious deformations. This made possible the ommipotence of Stalin and his entourage, and the wave of repressive measures and lawlessness. The command methods of administration that arose in those years had a direct effect on various aspects of development of our society. Rooted in that system are many of the difficulties that we experience to this day".[64] Realisation of this 'new truth' forces Gorbachev to take up necessary measures to put an end to command management system.

Before evaluating Gorbachev's position on bureaucracy, one should first seek answers for certain fundamental issues related to the socialist society in the USSR. The questions include : (1) What is the socio-economic basis of bureaucracy in Soviet Russia ? (2) How far was Stalin responsible for its growth? (3) What is the class character of the bureaucrats and professionals ? (4) What are the conditions necessary for total elimination of bureaucratic institutions? Let us examine these issues on the basis of Lenin's works.

Bureaucracy is not a phenomenon associated exclusively with Stalin and post-Stalin periods in the Russian history. It existed even at the time of Lenin. Though Lenin insisted that the old state machinery of the landlords and capitalists should be destroyed, because of the peculiar conditions that prevailed in Russia at the time of revolution, Lenin considered it impossible to throw out all the bureaucrats at one stroke. As Lenin himself put it, "In our country bureaucratic practices have different economic roots, namely, automised and scattered state of small producers, with his poverty, literacy, lack of culture, the absence of roads and exchange between agriculture and industry, the absence of connection and interaction between them".[65] Hence it requires many more years of consistent fight to overthrow the bureaucracy completely. To quote Lenin again, "When you are called upon to 'put a stop to bureaucratic practices' it is demagogy. It is nonsense, we shall be fighting the evils of bureaucracy for many more years to come and whoever thinks otherwise is playing demagogue and clearly cheating, because overthrowing the evils of bureaucracy requires handreds of measures, wholescale literacy, culture and participation in the workers and peasant inspection".[66]

Though workers and peasants took over political power from the Czar and the Russian bourgeoisie, they did not have the experience and capability to run the administrative and economic bodies. Hence there was a necessity to retain many bureaucrats and professionals who were till then working under the Czarist and Kerensky's governments. Lenin was not unaware of the bourgeois attitudeof such workers. He also knew that many Czarist and bourgeois elements which had lost their economic and political power, gradually entered the bureaucratic apparatus as managers and technicians. It was considered premature to give call for total elimination of such elements until and unless the working people gave birth to its own intelligentsia capable of handling all the administrative, economic and technical problems involved in socialist development. Association with bourgeois experts is seen as a condition essential for the proletariat to develop its own skills. The concessions that the bourgeois experts used to get in the initial years of development were viewed as the "price" that the working class pay for learning from them.[67] Though the bourgeoisie played significant role as experts for quite sometime, they could not consolidate their position forever With the complete elimination of the kulaks and the capitalists and with the gradual inflow of the educated people from the working class and peasantry, the strength of the bourgeoisie began to fall down. Charles Bettelheim's argument that the bourgeoisie consolidated its position as 'state bourgeoisie'[68] is against the historic reality. Mere existence of bourgeoisie in the state machinery or the predominance of bourgeois practices in administration cannot automatically turn the proletariat state into the state of the bourgeoisie, just as the presence of representatives of the proletariat cannot make the capitalist state into a proletariat state. Yet, owing to ideological backwardness and absence of cultural revolution, the representatives of the workers and peasants who entered into bureaucracy could not completely overcome the bourgeois practices of their predecessors. Hence in spite of the disappearance of the bourgeois class as economic category, bureaucracy as an ideology and as a method of working continued to affect the administrative process in the socialist Russia.

Stalin was first to detect this new development. He noticed that the bureaucratic method of functioning entered even within the party, komsomols, trade unions and economic bodies. It is incorrect to say that Stalin had no intention to fight out the bureaucratisation. In the case of bourgeois experts, he correctly handled their dual character before and after the civil war in the early 30s. However, he understood that it is not so easy to handle the communist bureaucrats. As he himself puts it, "If it were only a question of the old bureaucrats, the fight against bureaucratism would be very easy. The trouble is that it is not a matter of the old bureaucrats. It is a matter of the new bureaucrats, bureaucrats who sympathise with the Soviet government and finally communist bureaucracy with the title of party member. And unfortunately, we have quite a number of such communist bureaucrats".[70] Stalin had contempt for bureaucracy and he never wanted to rest the fortunes of socialism on the shoulders of socialist bureaucrats. However, his dependence on those elements became inevitable during the second World War where the prompt action was necessary to deal with the Fascist menace. The necessity of dealing with internal and external enemies was so much that Stalin could not but depend on bureaucracy which he himself desisted. It was true that some of the bureaucrats took advantage of the freedom they got and committed many mistakes in handling the extraordinary situattion. These stray incidents should not lead one to conclude that all the excesses committed by them had the sanction of Stalin. Stalin had no intention to cover the mistakes committed during the period, as Gorbachev or his predecessor, Khrushchev alleged. In the 18th Congress of the CPSU, Stalin himself admitted that "grave mistakes" took place during the purges. So while evaluating these exceptional situations in the Russian history, peculiar national and international conditions of that period should be taken into consideration. Stalin never argued that the state should continue to depend on the bureaucracy even in ordinary conditions. If the evils of bureaucracy continue to dominate the Russian society even 35 years after Stalin's dealth, it is the post-Stalin leadership—not Stalin who had to be blamed. Nothing would have stopped the post-Stalin leadership bent upon de-Stalinisation to wage a struggle against the bureaucracy. An impartial study shows that the so-called command-management method of working, which Gorbachev criticised, further spread its tentacles after Stalin's death. It is ridiculous to blame Stalin for the problems that the present society faces.

If Gorbachev truly desires to fight out bureaucracy, it is indeed a welcome step. If the new leadership attempts to increase the cultural and ideological consciousness of the people, encourage mass criticism of bureaucratic practices and initiate mass participation in public affairs, then definitely one can overcome the evils of bureaucracy. But if Gorbachev mistakes bureaucracy with central planning and locates the solution for the problems arising out of bureaucratisation in 'decentralisation', then he only demeans the socialist status of the central authority and help in decentralising the bureaucracy up to the local levels.

Party and Soviets in the System of The Dictatorship of the Proletariat

Mikhail Gorbachev who characterises the Communist Party as the party of the whole people expects the party to become a vehicle for implementing perestroika. Accordingly he proposes many reforms affecting the structure and functions of the party and party's relationship with the Soviets. It is already mentioned that Gorbachev is against excessive interference of the party in the affairs of the soviets and brands such intervetion as bureaucratic. Hence he argues for separation of powers between the soviets and the party. To justify his statement Gorbachev says, 'Lenin repeatedly pointed to the harmful nature of the notion that a governing party must directly administer, ignoring or replacing other organisations of working people. He insisted on the need to delimit much more precisely the functions of the party (and of its Central committee) from those of Soviet Government".[71] In addition to demarcating the restrictive roles of the soviets and the party, Gorbachev talks of cleansing the whole party of all its internal defects. He bitterly criticises command style method that developed within the party, especially during Stalin's regime. According to him "Our party was built by Lenin as an organisation of like minded members and free discussion of all probelms and joint actions once a decision has been made was a law in it. But when command style method of administration got established, the atmosphere of party comradeship was gradually giving way to relations based on orders and their execution, on the division of Party members into chiefs and subordinates, relations in which equality among the communists was flouted."[72] As a result, the principle of democratic centralism degenerated into bureaucratic centralism and many of the leaders began to consider that they are infallible and above criticism. This led to disappearance of comradeship within the party and loss of abilities among the rank and file members to infulence the party's activities.

Since the party and the soviets play important roles in the system of the dictatorship of the proletariat, one may first examine the Leninist understanding of the party and its relationship with the soviets and then evaluate Gorbachev's stand on these issues. According to Lenin the Communist Party is the highest form of class organisation of the proletariat, armed with a revolutionary theory and knowledge of the laws of revolution. The party is not something external to the working class. The party is a part of the class, closely bound up with all best elements of the working class, their experience, their selfless devotion to the cause of the proletariat. He was very critical of theories of khvotism and spontaneity in the working class movement. To Lenin, the party should act as the vanguard of the proletariat—as its general staff—which can guide the working class in its most complicated struggle against the rule of capital. Lenin considered that the party is an instrument in the hands of the proletariat for achieving and for consolidating and expanding the dictatorship of the proletariat. He holds that it is impossible to think of the proletarian dictatorship in the absence of the leading role of the party. To quote Lenin, "the Bolsheviks could not have maintained themselves in power tor two and a half months, let alone two and a half years, without the strictest, truly iron discipline in our party and without the fullest and unreserved support of the latter by the whole mass of the working class, that is, by all its thinking, honest, self sacrificing and influential elements capable of leading or carrying with them the backward strata".[73] He makes the same point clear when he says, "without an iron party tempered in the struggle, a party capable enjoying the conflidence of all that is honest in the given class, without a party capable of watching and influencing the mood of the masses, it is impossible to conduct such a struggle successfully".[74]

In spite of the significance he attributed to the role of the party, Lenin did not consider that the party is the only instrument in the system of the dictatorship of the proletariat. Along with the party there are many non party organisations like the trade unions, cooperatives, komsomols and the soviets. Among them, Lenin attributed state power to the soviets of the workers, peasants and soldier deputies. The soviets constitute the political base of the Russian socialist system. To quote him, "the democratism of Soviet power and its socialist nature are expressed in the fact that the supreme authority is vested in the soviets, which are made up of the representatives of the working people (workers, soldiers and peasants) freely elected and removable at any time by the masses, hitherto oppressed by Capital, that the local soviets freely amalgamate on the basis of democratic centralism into a single federal union as represented by the Soviet power of the Russian republic, that the Soviets concentrate in their hands not only the legislative power and supervision of law enforcement, but direct enforcement of the laws through all the members of the soviets with a view to gradual transition to the performance of the legislative functions and state administration by the whole working population".[75]

The party as well as the soviets constitute indispensable transmission belts in the system of the dictatorship of the proletariat. If the party is the class conscious organisation the soviets are the state power of the socialist Russia. Hence the study of their relationship turns into a study of the state and the conscious ruling class within the Socialist Russia. In capitalist and precapitalist societies characterised by the existence of antagonist interests within the dominant coalition, the state becomes relatively autonomous of the classes. Such autonomy is indeed necessary for all those societies. But, this need not be so in the socialist set up, where the dictatorship of the proletariat is well consolidated. Since there is absence of antagonistic interests within the ruling coalition led by the proletariat, the state in socialist set up can be transformed into direct instruments promoting the interests of the working class. As Marx said in his *Critique of Gotha Programme*, "It is by no means the aim of the workers to set the state free... freedom consists in converting the state from an organ superimposed upon society into one completely subordinate to it".[76] It, however, presupposes existence of a party of class conscious proletariat capable of understanding the short term and long term interests of the working class. Such a party should exercise ideological hegemony over all other mass organisations. It should be kept in mind that the soviets are not purely proletarian organisations. In addition to workers they also include peasants, soldier deputies and the intelligentsia. As in the case of other non party organisations, ideological and intellectual standard of the members of the soviets do not match that of its advanced detachment. Hence there arises the necessity of the leading role of the party. Since the soviets on their own cannot undertake all the tasks necessary for the development of communist society, continuous guidance from the party becomes essential. As Lenin points out, "To forget the distinction between the advanced detachment and the whole of the masses which gravitate towards it, to forget the constant duty of the advanced detachment of raise ever wider strata to this advanced level, means merely to deceive oneself, to shut one's eyes to the immensity of our tasks and to harrow down the tasks".[77]

The leading position of the party however does not negate the existence of non party organisations like Soviets. All transmission belts have their roles to play in the spheres allotted to them. Party combines the work of mass organisations of the proletariat and direct their activities towards the ultimate goal of communism. The relationship between the party and the soviets should be dialectical. It is the responsibility of the Party to see that non party organisations accept the leading role voluntarily and never feel that they are subordinated to the party. This aspect was beautifully explained by Stalin who clearly understood that "the party cannot lead the class if it is not connected with the non party masses, if there is no bond between the party and non party masses, if the party enjoys no moral and political credit among the masses".[78] He sees the possibility of conflict between the party and the ruling class, if party turns bureaucratic or if it ceases to be self critical or if the masses did not raise to a level where they can voluntarily accept party's viewpoint. In case the party imposes its decision arbitrarily then open conflicts may develop between the party and non party organisations, including the soviets.[79] In case of fulfilment of all necessary conditions, the soviets do not feel the party's guidance as unwanted intervention, since the party instead of demeaning their status would only encourage them to utilise all their powers in legislation, execution and implementation of party's policy. When the relationship is dialectical the party gets more and more benefited by the continuous feed back that it gets from the day-to-day experience of the Soviets and other mass organisations.

Here it needs to be mentioned that among other things, the ability of the party to raise to the status of a leader of the class is based on the way the party is organised. It is not merely the goals which separate a proletarian party from bourgeois and petty bourgeois parties. It is the structure, composition and the process of working which differentiate proletarian party from other parties. Unless the party is organised on the basis of democratic centralism and collective leadership, it cannot be called a Marxist Leninist party. What is the real essence of democratic centralism? General principles such as lower party bodies obeying the higher party bodies and and minority submitting to the majority do not constitute the 'essence' of democratic centralism as is generally conceived. They only refer the form in which the party has to be organised. Such principles, in formal sense, exist even in bourgeois and petty bourgeois parties. In Lenin's language democratic centralism means 'fusion of proletarian democracy with centralism'. It is the 'proletarian democracy' which distinguishes democratic centralism from bourgeois centralism. Democratic centralism is achieved when organisational centralism is built upon the foundations of proletarian ideological centralism. As such struggle to develop ideological centralism is the basic condition for the prevalence of democratic centralism in the party. In the words of Shibdas Ghosh, "this ideological centralism grows out of the struggle to develop one process of thinking, uniformity of thinking, oneness in approach and singleness of purpose based on Marxism Leninism and dialectical materialism, not only on economic questions but on all questions covering all aspects of life".[80]

Closely connected to this is the concept of collective leadership which is generally mistaken for the majority decision or the decision of all members of the party or of its higher bodies. According to Leninism collective leadership means the collective knowledge of all the members of the party. All members of the party contribute to collective knowledge of the party through their personal experiences and struggles. Since experiences and knowledge acquired therefrom differ from one to another, there should be freedom for all members to express their viewpoints without any inhibitions. In course of dialectical interactions among all members of the party, this collective knowledge of all members of the party gets expressed and personified in the highest form through one person. The criterion for the existence of collective leadership in the party is precisely this "concrete and personified form of expression—through an individual of the collective knowledge of all the members of the party derived through conflict and interaction of ideas and experience not only on political and economic questions but on question covering all aspects of life.[81] The views expressed by that leader is not going to be merely a personal view of that individual. It is the highest personified expression of the whole party. To recognise the leading role of the individual is not against collective leadership. To be more precise, collective leadership is negation of individualism. Individualism having its base in the private property mental complex does not allow whole hearted appreciation of a correct and valid idea in case they contradict the personal interests of the party members. In a true Communist party the members identify or at least voluntarily subordinate their personal interests to the interests of the party and the class. Here the leadership which emerges out of the internal struggle of the party in all aspects—organisational, intellectual and moral aspects—would be accepted by all conscious members of the party. Voluntary acceptance of the ideas of such leadership by other leaders and cadres is not an indication of blindness or hero worship: but it is a concrete manifestation of the development of proletarian democracy within the party.

After such elaborate discussion on party and other related questions it may be understood that,

1) Gorbachev was wrong in considering that the intervention of the party in all affairs is responsible for diminishing the status of the soviets and other mass organisations. If a party is really a proletarian party, then, its guidance is not inconsistent with the role of other non party organisations. Only when the party loses its leadership and turns bureaucratic in its attitude then alone will conflict develop between the party and other transmission belts. The solution then is not one of limiting the role of the

party but of overcoming its defects and of becoming a real vanguard of the people.

2. Lenin always saw the Communist Party as the highest class organisation of the proletariat. The concept of the Party of all people is alien to Leninism. Lenin considered that party is necessary so long the classes continue to exist and all the workers do not develop to the status of its advanced detachment.

3.Lenin's party is not merely a party of the like minded people, Lenin's concept of democratic centralism is not simply to discuss and then accept the decision of the majority. It is not proper to think of democratic centralism without securing ideological centralism in the party. So also, in the absence of ideological centralism it is futile to talk of collective knowledge within the party. Similarly, it is wrong to give populist slogans such as 'democracy' and 'freedom' without providing the people the knowledge as to what such terms should mean to the proletariat and how they differ from bourgeois and petty bourgeois interpretations. Confusing the workers with supra-class slogans is virtually a negation of the spirit of Leninism.

Conclusion

In the light of Gorbachev's 'Perestroika' an attempt is made in this chapter to arrive at a comprehensive understanding of the dialectics of state, economy and classes in the socialist set up. Historical evidences and classical Marxist sources are approached and cited to examine the socialist content of the economic and political reforms initiated by the new regime. The overall conclusion at which one is forced to arrive after such a thorough evaluation is that the Gorbachev's perestroika is a great leap backward in the advancement of socialism in Russia. Despite all his socialist rhetoric, Gorbachev's policy is a major deviation from Leninism.

We have not arrived at this conclusion just because some of the policies that Gorbachev initiated have no sanction in classical Marxist literature. We know that classics cannot provide solutions for each and every problem that may crop up in any and every society. No Marxist would deny the necessity of creative application of Marxism to the concrete conditions. However, every revisionist interpretation should not be justified as creative Marxism. How does a revisionist differ from a creative Marxist? A creative Marxist thinker is one who on the basis of Marxist Leninist methodology comprehends correctly the contradictions of the existing society. On the contrary a revisionist is one who deviates from the fundamentals of Marxist Leninist philosophical approach. A revisionist policy in praxis takes the society away from the goal of classless and stateless communist society.

We call Gorbachev a revisionist because he approaches the problems of developed socialism from non Marxist Leninist angle. There is no element of Marxist creativity in his reforms. What he actually does in the name of creative application of Marxism Leninism is the indiscriminate borrowing of the primitive methods which were relevant to the Russia of early 1920s to solve the problems of the modern advanced socialist Russia. In praxis, his reforms widen the sphere of commodity production and speculation, create an idea of profit motive among the workers, reestablish private ownership of land, weaken the central authority over all administrative and economic bodies and introduce bourgeois values and their rights and liberties in the name of socialist democracy.

While being critical of Gorbachevism for its anti Marxist-supra class approach to the problem of socialism, it should be admitted that it was not really Gorbachev who gave birth to revisionism in Russia. Modern revisionism started with the 20th Congress of the CPSU where Khrushchev introduced the concepts of the state and the party of all people. From Khrushchev onwards, the venom of anti-Stalinism was used time and again to implement the revisionist policies in the socialist Russia. However, credit should go to Gorbachev who could take advantage of the low level of consciousness among the people and party member and come out with a comprehensive revisionist attack on all aspects of socialist society. If his policies are left unchecked, it would further strengthen the elements of capitalism already introduced by Gorbachev's predecessors. Together all of them may lead to intensification of crises which the socialist system may find it difficult to manage in the future. Though there is not enough evidence to call Russia a 'capitalist' or 'social imperialist' state, if at any time, by taking advantage of the conditions created by the revisionist regimes, the relations of production and the motive force of production conducive to capitalism could develop and become dominant in the economy, then, in Russia the possibility of a counter revolution which would restore the rule of the bourgeoisie in the place of the dictatorship of the proletariat may not be overruled.

Notes and References

1. Gorbachev, Mikhail, *Perestroika,* Collins, London, 1987, p. 19.
2. Gorbachev, *Documents and Materials, 19th All Union Conference of the CPSU,* Novosti, Moscow, 1988, p. 39.
3. *Ibid.,* p. 77.
4. Gorbachev, *Perestroika, op. cit.,* p. 22.
5. Gorbachev, *Political Report of the CPSU (CC) to the 27th Party Congress,* Novosti, Moscow, 1986, p. 32.
6. Gorbachev, *Using the Potentials, of Cooperatives for furthering Perestroika,* Novosti, Moscow, 1988, p. 12.
7. Gorbachev, *Documents and Materials : 19th All Union Congress of the CPSU* (Hereafter referred as '19th AUC of CPSU'), *op. cit.,* p. 29.
8. Gorbachev, *Using the Potential of Cooperatives for Furthering Perestroika, op. cit.,* p. 12 (Hereafter book is referred as 'On Cooperatives').
9. *Ibid.,* pp. 19-20.
10. Gorbachev, *Political Report of the CPSU (CC) to the 27th Party Congress, op. cit.,* p. 50 (Hereafter 'Political Report to 27th Congress').
11. Gorbachev, *On Cooperatives, op. cit.,* p. 16.
12. Braginsky, M. *Joint Ventures : Benefit for All,* Novosti, Moscow, p. 3.
13. Gorbachev, *Political Report to the 27th Congress, op. cit.,* pp. 50-51.
14. Wadekin, Karl Eugen, 'The Re-emergence of the Kolkhoz Principle' *Soviet Studies,* Vol. XLI, No. 1, January 1989, pp. 33-34.
15. Gorbachev, *Political Report on the 27th Congress, op. cit.,* pp. 51-52.
16. *Ibid.,* p. 142.
17. Gorbachev, *Perestroika, op. cit.,* p. 84.
18. Gorbachev, *19th AUC of the CPSU, op. cit.,* p. 141.
19. *Ibid.,* p. 140.
20. *Ibid.,* pp. 58-59.
21. *Ibid.,* p. 58.
22. *Ibid.,* p. 83.
23. *Ibid.,* p. 43.
24. *Ibid.,* pp. 54-55.

24a. Gorbachev, *Perestroika, op. cit.,* pp. 25, 26.
25. *Ibid.,* p. 45.
25a. Gorbachev, *On Cooperatives,* Novosti, Moscow, 1988, p. 8.
26. Stalin, J.V., *Problems of Leninism,* Foreign Languages Press, Peaking, 1976, pp. 241-242.
27. Lenin, V.I., *Problems of Building Socialism and Communism in the USSR,* Moscow, Progress Publishers, 1981, p. 28.
28. Lenin, *ibid.,* pp. 7, 8.
29. Lenin, *Selected Works Vol. III,* Moscow, Progress Publishers, 1977, p. 540.
30. Quoted in Stalin, *Problems of Leninism, op. cit.,* pp. 510-511.
31. Lenin, *Selected Works Vol. III, op. cit.,* 541.
32. *Ibid.,* p. 699.
33. *Ibid.,* p. 702.
34. Gorbachev, *On Cooperatives, op. cit.,* p. 12.
35. Quoted in Stalin, *Problems of Leninism, op. cit.,* p. 542.
35a. Quoted in SUCI, *Perestroika and Glasnost,* Ganadabi, Calcutta, 1989, p. 145.
36. Stalin, *On Opposition,* Foreign Languages Press, Peking, 1975, p. 220.
37. Stalin, *Problems of Leninism, op. cit.,* pp. 473-474.
38. *Ibid.,* pp. 708-710.
38a. Dobb, Maurice, *Soviet Economic Developments since 1917,* Routledge and Kegan Paul, London, 1972, pp. 316-317.
38b. Clarke, R.A. *Soviet Economic Facts, 1918-81,* Macmillan, Hongkong, pp. 110-130.
39. Stalin, *Problems of Leninism, op. cit.,* pp. 297, 365, 495; also *On Opposition, op. cit.,* p. 220.
40. Stalin, 'Dizzy with Success' and 'Reply to Collective Farm Comrades' in *Problems of Leninism, op. cit.,* pp. 485, 493, 495, 497, 502.
41. *Ibid.,* pp. 412, 413.
42. Lenin, *Problems of Building Socialism and Communism in the USSR,* Moscow, Progress Publishers, 1981, p. 15.
43. Lenin, *On Workers Control and the Nationalisation of Industry,* Moscow, Progress Publishers, 1977, p. 183.
44. *Ibid.,* p. 186.
45. *Ibid.,* p. 55.
46. Lenin, *Selected Works Vol. III, op. cit.,* p. 89.
47. *Ibid.,* p. 310.
48. Stalin, *Economic Problems of Socialism in the USSR,* Foreign Languages Press, Peking, 1972, pp. 75, 76.
49. Lenin, *Selectecd Works Vol. III, op. cit.,* pp. 693-697 and 703.
50. Gorbachev, quoted in SUCI, *On Perestroika and Glasnost,* Ganadabi, Calcutta, 1989,

p. 10.
51. Kaushik, Devendra, *Soviet Political System : Perceptions and Perspectives,* Progress Publishers, Moscow, 1983, pp. 45, 46.
52. Stalin, *Problems of Leninism, op. cit.,* p. 295.
53. Lenin, *Selected Works Vol. III, op. cit.,* pp. 36-38.
54. Stalin, *Problems of Leninism, op. cit.,* p. 800.
55. Marx, *Selected Correspondence,* Moscow, Progress Publishers, 1982.
56. Lenin, *Selected Works Vol. III, op. cit.,* p. 565.
57. Lenin, *ibid.,* pp. 161, 162.
58. Lenin, *ibid.,* p. 172.
59. Lenin, *ibid.,* p. 310.
60. Gorbachev, *Perestroika, op. cit.,* pp. 19, 12, 24.
61. SUCI, *Perestroika and Glasnost, op. cit.,* p. 19.
62. SUCI, *ibid.,* pp. 22, 23.
63. Gorbachev, *Perestroika, op. cit.,* p. 46.
64. Gorbachev, *19th AUC of the CPSU, op. cit.,* pp. 38, 39.
65. Chakarbarti, B. (ed). *Stalin Question,* Kathashilpa, Calcutta, 1979, pp. 159-160.
66. Chakrabarti, *ibid.,* pp. 157, 158.
67. Lenin, *Selected Works Vol. III, op. cit.,* pp. 555-556.
68. See Bettelhim, Charles, *Class Struggles in the USSR,* M.R.P., 1976, pp. 22, 139, 141, 253.
69. Chakarbarti, *op. cit.,* p. 177.
70. Chakarbarti, *op. cit.,* p. 179.
71. Gorbachev, *19th AUC of the CPSU, op. cit.,* p. 84.
72. Gorbachev, *ibid.,* pp. 76, 77.
73. Quoted in Stalin, *Problems of Leninism, op. cit.,* p. 108.
74. Stalin, *Problems of Leninism, ibid.,* p. 109.
75. Lenin, *On Workers Control and Nationalisation of Industry, op. cit.,* p. 186.
76. Marx, *Critique of Gotha Programme,* Moscow, Progress Publishers, 1978, p. 25.
77. Lenin quoted in Stalin, *Problems of Leninism, op. cit.,* p. 101.
78. Stalin, *ibid.,* p. 100.
79. Stalin, *ibid.,* p. 195.
80. Ghosh, Shibdas, *Why SUCI is the only Genuine Communist Party in India,* Ganadabi, Calcutta, 1985, p. 25.
81. Ghosh, *ibid.,* p. 22.

Chapter VII

PRESENT STAGE OF REVOLUTION
Obstacles and Options

Introduction

The basic thrust of the book is to throw light on the nature and dynamics of state in different social formations. In the changed social, economic and political conditions of the post-war world, how do the form and functions of the state change in course of its interaction with the economy and the classes that emerge out of it—finding answer to this question is precisely the aim of the present work. Keeping it in mind, attempt is made in the previous chapters to critically review the contemporary Marxist theories of state. In course of evaluating the contributions of different Marxist theoreticians, efforts are made to perfect our knowledge of different issues related to the state, classes and economy. Since all of them play determinant roles in historical development, a clear understanding of their nature and dynamics is indeed desirable. However, it needs to be mentioned here that the actual course of development of human history depends on many other social, ideological and psychological factors. Though we may say that History is the product of complex interactions of many structures and social forces, what really makes the dynamics of the human society different from other animate or inanimate things in nature is the conscious role that human beings can play in bringing about the desired changes. In the ultimate analysis the material contradictions take the shape of conflicts among different groups of persons and the history of the given society is shaped by the conscious role of human beings. It is precisely what Engels wrote to J.Bloch : "history proceeds in such a way that final result always arises from conflict between many individual wills and every one of them is in turn made into what it is by a host of particular conditions of life. Thus there are innumerable intersecting forces, an infinite series of parellelograms of forces which give rise to one resultant—the historical event." Those all dialecticians interested not only in understanding particular relationship but also in influencing the course of human history should try to comprehend these "innumerable intersecting forces" and "series of parellelograms of forces". Such a study should examine each social formation in itself, in its interrelationship with others, in its origins, development and transformation.

The scope of the book does not allow such a comprehensive study of all factors influencing the process of change in each social formation. Yet complete omission of the issue concerning change, creates a great void in the present work. To overcome this limitation, at least partially, effort is made in this concluding chapter to throw light on possible outcome of the contradictions of the contemporary world. Basing ourselves on the Marxist methodology that we could perfect in course of our evaluation of different theoreticians, we may look at the prospects of change in each social formation. Instead of merely reflecting on how the contradictions unfold themselves, we may also search for the conscious role that men should play to bring about revolutionary transformation of the contemporary world.

Advanced Capitalist Society : Crises or Compromise

Capitalism with a history of over five centuries, underwent different stages of development. The later phase of capitalism cannot be understood without a clear comprehension of its previous stages. Hence before passing comments on the prospects of change in the advanced capitalist societies, an attempt is made to understand how the previous stages unfolded themselves into the present stage of capitalism.

Progressive Era

The progressive era of capitalism which Marx and Engels so beautifully portrayed in their *Communist Manifesto*, continued up to 1830. During this period while trying to create national markets the bourgeoisie were also striving to extend their area of operation beyond their national boundaries. The obstacles in the path of capital accumulation were the continuing feudal relations of production, feudal values and the political power of the nobles. The bourgeoisie then trying to achieve dominance in the society were objectively in need of a new ideological and political superstructure. The bourgeois humanist values such as individualism, secularism, nationalism, liberty and equality (in bourgeois sense) appeared to replace the absolutist state into nation states. In the countries like England, U.S.A. and even during the first stage of French Revolution, with varying degrees, the 'states' were moulded based on the principles of rule of law, constitutionalism, parliamentary form of government, independent judiciary and a system of checks and balances. During this period, the main contradiction revolved round the ascending bourgeoisie and the declining feudal power. Unorganized working class didn't pose any kind of threat to the survival of the bourgeoisie. Hence national army and bureaucracy though made their appearance fclt at that time itself they did not become strong oppressive branches of the state apparatus. In economy, though the state always helped to create external conditions necessary for capital accumulation, the possibility and the historical necessity of *laissaiz-faire* economy made direct state intervention in the economy unnecessary. Both in content and form, the nature and functions of the state were in accordance with the interest of the emerging bourgeoisie.

Transitional Era

This is the period of expanding capitalism. During this period (which roughly extends from 1830s to 1870s) capitalism consolidated its roots nationally and brought many non-European parts of the world under its embrace. Though free competition was still continuing, the development of capitalism and the necessity of division of labour brought into existence a number of factions within the bourgeoisie. During the same period the exploited workers gradually began to organise themselves against capital domination. Socialist ideas of different colour made their appearance. The economic discontent began to take the shape of political class struggles. Political parties and trade unions representing the working class and other labouring masses emerged, though not legally recognised, to fight for their political and economic rights. National parliaments composed of various antagonistic factions of the bourgeoisie could not successfully meet the new challenge. Wherever universal adult franchise was introduced, parliament began to lose its significance as a means to promote the interests of the bourgeoisie. So the objective necessity of the bourgeoisie demanded a strong independent executive power backed by powerful military and bureaucracy. The threat of class struggles and inefficiency of the individual capitalist to realise their long term interests demanded the state to become relatively autonomous of the capitalists and make its appearance as a neutral third force in the society. While the state conceded demands of the working class to serve the long term interests of the bourgoisie, it did not hesitate to curb the working class struggles when they posed a real threat to the capitalist system itself. This transitional era, where the capitalist state was taking its clear cut shape is well portrayed by Marx and Engels in their analyses of the Chartist movement, Bonapartism and the British parliament Acts on labour.

Era of Monopoly Capitalism and Imperialism

In course of capitalist development, there emerged within capitalism the system of monopolies. This happens either due to combination of production or swallowing of small capitalists by bigger capitalists. Monopolies with huge concentration of capital and control over market, though began to appear after 1880s, they became the characteristic features of all advanced capitalist countries during the next three decades. The birth of finance capital, signifying the beginning of the era of imperialism, put an end to *laissaiz-faire* economy. Though 'pure firms'[2] still continue to exist because of their inferior economic position, they get eliminated or survive without much significance or began to play subordinate role to monopolies. By then, the state which had entered production, some time back could also become a kind of monopoly. Since the protection of the whole bourgeoisie from economic and political crises and as such the survival of capitalism itself demanded, the state had to merge with monopolies.[3]

During this period, even class positions underwent a significant change. The monopolists fraction because of their identification with monopoly, achieves a superior power and status within the bourgeoisie.[4] Though exploitation of the working class as such didn't cease, the monopolists earning superprofits in their colonies, could provide better economic benefits to certain layers of the working class and could co-opt them into the system. This 'aristocracy of labour' or 'bourgeoification of workers' somewhat weakened class struggles in the U.S.A. and Britain. But in Italy and Germany class struggles could not be handled by the old forms of state. Sporadic development of capitalism and the necessity to check the working class and its party, reorganise the national economy in the direction of state monopoly capitalism and struggle to redivide the world market demanded the advent of fascist regimes in Italy and Germany.

The essential characteristic features of the state in fascisms are extreme concentration of political power, diminishing significance of parliamentary and liberal democracy, idea of superman and superclass state, growth of military and bureaucracy, loss of independence of judiciary, birth of committed bureaucracy and extreme inflation of executive power. Though these features appeared in some degrees in other capitalist states as well the peculiar class coalitions and the ideological tradition of Italy and Germany gave their states authoritarian forms. It was the only form of state available to protect and promote the interests of the bourgeoisie then. When there was world wide economic crisis in capitalism during the early thirties, in the U.S.A. there was governmental intervention in economy on a massive scale to boost up the purchasing power of the consumers. The effect of the New Deal programme gave a new base of life to paralysed capitalism.

The Post World War Era

The capitalist state of this era took its form on account of the problems created by the two world wars, emergence of socialist regimes in one third of the world and the liberation of many colonies. These events weakened imperialism. Capitalism began to lose even that relative stability which it enjoyed before the world war. The possibilities of further crisis in economy and the danger of working class becoming class conscious were there. Under such conditions the bourgeoisie found alternatives for its survival in the revival of Keynesian economics, militarisation of economy, dependency and neo-colonialism. The state monopoly capitalism under the mixed economy doctrine has become the order of the day. The state is forced to undertake multifarious functions in economic fields in the aggregate interests of the bourgeoisie.[5] The states are forced to militarise economy to give artificial stimulation to the sagging capitalist economy.[6] Social democratic welfare measures began to be undertaken to curb the discontent of the people on the one hand and to create an artificial demand by increasing the consumption capacity of the people on the other.[7] In ideological sphere, it helped the state to project itself as neutral welfare state. Though it could bring relative stability for nearly two decades, after the sixties the contradictions within the welfare state made its further continuance difficult. The welfare policies and the corporate policies that the state had to undertake increased the deficit in the budgets. The capitalist state unable to fill the budgetary gaps and solve the fiscal crisis, started throwing burden on the citizens in the form of heavy taxation.[8] Added to this are the mounting economic problems such as inflation, stagnation in growth and unemployment. As a response to the increasing demands of the corporate sectors the budget allotment for social welfare measures are being cultailed gradually. Reagonomics and Thatcherism or supply side economic have come to substitue Keynesianism.[9] Under such circumstances all the states in the advanced capitalist countries, in spite of maintaining the facade of two party system or parliamentary democracy started gradually acquiring certain features of anit-liberal states. Though all-out fascims embracing all aspects of capitalist society is yet to come, certain symptoms are already visibile.

On the other side, one can see, in almost all these countries consumers, workers and other weaker sections who were affected by the developments mentioned above, are forced to come to the streets to agitate for their demands. However, simply based on these stray incidents one cannot draw conclusins that the days of the bourgeois state are over. The state in the advanced capitalist society is still secure, for the simple reason that the workers are not conscious of their real interest. However intense may be the people's democratic struggles, without socialist consciousness among the workers and without the develoment of a revolutionary vanguard of the proletariat[10] one cannot dream of destroying the capitalist societies. Where the parties calling themselves communists have fallen victims to nationalism, economism and petty bourgeois individualism, working class cannot break away with the capitalist system. In this sense, the bourgeoisie is still in an advantageous position. Hence the capitalist state finds alternatives to serve the bourgeoisie without resorting to all out fascism immediately. Prospects of revolution in such countries depend on many factors such as the weakening of imperialism, birth of revolutionary Marxist-Leninist parties, defect of economics and national jingoism, de-bourgeoisification of the working class and development of a strong proletarian cultural hegemony that can overcome the bourgeois cultural domination in the capitalist societies.

Third World : Revolution At The Cross Roads

Extreme complex is the problem of determining the present stage of development in the Third World. This complexity is the consequence of variations in social, economic and political structures in the developing nations. Whereas the contradictory role played by the social institutions like religions, tribes and castes which have their origins in the precapitalist social structures contribute to certain amount of confusions, the process of economic development also made it difficult to come to general conclusions about the nature of the state in the Third World. Though capitalism made inroads in to almost all the countries of the Third World, in certain countries like Bhutan precapitalist modes of production still dominate. Among those which are wholly integrated into the world capitalist system, many countries of Africa and Latin America[11] remained single commodity exporting economies wholly depending on the mercy of the foreign capital and foreign markets. Yet there are countries like India which have considerably diversified their trade and secured different sources of foreign capital, so much so that no single imperialist power can coerce them to submit the fate of their economies totally to the dictates of imperialism. From among such countries, there exist some states which are emerging as mini-imperialist power exporting even finance capital to other foreign countries.[11a] In view of such variations, one should avoid making generalisations about the stage of development of economy in all developing nations.

The same is true even in the case of determining the class character of the state in the Third World countries. Since the correlation of the class forces that led anti-imperialist struggles and the changes that took place after decolonisation differed from one country to another, nature and dynamics of the states cannot remain the same everywhere. In view of all these peculiarities, determining the stage of revolution in these countries indeed becomes problematic. The solution that different brands of Marxist theoreticians prescribed so long appear to be simplistic. Here it may be recalled that the Dependency theorists attribute the cause of underdevelopment of the Third World to the status, it acquires in the world economic system as the satellite countries. They characterised the bourgeoisie in the developing nations in different ways. Whereas a few call it 'lumpen' there are others who named it as 'national' and sometimes even 'comprador'. Yet all of them say that all countries are on the stage of socialist revolution. Such a stand is typical of Trotskyites who prescribe anticapitalist socialist revolution to all countries irrespective of the class character of the state. On the other extreme we see the Maoists. At one time the theoreticians like Lin Biao argued that Mao's thought had universal validity and that all Third World countries should follow the path of 'New Democratic Revolution'.[12] Since it was considered that all developing nations are semi-feudal and semi-colonial, they thought that the basic enemies in all these countries are feudalists, imperialists and the comprador bourgeoisie. However, after the sixties, the Chinese leadership itself recognised that most of the countries in the Third World are politically independent and that they can play an important role in fighting the super power hegemony in the world.[13] As far the Soviet Marxists are concerned, they give altogether a different picture of development of these transitionary societies. Khruschev at one time thought that in countries where the national bourgeoisie which played leading role in the anti-imperialist struggle could come to the state power, there it is possible to pass over to socialism, peacefully, through parliamentary means—that too in collaboration with the national bourgeoisie.[14] Though no country in the post colonial societies could fulfill the dream of Khruschev, the theory of 'national democratic revolution' still remains valid in Soviet Marxism. The theory of 'non capitalist path of development'[15] is a more sophisticated version of Khruschevite idea. The people of the U.S.S.R. believe that many of the Afro-Asian countries where capitalism has not penetrated deeply and the petty bourgeois elements remain dominating force in economy and politics, it is possible to think of non capitalist path of development. It is conceived that with the help of socialist countries the petty bourgeois radicals can take up anti-feudal and anti-imperialist measures. By developing state sector and by restraining the growth of private monopoly, it is possible to pass over to socialism without the necessity of developing capitalism. Notwithstanding the arguments they put forward to justify this path on the basis of classical Marxist literature, they cannot escape answering certain practical questions. How far the experience of Siberia or Mongolia which were under direct political control of the Russian proletariat dictatorship be imposed on the Afro-Asian countries which still suffer from direct or indirect imperialist exploitation? Do socialist countries really have enough potentialities to give adequate economic support to all their nations to overcome their dependence on imperialist finance capital? How many of the countries in the Third World can still be claimed as nations where the bourgeoisie—national or comprador—is kept out of state power? Is this non capitalist path of development valid even in those countries where the indegenous capitalist development has given birth to monopolies?

As we have pointed out earlier all these theories suffer from temptation to project the experiences of a few countries as the experience of all the countries of the Third World. Moreover in some of them, there is certain amount of economic determinism, in the sense that the stage of revolution is judged on the basis of their understanding of the economic development of particular countries. In the main, the classes are seen as mere economic categories, and their nature is determined by concentrating particular aspect of their actual dynamics.

As such all these theories fail to give a comprehensive understanding of the contradictory role that the state performs in the Third World countries.

To our mind the dynamics of the Third World can be understood only when we correctly comprehend the contradictions between imperialism and the newly emergent nation state. The World War II weakened the imperialist hold, main enemy being imperialism, all patriotic forces opposed to colonialism fought together for the sake of independence of the nation. Since class correlations and economic development differed from one country to another, the classes or social force that attained state power after independence differed from one country to another. Whatever may be the class character of particular states, under the present historical context, broadly speaking there are only two options left for them to develop their economy. They have to choose either socialist path or capitalist path. Other than in countries like China, Vietnam and Cuba where the anti-imperialist struggles were led under the leadership of the proletriat, many post colonial societies chose capitalist path of development. Since socialism demands radical transformation of the existing socio-economic structures, many countries where the classes other than the proletariat came to power cannot but opt capitalist path of development. But this alternative has its over price. The world capitalist system being dominated by the imperialist powers the newly liberated countries which allow themselves to be integrated in the imperialist chain cannot but pay the due price. Economic compulsions which force these countries to depend on the metropolis for capital and technology drive them into the vortex of imperialist exploitation. However, what prevents the developing nations from becoming neocolonies is the existence of a powerful socialist block along side the imperialist powers. As is seen, the Third World countries entertain dual relationship with imperialism. While its own class character drives them to opt for capitalist path of development, their colonial past and their subordinate status in the present capitalist system force them to take anti imperialist stand. Had there been only imperialist powers along side the newly liberated nations, despite all their intentions to the contrary, the developing nations sooner or later become neocolonies of the metropolis. But the existence of anti-imperialist socialist block throws opportunities for the Third World to survive as independent nations. Though the devloping nations may not prefer socialist transformation, in the international sphere they maintain friendly relationship with the socialist countries. Friendship with the socialist block may be used as a lever to protect their political independence and promote their economic development by restraining the imperialist economic domination. However, the developing countries continue to seek the help of the imperialists whenever they face troubles from the radical forces inside their countries. Such manoeuvrability can be used to get economic aid from both the blocks so that they can initiate independent economic development without submitting to any one power.[16]

However, it should be remembered that mere existence of certain opportunities should not lead to the conclusion that the same can be utilised equally by all the developing nations. Though all the UDCs may try to take advantage of the new correlation of forces in the international arena how far the available opportunities are effectively utilised by each state depends on the class character of the state, present stage of economic development, geographical and strategic significance of those areas, political maturity of the leadership and diplomatic manoeuvres of the governing elites in the respective countries.[17] All these factors contribute to substantial differences in the economic development of the countries concerned. Only those countries which could effectively utilise their potentialities succeeded in making considerable progress towards economic self reliance. But many other nations which have no potentialities or failed to use potentialities remained underdeveloped.

At this moment it needs to be said that though there are variations in economic development, no Third World country could completely extricate itself from imperialist domination. In different degrees all are victims of unequal exchange and world debt trap.[18] Basic problems of poverty, unemployment, illiteracy and economic inequalities continue to be unresolved in all these countries. As such though the international conditions may ensure political independence of the nations and permit certain degree of economic growth, they cannot solve the fundamental problem of life. Without a revolution that could bring structural changes in economic and social conditions, these countries cannot completely overcome economic dependency. For the oppressed masses of the developing societies the only alternative is a political revolution that would establish the rule of the proletariat. But how to accomplish the revolution ? Khruschevite belief in peaceful revolution can be ruled out, for, under the given conditions no classes in power would voluntarily transfer their state power to the proletariat sacrificing their privileged positions in the existing system. If violent revolution is accepted as inevitable, what is the strategy of revolution to be adopted in all countries of the Third World? Generally the stage of revolution is determined by the stage of economic development, correlation of class forces and the nature of the state. It is not difficult to identify the stage of revolution in the advanced capitalist countries where all structures—social, economic and political exhibit capitalist features. But in the UDCs where precapitalist structures are still dominant and capitalism is very unevenly developed, indentification of the stage of revolution indeed become a problem. Even Lenin had to face the problem in Russia. Even though the state power was passed on to the capitalists after the February Revolution, the social and economic structures were then predominantly semifeudal. French finance capital had considerable hold over the Russian industry.[19] Under such circumstances Mensheviks and the Socialist Revolutionaries considered that at that stage it was necessary to develop capitalism. To them only after fulfilling the democratic tasks of bourgeois revolution one can expect to pass over to the stage of socialist revolution. Such arguments were refuted by Lenin. In his historic document, namely, *The April Theses* he argued that fundamental question of every revolution is state power. Which class or classes hold state power, which class or classes are to be overthrown and which other classes are to come to power—such understanding he asserted that once the bourgeoisie achieved the state power, no matter whether all other tasks of democratic revolution are finished or not, politically Russia reached the stage of socialist revolution.[20] Hence notwithstanding the feudal hangovers and imperialist exploitation, Lenin gave call for anti-capitalist socialist revolution in Russia. These teachings of Lenin are of great significance to the revolutionaries of the Third World. In the post-colonial societies where the classes that hold state power differ from one country to another, temptation to generalise the stage of revolution on the basis of social and economic structures amounts to clear violation of the basic principles of Leninism. Since the class character of the state differs from one country to another, the stage of revolution is also bound to be different. In nations where the national bourgeoisie consolidated its position in the state power, the strategy of anti-capitalist socialist revolution is to be followed. In countries where the feudal classes constitute the ruling class, 'people's democratic revolution' will be the alternative. But in those societies where the political independence is only formal and the real state power is shared by the comprador bourgeoisie and the landlords along with their imperialist bosses then 'new democraric revolution' is the correct strategy. So the basic tasks of Marxists of the Third World is to indentify correctly the class character of the ruling classes in each particular country and to develop appropriate tactics to fight against the real enemies by mobilising all possible forces against the classes holding the state power. Ultimately the future of the underdeveloped countries precisely depends on the ability of the Marxists to apply the principles of Marxism-Leninism creatively to the concrete conditions.

Socialist States: Revolution or Counter Revolution?

Role of the state in socialist societies qualitatively differs from that of the states in the advanced capitalist countries and developing nations. Like other states, the socialist state as a political superstructure is relatively autonomous of the economic base, so much so that by its conscious action it can change the old economic relations for creating conditions necessary for the development of socialism. However, if one examines relative autonomy in relations to the ruling classes and the class struggle, it should be said that what is applicable to the state in advanced capitalist countrires and the developing nations need not be true of the proletarian state. Due to absence of antagonistic contradictions within the system of the dictatorship of the proletariat and establishment of absolute superiority over the exploiters, the socialist state should become a direct instrument of the proletariat.[21] To make the state an instrument in that sense it is necessary to have a class conscious party capable of comprehending the short term and long term interests of the proletariat. Without continuous guidance from the vanguard party, the state on its own cannot accomplish the goal of communism. If the ordinary proletarians and other labouring masses are given absolute freedom to run the state machinery there is every possibility of misdirecting the course of proletarian revolution.

The dictatorship of the proletariat being a transitory stage between capitalism and communism, the socialist state inherits the birth marks of the old bourgeois society. Even after the capture of state power, the remnants of feudal and capitalist structures exist for sometime. As far the small commodity production is concerned—no direct attack on it is possible for long. The socialist system has to bear with the small scale production for many decades. Even if feudal and capitalist classes are eliminated from the economy, ideas and ideologies corresponding to them may continue to influence the minds of the people. In the absence of periodic cultural revolutions non-proletarian values and culture gradually pollute the entire society. The absurdity of the argument that the relevance of the dictatorship of the proletariat is lost with the elimination of the exploiting classes is revealed when the masses polluted with non-proletarian outlook could pose serious threats to the socialist system. Mass uprisings in Hungary, Czechoslovakia, Poland and recently in China show that if the masses including the proletariat fall victims to the bourgeois culture, they themselves become the enemies of revolution. Mere suppression of or elimination of the exploiting classes is not a sufficient condition for uninterrupted socialist development. As Lenin points out class struggles exist even in the dictatorship of the proletariat. During this period classes do not disapper; they merely change their forms.[22] The enemy that was once visible to all, now starts confronting the proletariat from within. The task of fighting out such internal enemy is more difficult than conducting struggles against the exploiters. It is impossible to conduct such a complicated struggle without the help of a class conscious party of the revolutionary proletariat.

However, if at any time the party itself falls victim to bourgeois or petty-bourgeois ideologies and deviates from the path of Marxism Leninism, then the party degenerates into a revisionist party. Once the party becomes revisionist, it cannot but take non-proletarian line in determining the economic, political and cultural tasks of revolution. If the cultural and ideological standard of their mass organisations remain at low level and the proletariat out of ignorance continue to consider such party as a true Marxist party, then revisionism spreads into all walks of life diluting proletarian content everywhere. In such conditions the state or other mass organisations of the proletariat may try to assert their independence or party itself may lose its hegemony over the proletarian state and other mass organisations. It is precisely what is happening in the contemporary socialist world.

Though the book examined the dynamics of only one socialist state *i.e.*, U.S.S.R. the same trend exists in almost all countries of the socialist camp. Modern revisionism which started with Tito of Yugoslavia got strengthened by Nikita Khruschev. The 20th Congress of the CPSU led by him opened the flood gates of revisionism on a world scale.[23] His non-Marxist approach and his inability to exercise ideological hegemony over the world communist movement gave birth to Eurocommunism in the Western Europe and socialist individualism in the East European countries. At that moment Mao-Tse-Tung upheld the banner of Marxism Leninism and tried to expose the revisionist policies initiated by the post Stalin leadership in the USSR. Understanding the necessity of elevating the cultural and ideological standard of the rank and file members of the party and also of the general masses, the CPC under Mao's leadership initiated cultural revolution in China. At a time when the nuclear war phobia made Khruschev ignore the necessity of standing by the side of anti-imperialist struggles taking place in the world, it was again Mao who upheld the banner of proletarian internationalism. In spite of certain mistakes, the CPC led by Mao remained a centre of revolutionary communist movement for a long time.

However, after the death of Mao, Deng Xiao Peng and Hu Yao Bang who were at one time discarded as revisionists in the party, could gradually assert their leadership in the Party and the state apparatus. As a result even the CPC turned into a revisionist party. After assuming power, Deng's leadership neglected the cultural tasks and ignored its international responsibility and gave full attention on the ways and means of using modern technology by collaborating with the Western nations. As in the USSR, market mechanisms were widened and the policy of financial incentives were introducted.[24] No doubt such measures contributed to increase in production. But along with production they also led to introduction of liberal values and western styles of living. Since then, people started becoming individualistic and liberal in their outlook. Massive protest of the students against the Communist Party and the state in China is a logical consequence of such development. The youth which at one time supported Mao's cultural revolution now started demanding 'democracy' and 'freedom' without clearly understanding the class essence of such concepts. It was the Chinese leadership which introduced economic reforms conducive to the development of bourgeois thinking. But now it expects to set limits to introduction of reforms in the field of politics. Such an attempt is bound to fail if the proletarians and other labouring masses themselves fall victims to non-proletarian ideologies. Then the only possible alternative left for the party is to suppress the mass protests by using the state violence. It was precisely what happened recently in China and at one time in Hungary and Czechoslovakia. If the USSR goes forward with Gorbachev's 'perestroika' and 'glasnost' and brings about economic and political changes conducive to the non-proletarian ideological outlook among the workers and peasants, there is every possibility of organised counter revolution which cannot be handled by the Russian state except by applying force against its own people. Such counter revolutions can be avoided only when the revisionist leaderships holding power in all these socialist states are overthrown by the class conscious proletariat. Such a step presupposes ideological awareness of the masses, dialectical interactions between the rank and file members of the party and cultural hegemony of the proletariat. Only when the revolutionary proletariat could reorganise the party on the basis of genuine Marxist-Leninist principles and reverse the continuing non-proletarian practices in the goverment, economy and civil society, one can dream of passing over to higher stage of socialism *i.e.* communism.

Notes and Reference

1. Marx and Engels, *Letters on Historical Materialism*, Progress Publishers, Moscow, 1977, p. 12.
2. Lenin calls the non-monopoly sector as "pure firms", O'Connor calls the same as competitive sector. See Lenin, "*Imperialism the Highest stage of Capitalism*" in *Selected Works Vol.II*, Progress, 1977, p. 178; also O' Connor's 'Competitive Capital and Monopoly Capital' in Edwards R.C. ed., *Capitalist System*, Prentice Hall, New Jersey, 1977, p. 159.
3. Lenin observed in 1917-"The imperialist war has immensely accelerated and intensified the process of transformation of monopoly capitalism into state monopoly capitalism. The monstrous oppression of the working people by the

state, which is merging more and more with all powerful capitalist associations is becoming increasingly monstrous'. See Lenin's *Selected Works Vol.II, op. cit.*, p. 263. After three decades Stalin considers that "merging process is not simply a process of coalescence, but the subjugation of the state machine to the monopolies." See Stalin, *Economic Problems of Socialism in the U.S.S.R.*, Foreign Languages Press, Peking, 1972, p. 38.

4. See that the term 'monopoly' is used to denote the economic system, whereas the 'monopolist' to denote the faction of the bourgeoisie (not an individual capitalist).
5. O'Connor, James, 'the Expanding Role of the State' in Edwards R C, ed., *op.cit.*, p. 235.
6. Reich, Michael, 'Military Spending and Production for Profit' In Edwards, R.C. *op.cit.*, p. 410.
7. Skidelsky, R. 'The Decline of Keynesian Politics' in Crouch, Collin, ed., *State and Economy in Contemporary Capitalism*, Croomhelm, London, 1979, p. 61
8. O'Connor, 'Fiscal Crisis of the State' in Quinney, Richards, *Capitalist Society*, The Dorsey Press, Illinois, 1979, p.288.
9. Mishra, Ramesh, *The Welfare State in Crises*, Harvester Press, 1984, p. 20. Also Skidelsky, *op.cit.*, p. 81.
10. Stalin observed at the Seventh Congress of the CPSU ; "The Victory of Revolution never comes of itself. It must be prepared for and won. And only a strong revolutionary party can prepare for and win. Moments occur when the situation is revolutionary, when the rule of bourgeoisie is shaken to its very foundation and yet victory of revolution does not come, because there is no revolutionary party of the proletariat.".
11. For example, Ivory Coast and Ghana heavily export Cocoa, Zaire and Zambia depend on the export of copper, Mauritius earns most of its foreign exchange from sugar and Sudan from cotton. See Lancaster, Carol, *The Search for a growth Strategy for Africa*, Africa Report, March-April, 1984, p. 50.

11a. See Krishna Kumar and Macleod, Maxwell, G.ed. *Multinationals from Developing countries*, Lenington Books, Toronto, 1981; also Khan Khushim, *Multinationals of the South*, Francis Pinter Publishers, London, 1986.

12. See Dhanapala, Jayantha, *China and the Third World*, Vikas, Delhi, 1985, pp. 40-41.
13. Teng Hsio Peng's speech at the UN General Assembly, April 1974, published in *Peking Review*, No.16, April, 19, 1974, pp. 6-11.
14. Khruschev said, "it is quite probable that forms of transition to socialism will become more and more varied; Moreover, achieving these forms need not be associated with civil war... it is not true that we regard violence and civil war as the only way to remake society". He also said, "In present day conditions the working class in many capitalist countries has genuine opportunity to unite the overwhelming majority of the people under its leadership and to ensure that means of production are placed in the hands of the people...(Uniting with) the working peasantry, intellectual and patriotic forces (it) has an opportunity to turn the parliament into an agency of genuine democracy". Quoted in Emberee, G.D., *Soviet Union between the Nineteen and Twenty Party Congress 1952-56*, The Hague, Martinum Nijhoff, 1959, pp. 301-302.

16. Ghosh, Shibdas, *Selected Works Vol. I*, Ganadabi, Calcutta, 1988, p.410.
17. Srikanth H., 'Political Economy of India's Nonalignment', Paper submitted at the National seminar on *Jawaharlal Nehru and India's Foreign Policy*, Mahatma

Gandhi University, Kottayam, 1989.

18. The aggregate external debt of developing nations zoomed from 755 billion dollars in 1981 to a whopping 1, 190 billion dollars in 1987. Developing countries debt grew at an annual rate of 81 billion dollars in 1970 to 580 billion dollars in 1980. According to Deutsche Bank estimates they were scheduled to pay an estimated $80 billions as interest on their short and long term external debt in 1987. Countries like Argentina, Bolivia, Brazil, Chile, Columbia, Ecuador, Ivory Coast, Mexico, Morocco, Nigeria, Peru, Philippines, Uruguay, Venezuela and Yugoslavia together account for roughly half of the interest to be dispersed by all developing countries. See *PTI Economic Service*, New Delhi, May 1988.
19. Stalin, *Problems of Leninism*, Foreign Languages Press, Peking 1976, p. 35.
20. Lenin, *Selected Works Vol. II* Progress Publishers. Moscow, 1977, p.35.
21. Marx clearly says, "It is by no means the aim of the workers... to set the state free.. Freedom consists in converting the state from an organ superimposed upon society into one completely subordinate to it". See Marx, *Critique of Gotha Programme*, Progress Publishers, Moscow, 1978, p. 25.
22. Lenin, *Selected Works Vol. III,* 1977, pp. 161-62.
23. See Ghosh, Shibdas, *Selected Works Vol. I, op.cit.*
24. SUCI, *On C P C,* Ganadabi, Calcutta, 1986.

Bibliography

Alavi, Hamza (1972), 'State in Post-colonial Societies : Pakistan and Bangladesh', *New Left Review*, No. 74, July-August.

Alimov Yuri (1987), *The Rise and Growth of Nonaligned Movement*, Progress Publishers, Moscow.

Althusser, Louis (1971), *Lenin and Philosophy*, Monthly Review Press.

------ (1973), *For Marx*, Penguin.

Altvater, Elmar (1978), "Some Problems of State Intervention". In Holloway, J & Picciotto, S. (ed) 1978.

Balibar, E. and Althusser, L. (1970), *Reading Capital*, NLB

Baran, Paul, (1957), *Political Economy of Growth*, MRP, New York

--------, 1970, 'On Political Economy of Backwardness'. In Rhodes, Rober I, (ed.,). 1970.

Blanke B., Jurgens, U., and Kastendiek (1978), "The Analysis of Form and Functions of the State", Holloway & Picciotto, ed., 1978.

Braumuhli, G. (1978), 'Bourgeois Nation state within the World Market Context' in Holloway & Picciotto, (ed) 1978.

Chirkin, Veniamin (1985), *Constitutional Law and Political Institutions*, Progress Publishers, Moscow.

Dos Santos, T. (1970), 'Structure of Dependence', *American Economic Review*, vol. 60, No.2, May 1970.

Engels, Frederick (1978), *Anti Duhring*, Progress Publishers, Moscow.

Flatow and Huisken (1973); "Zuon Problem der Alibeitung des Bourgerlichen States", *Problems de Klasscampts*, No. pp. 83-129.

Frank, A.G. (1970), 'Development of Underdevelopment'. In Rhodes, Rober, I., ed., 1970.

Gerstenberger, H. (1976), "Theory of State: Special Features of Discussion in the Federal Republic of Germany". In *German Political Studies*, Vols. I&II, Sage, London.

--------,1972, *Lumpen Bourgeoisie and Lumpen Development*, MRP

Ghosh, Shibdas (1985), *Why SUCI is the only Genuine Communist Party in India*, Ganadabi, Calcutta.

--------(1988) *Selected Works Vol.I*, Ganadabi, Calcutta.

Gorbachev, Mikhael (1986), *Political Report of the CPSU (CC) to the 27th Party Congress*, Novosti, Moscow.

--------(1987), *Perestroika*, Collins, London

--------(1988), *Documents and Materials: 19th All Union Congress of the CPSU*, Novosti, Moscow.

----------(1988) *Using the Potentials of Cooperatives for Furthering Perestroika*, Novosti, Moscow.Goulbeurne, H., (ed)., 1979, *Politics and State in the Third World*, Macmillan, London.

Hirsch, J. (1978), "The State Apparatus and Social Reproduction". In Holloway and Picciotto, (ed). 1978.

Holloway, J. and Picciotoo, S., (1975), "Capital crises and the state". In *Capital and Class*, No.2

----------(ed) (1978) *State and Capital*, Edward Arnold, London.

Kalecki, Mikhael, (1972), *Selected Essays in the Growth of Socialist and Mixed Economics*, Cambridge University Press, London.

Klachovsky, L.L. (1974) *The Economics of the Countries of Latin America*, Progress Publishers, Moscow.

Lenin (1967), *Collected Works*, Progress Publishers, Moscow.

Lenin, (1977), *Selected Works Vols. I,II and III*, Progress Publishers, Moscow.

Levkovsky Alexei (1987), *The Developing Countries Social Structures*, Progress Publishers, Moscow.

Mao-se-Tung (1971), *Selected Readings*, Foreign Languages Press, Peking.

Marx, Karl (1978), *Capital Vol.I*, Progress Publishers, Moscow.

Marx, Karl (1977), *Capital Vol.III*, Progress Publishers, Moscow.

Marx and Engels (1976), *Selected Works Vols. I &II* Progress Publishers, Moscow.

Marx and Engels (1977), *Selected Works Vol. III*, Progress Publishers, Moscow.

Marx, Engels and Lenin (1977), *On Dialectical Materialism*, Progress Publishers, Moscow.

Miliband, Ralph, (1970), *The State in Capitalist Society,* Weidenfeld and Nicholson, London.

----------(1970) 'The Capitalist State : A Reply to Nicos Poulantzas', *New Left Review*, London.

----------(1973) "Poulantzas and the capitalist State', *New Left Review*, No. 82.

--------(1977) *Marxism and Politics,* Oxford University Press.

--------(1982), *Capitalist Democracy in Britain*, Oxford University Press.

Muller, W & Neususs, c. (1970), "The Illusion of State Socialism and the Contradictions between Wage Labour and Capital", *Teles, No.25.*

------(1979), "Welfare State : Illusion of state socialism and contradictions between wage labour and capital", In Holloway and Picciotte, ed., 1978

Myrdal, Gunnar (1960) *Beyond the Welfare State*, Yale University Press, New York.

-------- (1967) *Asian Drama*, Pantheon.

--------, *Challenge of the World Poverty*, Vintage Books New York.

Pashukinas, E. (1978), *Law and Marxism - A General Theory*, Ink Links, London.

Picciotto, S. (1979), "The Theory of State, Class Struggle and the Rule of Law", B.S.A. Conference, Warwick.

Primakov, M.Ye. (1988) *The East After the Collapse of the Colonial System*, Progress Publishers, Moscow.

Poulantzas, Nicos (1969) "The Problem of Capitalist State", *New Left Review*, No. 58.

----------(1972), *Political Power and Social Science,* Verso.

--------(1976) "The Capitalist State : A Reply to Miliband and Laclau", *New Left Review*, No. 95

----------(1979) *Fascism and Dictatorship,* Verso, London.

----------(1979) *Classes in Contemporary Capitalism*, Verso.

Reichelt, H. (1978) "Some Comments on Flatow and Huisken" in Holloway and Picciotto, ed., 1978.

Rhodes, Robert I. ed (1970) *Imperialism and Underdevelopment : A Reader*, MRP, New York.

Simoniya, N.A. (1985), *Destiny of Capitalism in the Orient*, Progress Publishers, Moscow.

Stalin, J.V. (1975) *On Opposition*, Foreign Languages Press, Peking.

Stalin, (1976), *Problems of Leninism*, Foreign Language Press, Peking.

Stalin, (1972), *Economic Problems of Socialism in the USSR*, Foreign Languages Press, Peking.

Stanis, V.F. & Khromushin, G.D., ed (1976) *The Role of the State in Social and Economic Reforms in the Developing Countries*, Progress Publishers, Moscow.

Agger, Ben, ed (1979) *Western Marxism. An Introduction*, Goodyear Publishing Co, Inc., California

Arghiri, Emmannuel (1972) *Unequal Exchange*, Monthly Review Press

Babu, A. M. (1985) *African Socialism or Socialist Africa*, Zed Press, New York.

Barone, Charles A, *Marxist Thought on Imperialism*, Macmillan, Michigan.

Bettelheim, Charles (1976) *Class Struggles in the USSR Vol. I & II*, Monthly Review Press.

Bhattacharya, Sisir (1985) *Social Darwinism in India's Welfare State*, Hyderabad.

Blackburn, R. (1971) *Ideology in Social Sciences*, Fontana/Collins.

Bloc, Fred (1979) "The Ruling Class does not Rule". In Quinney, Richard, ed., *Capitalist Society*, Illinois, Dersey Press.

Braginsky, M. (1988). *Joint Ventures: Benefit for All*, Novosti, Moscow.

Braverman (1974). *Labour and Monopoly Capital*, Monthly Review Press, New York.

Burnham, James (1941), *The Managerial Revolution*, New York.

Chakrabarti, B., ed., (1979). *Stalin Question*, Kathashilpa, Calcutta.

Clarke, S. (1977). "Marxism, Sociology and Poulantzas : Theory of State", *Capital and Class*, No.2.

Clarkson, Stephen, (1980), *The Soviet Theory of Development : India and the Third World*, Macmillan, London.

Crouch, Collin, ed. (1979), *State and Economy in Contemporary Capitalism*, Croomhelm, London.

Dahrendorf, Ralf (1976), *Class and Class Conflict in Industrial Society*, Routledge and Kegan Paul.

Desai, A.R. (1979) "Economic Function of the State in the Third World" and "India's Capitalist Class and Immperialism" in his *India's Path of Development*, C.G. Shaw Memorial Trust Publications, Bombay.

Dhanapala, Jayantha (1985), *China and the Third World*, Vikas.

Dobb, Maurice (1972), *Soviet Economic Developments Since 1917*, Routledge and Kegan Paul.

------(1976), *Welfare Economies and Economies of Socialism*, Cambridge University Press.

Domloff William (1978) "Capitalist Control of the State". In Edwards, Richard C., ed., *Capitalist System*, New Jersey. Printice Hall.

Draper, Hal (1977), *State and Bureaucracy*, Monthly Review Press

------, (1978), *The Politics of Social Classes*, Monthly Review Press.

Dowes, Douglas, (1978), 'Capitalist Control of the State'. In Edwards, Richard C, ed., *Capitalist System*, Printice Hall.

Dyson, Kenneth (1978) "Logic of Capital Accumulation". In Edwards, Richards C, ed. 1978.

Edwards R.C. Reich. M.E. & Weisskopf. E., ed (1978). *The Capitalist System*, Printice Hall, New Jersey.

Emeree, G.D. (1959), *Soviet Union between 19th and 20th Party Congresses*, Martinum Nijhoff, Hague.

Ferguson, T. (1988), *The Third World and the Decision Making in the IMF*, Pinter Publishers, London.

Galbraith, J.K. (1969), *The New Industrial Society*, Penguin.

Giddens, A. (1977), *Class Structure of the Advanced Societies*, Hutchinson, London.

Ginsberg (1979), *Class, Capital and Social Policy*, Macmillan.

Gough, Ian, (1975). "State Expenditure in Advanced Capitalism" *New*

Left Review, No. 92.

------ (1979) *Political Economy of the "Welfare State"*, Macmillan, London.

Haberman, J. (1975), "A Reply to Muller And Neususs: *Telos* NO. 25.

Habsbawn, E. (1978), *Capitalist Crises in Historical Perspective*, Edwards, R. C. ed., 1978.

Ham, C & Hill M (1984), *The Policy Process in the Modern Capitalist State,* Wheatsheaf Books, London.

Harris, Marvin (1979), *Cultural Materialism*, Random House, New York.

Hirsch, Fred (1977), *Social limits to Growth*, Roultedge and Kegan Paul.

Hirschhorn, Larry (1978), *Contemporary Crises*, Netherlands.

Hoogvelt, A. (1982), *Third World in Global Development*, Macmillan, London.

Huge, Mosley (1982), "Capital and State : West German Neo-ortheo-dox Theory", *Review of Radical Political Economy*, Spring.

Hyme, Stephen, (1978), "The Evolution of the Corporation" in Edwards, R. C. ed., 1978.

Jessop, B. 1977 (1982), *Capitalist State : Marxist Theory and Methods*, Oxford Martin Robertson.

------(1977) :Recent Marxist Theories of the Capitalist State", *Cambridge Journal of Economics*, No.1.

Jorden, U.J. and Richardson, J.J. (1979), *Governing Under Pressure,* Martin Robertson, Oxford.

Kenet, Roger E, 1975, *Soviet Union and the Developing Nations,* John Hopkins University Press.

Kaushik, Devendra (1983), *Soviet Political System : Perceptions and Perspectives*, Progress Publishers, Moscow.

Kiernman, V.G. (1974), *Marxism and Imperialism*, Edward Arnold, London.

Kublakova, V. and Cruickshank, A.A. (1980), *Marxism and Theory of International Relations*, Routledge & Kegan Paul, London.

Lalhem, E. (1952) *Group Basis of Politics*, Cornwell University Press.

Levi Strauss, Claude (1969), *Elementary Structures of Kinship*, Boston, Bascon.

--------(1978) *Structural Anthropology*, Harmondsworth, Penguin.

Lindblum, C. E. (1977), *Politics and Markets*, Basic Books, New York.

Magdoff, Harry (1979), "American Empire and the U.S. Economy". In Rhodes, R.T. ed., *Imperialism and Underdevelopment : A Reader*, Monthly Review Press.

Mandel, E (1978), *Marxist Theory of State*, Bombay.

-------- (1979), *State in the Age of Late Capitalism*, Bombay.

Middlemas, K. (1979), *Politics in Industrial Society*, Andre Deusch, London.

Millier, Diana, ed., (1974) *The Political Economy of Capitalism*, Progress Publishers, Moscow.

Mills, C.W. (1977), *The Power Elite,* Oxford University Press.

--------(1977) *The Marxists*, Penguin.

Mishra, Ramesh (1984), *The Welfare State in Crisis*, Brighton, Wheatseaf Books.

Nathanson, C, (1969), "Militarisation of the American Economy". In Horowitz, ed., *Corporations and the Cold War*, Monthly Review Press.

Offe, Clause (1974), "Structural Problem of the Capitalist state". In K. Ven Beyne, ed., *German Studies*, Vol. I, Sage, London.

--------(1975) "The Theory of Capitalist State and the Problem of Policy Formation". In Lindberg, L, ed., *Stress and Contradiction in Modern Capitalism*, Lexington Books.

Parkins, F (1978), *Class inequalities and Political Order*, Grenada Publishers, London.

Philip, Andre (1955), *La democratic Industrialle*, Paris .

Quinney, Richard, ed (1978), *Capitalist Society,* Dorsey Press, Illionois.

Reich, Michael (1978) "Military Spending and Production for Profit". In Edwards, Richard C., ed, 1978.

Robson, William A., (1976). *Welfare State and Welfare Society : Illusion and Reality*, George Allen and Unwin, London.

Samhoff,J. (1982), "Class , Class Conflict and the State in Africa", *Political Science Quarterly,* Vol. 97, November, Spring.

Saul, J.S. (1978). "The State in Post-colonial Socieites : Tanzania". In Goulbourne, ed, 1979.

Schmitter, P. (1974), "Still the Century of Corporation" Review of Politics, No. 36.

Skidelsky, R (1970), "The Decline of Keynesian Politics". In Crouch, Collin, ed., 1979.

Smith, Anthony D. (1983), *State and Nation in the Third World*, Wheat Sheaf Books, Sussex.

Srikanth, H, (1988), "Nature of Indian State". In Chaubey, N.P. ed. *Indian Society at the Turn of the Century*, Allahabad.

Stratchey, J. (1956). *Contemporary Capitalism*, New York.

Sweezy, P.A. "Reproduction and the Capitalist State" in Edwards, R.C. ed., 1978.

Urry, John, (1981), *The Anatomy of the capitalist Societies,* Macmillan.

Urry, J. and Abercrimbie, N, (1976) "Class State and Fascism : The Work of Nices Poulantzas" *Political Studies* No.24.

Weiner, Richard, R. (1981), *Cultural Marxism and Political Sociology* Sage Publications, London.

Weinstein, J, "Corporate Liberalism and Monopoly Capitalist Societies" in Edwards, R.C., ed., 1978.

Wells, David (1983). *Marxism and the Modern State,* Select Books Service Syndicate, New Delhi.

Westergard, J. and Bester, H (1978). *Classes in Capitalist Society*, Penguin.

Wirth, M (1977), "Towards a Critique of the Theory of State Monopoly Capitalism", *Economy and Society*, No.6

William, G. (1987), *Third World and Political Organisation*, Macmillan.

Wright, E. O. (1979), *Class, Crises and the State*, Verso, London.

Wright, E.O. Anderson and Friedland, (1976), "Modes of class Struggle and the Capitalist System", *Kapitalistate*, No. 4-5.

Wynia, Gary, (1985). *The Politics of Latin American Development*, Cambridge University Press, New York.

Yaffe, D, (1975), "The State and the Capitalist Crises", VESV Conference, Amesterdam.

Index

U

V

W

Y

Z